Understanding, Managing and Implementing Quality

This book considers strategic aspects of Quality Management and self-assessment frameworks, and provides an in-depth and systematic examination of a number of the main quality improvement tools and techniques.

Incorporating a critical orientation, the text reviews the implementation of a variety of Quality Management programmes across a range of organizational contexts, including manufacturing, higher education, health care, policing and retailing.

With case studies illustrating good practice in all contexts, including manufacturing and service organizations, critiques and further reading, *Understanding, Managing and Implementing Quality* is a highly useful resource for students, researchers and those studying for professional qualifications.

Jiju Antony is a Senior Teaching Fellow at the International Manufacturing Centre of the University of Warwick.

David Preece is Professor of Technology Management and Organization Studies and Head of the Human Resource Management Corporate Strategy Group at the Business School of the University of Teesside.

Understanding, Managing and Implementing Quality

Frameworks, techniques and cases

Edited by Jiju Antony and
David Preece

London and New York

First published 2002
by Routledge
11 New Fetter Lane, London EC4P 4EE

Simultaneously published in the USA and Canada
by Routledge
29 West 35th Street, New York NY 10001

Routledge is an imprint of the Taylor & Francis Group

© 2002 Jiju Antony and David Preece, selection and editorial matter;
individual chapters, the contributors.

Typeset in Times by Wearset Ltd, Boldon, Tyne and Wear
Printed and bound in Great Britain by Biddles Ltd, Guildford and
King's Lynn

British Library Cataloguing in Publication Data
A catalogue record for this book is available from the British Library

Library of Congress Cataloging in Publication Data
A catalog record for this book has been requested

ISBN 0-415-22271-0 (hbk)
ISBN 0-415-22272-9 (pbk)

This book is dedicated to:
Frenie and Evelyn and
Maureen, Laura and Jamie

Contents

**10 Changing supervisory relations at work: behind the success
stories of Quality Management initiatives** **211**
PATRICK DAWSON

Figures

Tables

Contributors

Jiju Antony is a Senior Teaching Fellow at the International Manufacturing Centre of the University of Warwick, Coventry, UK.

Nick Capon is a Senior Lecturer in Operations and Quality Management, Portsmouth Business School, University of Portsmouth, UK.

Patrick Dawson is a Professor in the Department of Management Studies, University of Aberdeen, Aberdeen, Scotland, UK.

Ceasar Douglas is a Professor of the Department of Management, Seidman School of Business, Grand Valley State University, Michigan, USA.

Andreas J. Frangou is a Business Modeller within the Modelling Services Group, DHL Worldwide Express, Hounslow, Middlesex, UK.

Harriet Jefferson is a Senior Research Fellow in the School of Nursing and Midwifery, University of Southampton, UK.

Graeme Knowles is a Senior Teaching Fellow in Quality & Reliability, Warwick Manufacturing Group, University of Warwick, Coventry, UK.

Ashok Kumar is an Assistant Professor of the Department of Management, Seidman School of Business, Grand Valley State University, Michigan, USA.

Glenn Mazur is an Executive Director of QFD Institute, an adjunct lecturer of TQM and President of Japan Business Consultants Ltd, Michigan, USA.

Vivien Mills is a retired Superintendent from Sussex Police.

Jaideep Motwani is a Professor in the Department of Management, Seidman School of Business, Grand Valley State University, Michigan, USA.

David Preece is Professor of Technology Management and Organization Studies and Head of the Human Resource Management Corporate Strategy Group at the Business School of the University of Teesside.

Gordon Steven is the Managing Director of Betting Direct.

Valerie Steven is a Senior Lecturer in Human Resource Management of Coventry Business School, Coventry University, UK.

Michael Wood is a Principal Lecturer in Portsmouth Business School, University of Portsmouth, Portsmouth, UK.

Acknowledgements

As editors and as chapter authors, we have benefited from the advice and help of a number of people in the preparation of this book. At Routledge, the book was conceived during Stuart Hay's stewardship of the Business and Management list, carried forward by his one-time assistant and subsequent successor, Michelle Gallagher, and the manuscript was submitted to one of her successors, Francesca Lumkin. We thank them for their encouragement and forbearance and we also thank the two reviewers appointed by Routledge to comment upon earlier drafts of the chapters.

This collection of ideas on Quality Management and quality engineering was conceived during the year 1998–99 when Jiju had finished writing his book on *Experimental Quality*. When he took his ideas to David, he foresaw the potential which resulted in the present volume. Jiju's work on this book reflects his experiences and lessons learned from his previous book as mentioned above. He would like to thank Dr Hefin Rowlands of the University of Wales Newport and Dr Ranjit K. Roy of Nutek, Inc. for their critical comments on the earlier drafts of his chapter. Special thanks also go to the members of the Quality and Reliability Group of the University of Warwick for facilitating his work.

David's work on the book was greatly facilitated by the sabbatical he enjoyed during the second semester of the 1999–2000 academic year, and he would like to thank his colleagues in the Department of Business and Management at the University of Portsmouth for their support, particularly Peter Scott who took over most of his teaching for that semester. In addition, a number of people from public house retailing companies were only too pleased to divert their time to responding to questions and observations on Quality Management matters; it is a pity they cannot be mentioned by name for reasons of confidentiality.

Glossary

AHP	Analytic Hierarchy Process
AI	Artificial Intelligence
ANOVA	Analysis of Variance
BEM	Business Excellence Model
BPR	Business Process Re-engineering
CA	Clinical Audit
CBR	Case-based Reasoning
CEO	Chief Executive Officer
COQ	Cost of Quality
EFQM	European Foundation for Quality Management
EQA	European Quality Award
ESAS	Enterprise Strategic Advisory System
HEIs	Higher Education Institutions
HMIC	Her Majesty's Inspectorate of Constabularies
ISO	International Organization for Standardization
MBNQA	Malcolm Baldridge National Quality Award
OA	Orthogonal Array
OFAAT	One Factor At A Time
QA	Quality Assurance
QCIM	Quality Competitiveness Index Model
QFD	Quality Function Deployment
ROI	Return on Investment
SERVQUAL	Service Quality
SNR	Signal-to-Noise Ratio
SPC	Statistical Process Control
SPM	Statistical Process Monitoring
TQM	Total Quality Management
WPC	Worker Participation Committee

Introduction

In the pursuit of continuous improvement of product and service performance, quality is a major focus for contemporary organizations. This book is designed to provide the reader a critical appreciation of key Quality Management tools, techniques and implementation into both manufacturing and service organizations through drawing upon the research findings of a range of specialist scholars who have gathered together an extensive range of new data from organizations in the manufacturing, healthcare, higher education, policing, and leisure retailing sectors across a number of countries.

Given that the subject of Quality Management has become quite broadly based and generated a considerable number of tools, techniques and frameworks, we have had to be rather selective in the particular tools, techniques and frameworks we have chosen to review and evaluate. All the more so because, in any event, this is not a textbook, but rather is centrally concerned to explore the challenges faced and issues raised when those tools, techniques and frameworks are *applied* in organizations – and how, if at all, attempts were made to resolve those challenges. What we are arguing, then, is that Quality Management can only really be understood through a critical examination of its implementation, and that this necessitates a research design which incorporates an attempt to 'get close to the action' of everyday practice (see also Wilkinson and Willmott, 1995; Wilkinson *et al.*, 1998). This is not to argue or imply that the strategic dimension should or can be ignored in focusing upon implementation for, while we are primarily interested in the latter, we recognize that some at least of this activity takes place within a context which is framed by wider, especially managerial, considerations relating to such matters as corporate, business unit, human resource management, and manufacturing/service quality strategies. Hence, we felt it important to begin the book with two chapters which concentrate upon this strategic dimension of quality and which provide some frameworks and means for developing or extending an organization's strategic Quality Management capability (that is, by using case-based systems or self-assessment frameworks).

There are an extensive number of texts and textbooks on Quality Management (see, for example, Beckford, 2001; Dale, 1994; Oakland, 1993; Kolarik, 1995; Bergman and Klefsjo, 1994). What we are offering here is not another textbook, but rather a book which will allow the reader to appreciate some of the complexities and problems associated with the implementation of some of the key tools, techniques and frameworks of Quality Management in contemporary organizations. Thus, it is assumed that readers are already acquainted with the broad subject matter of Quality Management though having taken an introductory course and/or relevant work experience and reading. The present book is designed to build upon this grounding by offering a more specialist treatment of certain aspects of Quality Management which are either not covered or only summarily covered in the textbooks. This treatment is facilitated through the brief overview which is provided by the chapter author(s), where appropriate, of that particular tool, technique or framework, followed by a critical review and case study application, along with a guide to further reading. The references for each chapter are gathered together, chapter by chapter, at the end of the book, in order that the reader can more readily gain an overview of all the secondary material referred to in the book.

The book, then, focuses upon Quality Management implementation issues and challenges. It adopts a critical orientation, one which is based upon an engagement with practice through case study research. It also provides a systematic approach for both understanding and assessing the implementation of quality tools and techniques in a variety of business contexts. Many of the texts available in the area adopt a technicist/rationalistic approach: 'If only people in organizations acted more rationally and followed the tools and techniques to the letter, then most quality problems could be resolved.' They also commonly have a limited anchorage in the organizational literature and/or make no or only very limited use of primary data. Our view is that this leads to both a poor understanding of practice and (hence) a weak basis upon which to intervene in or manage Quality Management initiatives. It is intended that the material presented in the first two chapters should provide a strategic orientation of quality. It should be added at this juncture that the data has been gathered from organizations in three countries: the United Kingdom (Chapters 1, 3–5, 7–9), the United States (Chapters 2 and 6) and Australia (Chapter 10), although there is, of course, quite a bit of 'overlapping' of the countries implied or considered at various points. Given that many of the literature reviews are cross-national, there is, then, an international flavour to the overview and evaluation of Quality Management implementation presented here.

The book is carefully designed and presented so that it will be suitable for a wide spectrum of readers, ranging from undergraduates to Quality Management practitioners in the field of Quality Management. To illustrate, we are thinking of courses such as BA/BSc Business/Management Studies/Business Administration, International Management, Mathematics and Statistics, BEng Mechanical, Chemical, Electrical, Electronic, Manufacturing, Engineering, where Quality Management is taught as either a core or optional subject or forms an important part of a wider subject, and covered typically in the final year of the programme, following groundwork studies in earlier years. With respect to postgraduate programmes, we are thinking particularly of Masters/courses in Business

Administration, Quality Management, Quality and Reliability, Manufacturing Management/Engineering Business Management, Industrial and Systems Engineering/Manufacturing Systems Engineering. The book will also be of relevance for people who are studying programmes leading to professional examinations/membership in cognate areas such as the Institute of Quality Assurance, Certified Quality/Reliability Engineer/Technician.

Provided below is an overview of the chapters which make up the rest of the book. We move from a consideration of some key strategic issues associated with Quality Management, through an in-depth examination of certain key Quality Management tools, techniques and frameworks, to five case study chapters which relate, evaluate and comment upon the implementation of Quality Management in a variety of sectors, both public and private: manufacturing, higher education, healthcare, police, and public house retailing. These chapters illustrate many of the challenges and problems which are posed when the various tools and techniques are applied, and how actors in the relevant organizations have attempted to overcome them – and whether indeed (and if so in what senses) they can be said to have succeeded.

More specifically, then, Part I of the book consists of two chapters: Chapter 1 addresses the strategic issues of Quality Management using the application of AI techniques such as Case-Based Reasoning (CBR) and Chapter 2 provides a comparative evaluation of self-assessment frameworks for business organizations for developing and facilitating change. Part II consists of three chapters – all of them are arranged in a sequential order for designing quality into products and processes. The contents in these chapters are essential for organizations embarking on what we call today Six Sigma Business Improvement Strategy. The techniques and tools presented in Part II provide invaluable guidance for designing, optimizing and controlling product and process quality. Part III, which consists of five chapters, centres around the presentation and analysis of case study research into the implementation of some of the tools, techniques and/or frameworks, considered in the previous two main sections of the book, in contemporary organizations. While this is also the case in many of the previous chapters, here there is a focus upon a particular sector, such as healthcare or higher education, and more attention is devoted to the organizational, people and managerial issues and contexts associated with implementation. In other words, while the tools, techniques and/or frameworks are foregrounded in the first two sections, in this last section it is the organizational issues which are foregrounded, with the tools etc., being backgrounded. It is also the case that the majority of the illustrative/primary material presented in Part II is drawn from the manufacturing sector, whereas in Part III non-manufacturing sectors are represented much more strongly, in particular policing, leisure retailing, healthcare and higher education.

Chapter 1 introduces the reader to general Artificial Intelligence (AI) techniques and explores the notion of strategic quality from the perspective of continuous improvement and business performance. The chapter also describes in detail the development and evaluation of a case-based intelligent system to encourage the application of case-based reasoning methodology to quality and business.

Chapter 2 examines critically the topic of self-assessment in relation to five diverse frameworks: Malcolm Baldridge National Quality Award model, Business Excellence model, Continuous Improvement model, Quality Management systems model and Quality Competitiveness Index model. A comparative evaluation of these five frameworks over several desirable attributes is also presented.

Chapter 3 establishes the core principles of Quality Function Deployment (QFD) as a technique to design and develop products or services which is driven by the needs of the customer. The chapter also elucidates the strengths and limitations of the technique, the critical factors for the successful implementation of the technique and also throws light on the issues around the team formation for the application of QFD.

Chapter 4 illustrates the importance of experimental design technique in particular Taguchi approach to industrial experimentation. A systematic methodology for design/process optimization is also presented in order to assist people in organizations with limited skills in experimental design techniques. A case study from a hot forming process is presented. The chapter concludes by revealing a critique of experimental design advocated by Taguchi.

Chapter 5 provides a brief overview of Statistical Process Control (SPC) and explains its potential benefits and underlying assumptions. The chapter also looks at the difficulties in the application of SPC (or more accurately SPM – Statistical Process Monitoring) and possible ways of resolving them. A case study from a manufacturing company is presented to illustrate various issues involved in the implementation of SPM.

Chapter 6 discusses the implementation of TQM in Higher Education Sector. The chapter fundamentally explains a case application of QFD in designing a new course in TQM at the University of Michigan, USA.

Chapter 7 discusses whether a customer centred approach to Quality Management is appropriate in UK policing. The paper describes the application of SERVQUAL (or the so-called GAP model) in assessing service quality. The chapter concludes that apart from the Gap model, other methods such as process mapping and the Business Excellence model need to be used to improve value quality and technical quality respectively.

Chapter 8 introduces the evaluation of quality in the healthcare sector in particular the National Health Service (NHS) in UK. The paper reveals the difficulties in the successful application of TQM principles in the NHS.

Chapter 9 focuses upon Quality Management initiatives within the UK public house retailing sector. It was found that QC/QA orientation predominates within the sector and that a TQM project introduced in the early 1990s did not become embedded within the organization, although a number of public house managers were predisposed towards it and were beginning to adopt TQM-type practices within their pubs.

Chapter 10 emphasizes the importance of supervisory relations at work in organizations. The chapter highlights the more complex process of supervisory change by drawing longitudinal data from a National Programme of Australian research. The chapter concludes that there are no simple prescriptions for the development of harmonious quality cultures or one-minute recipes for implementing new forms of industry democracy at work.

References

Beckford, J. (2001) *Quality: A Critical Introduction*, 2nd edn. London: Routledge.

Bergman, B. and Klefsjo, B. (1994) *Quality – from Customer Needs to Customer Satisfaction*. McGraw-Hill, UK.

Dale, B. (1994) *Managing Quality*, 2nd edn. Hemel Hempstead: Prentice Hall.

Kolarik, W. (1995), *Creating Quality: Concepts, Systems, Strategies and Tools*. New York: McGraw-Hill.

Oakland, J. (1993) *Total Quality Management: The Route to Improving Performance*. London: Butterworth-Heinemann.

Wilkinson, A. and Willmott, H. (1995) *Making Quality Critical: New Perspectives on Organizational Change*. London: Routledge.

Wilkinson, A., Redman, T., Snape, E. and Marchington, M. (1998) *Managing with Total Quality Management: Theory and Practice*. Basingstoke: Macmillan.

Part I

Developing a strategic orientation for Quality Management

1 Promoting a strategic approach to TQM using a case-based intelligent system

Andreas J. Frangou

Introduction

Intelligent systems research is an area of artificial intelligence (AI) dedicated to the study and development of machines (notably computers) that can display and replicate human intelligent behaviour such as understanding, learning, reasoning and problem-solving (Michalski and Littman, 1991: 64; Schank, 1990). Traditionally AI research is concerned with the broad study of human intelligence and its replication. This can have more theoretical, technical and philosophical implications for AI research such as the following:

- the nature of intelligence itself (i.e. what is intelligence and what are its components);
- the development of models of human reasoning, problem-solving, knowledge representation and cognition;
- the development of tools and techniques such as AI programming environments (i.e. LISP and PROLOG) and learning algorithms to assist knowledge elicitation.

The field of intelligent systems is distinct from other areas of AI, only in that it focuses on the advancement of methodologies and tools that can aid in the development, application and evaluation of systems to real world systems. This chapter therefore does not aim to provide a deep theoretical and philosophical understanding of AI, rather, it focuses on the application of intelligent systems to business, by reporting on research into the development and evaluation of a prototype intelligent system called ESAS (Enterprise Strategic Advisory System). ESAS is a case-based intelligent system[1] designed to provide support for TQM and competitive advantage. The overall goal of the system is to encourage proactivity and creativity in organizations during strategic quality problem-solving and decision-making.

In sharing the experiences of developing and evaluating ESAS, this chapter aims to demonstrate to the reader the potential of AI and intelligent systems for business through the following:

- an analysis of the strategic significance of quality to firm performance, and the potential benefits of using intelligent systems to promote and encourage strategic thinking within organizations;
- an introduction to some of the theoretical and technical issues in developing intelligent systems, including a detailed discussion of the appropriateness of case-based reasoning for TQM applications;
- a description of ESAS's scope and development process, including the systems evaluation;
- a summary and conclusion discussing both what has been learnt from ESAS's development, and the future potential of such systems to business.

Linking TQM and performance: a strategic perspective

TQM and competitive advantage

Quality as a means of creating and sustaining a competitive advantage has been widely adopted by both public and private sector organizations (Frangou *et al.*, 1999). This strategic stance has been fuelled by the growing attention to strategic quality (Leonard and Sasser, 1982; Jacobson and Aaker, 1987; Brown, 1996; Wilkinson and Willmott, 1995) arising from the international successes of Japanese and other South Eastern Asian countries (Powell, 1995) and research that has focused on the link between quality (TQM) and business performance (Reed *et al.*, 1996; Powell, 1995; Buzzell and Gale, 1987; Jacobson and Aaker, 1987; O'Neal and Lafief, 1992; Capon *et al.*, 1990; Curry, 1985). Furthermore as Morgan and Piercy (1996: 231) state 'Consequently, quality improvement has been widely cited as a basis for achieving sustainable competitive advantage.'

To improve quality, businesses have applied 'Total Quality Management' (TQM) to their organizations to help them plan their efforts. The promise of superior performance through continuous quality improvement has attracted a wide spectrum of business to TQM, with applications reported in domains such as: finance (Wilkinson *et al.*, 1996), utilities (Candlin and Day, 1993), federal agencies, healthcare, education and research, environment and manufacturing (Lakhe and Mohanty, 1994).

A number of studies have focused on the effectiveness of TQM initiatives (in particular the use of self-assessment frameworks) in improving performance (General Accounting Office (GAO), 1991; Wisner and Eakins, 1994; Davis, 1992; Johnson, 1993). The US General Accounting Office (GAO) in 1991 studied the performance of the twenty highest scoring Baldridge Award applicants. It found that organizations had achieved improvements in the following areas: employee relations, quality, costs, market share, profitability, and customer satisfaction. The GAO also identified common features among these organizations which included strong leadership, employee involvement, customer focus, open cultures, and partnership programmes (Powell, 1995). An International Quality study conducted jointly by the American Quality Foundation and Ernst & Young sampled over 500 organizations operating in various industries such as computer, automobile, banking and healthcare (American Quality Foundation, 1991). Their findings showed that process improvement and supplier accreditation practices did improve performance.[2]

Although evidence exists which supports the effectiveness of TQM initiatives, a large number of studies have shown that between 60 per cent and 80 per cent of TQM initiatives fail, or fail to show significant impact on business performance. Wilkinson *et al.* (1996), state that a recent survey of 80 major financial institutions conducted by KPMG Management Consulting found that 80 per cent of participants had implemented some form of quality initiative that had little impact on 'bottom-line profits'. They also point out that another survey conducted by Tilson (1989) showed that few initiatives 'had any significant impact, either on customer perceptions or commercial results'. Wilkinson *et al.*'s (1996) own survey of quality initiatives within the financial services sector (122 companies being surveyed) highlighted the lack of impact on financial benefits with only 35 per cent of respondents reporting that profitability had improved. Knights and McCabe (1997: 38) point out that 'management may not always understand the implications or appropriateness of the quality initiatives they adopt'. Their study of TQM initiatives within the financial sector also highlighted the 'conformance to requirements' approach taken during quality improvement programmes, which they state is inconsistent with the strategic intentions of the business which should focus on 'customers' and 'culture'.

Tatikonda and Tatikonda (1996) report on surveys of quality improvement programmes carried out by the Boston Consulting Co., McKinsey Co. and the Electronic Assembly Association. These surveys highlighted the problems associated with TQM implementations, the high rate of failures and lack of impact on performance. Boston Consulting Co. (Schaffer and Thomson, 1992) found that only one-third of the organizations attributed their improved competitiveness to TQM. Tatikonda and Tatikonda's (1996) own findings suggest that in many cases TQM programmes lack focus on critical business areas that have a good 'return on quality'. Tatikonda and Tatikonda's (1996: 7) argue that organizations must measure the 'cost of quality' (COQ), otherwise there is a danger that resources are spent on improvements customers do not care for, and pick projects with only marginal benefits. They also advocate extensive COQ reporting as a means of accurately communicating the impact of quality projects on the business, thus enabling the prioritizing and coordination of valuable resources, and the motivation of personnel. Other commentators also report on the poor rate of quality initiatives, and have suggested the reasons shown in Table 1.1.

The suggested reasons for the reported failures summarized in Table 1.1 raise some important issues for TQM. Writers have identified a lack of focus and effective enterprise guidance in targeting critical areas for change during quality improvement programmes. Thus for programmes to be successful, organizations need concise guidance to implement quality improvements effectively. They also need to assess the costs of the programme and its potential outcomes (Tatikonda and Tatikonda, 1996). Furthermore, the lack of strategic focus and integration shown in TQM suggests that quality initiatives are carried out in

Table 1.1 Reasons for TQM failures

The lack of 'top management commitment' (Atkinson, 1990)

The implementation of changes that are only internally focused, with little external or customer focus (Foster and Beardon, 1993)

'Continuous improvement' did not permeate the strategic process (Gallaher, 1991; Walker, 1992; Boyce, 1992)

Lack of focus on critical business processes, no resource support for long term improvement efforts, and a lack of synergy between quality programmes and overall strategy (Erickson, 1992)

Poor timing and pacing of TQM initiatives, that are generally crisis led (Brown *et al.*, 1994)

Lack of measurement in all key areas, but particularly at a strategic level (Dyason and Kaye, 1996)

TQM concepts and terminology are barriers to success, because there is no consensus on their meaning (Foster and Whittle, 1989)

No supporting infrastructure for cultural change and people issues (Seddon, 1992)

Managerial or organizational 'mind-sets' that are inconsistent with the TQM philosophy (Hubiak and O'Donnell, 1996)

---

isolation, and do not involve other departments and functions such as marketing and strategic planning (Schmalensee, 1991). For example, Law and Cousins (1991) claim that marketing and business strategists are usually neglected in quality improvement programmes which are considered to be primarily the concern of manufacturing. This approach may affect whether or not critical/ strategic areas are focused on, where there is the greatest potential for return on investment (ROI) (Tatikonda and Tatikonda, 1996), bearing in mind that it is mainly the marketing function that gathers strategically important market intelligence (Butz, 1995). Hubiak and O'Donnell (1996: 20) argue that American organizational 'mind-sets impose serious constraints on the implementation of TQM', because they are usually individualist in nature, internally competitive, problem-solving and crisis orientated, linear thinking, and control orientated. Furthermore, they claim that management practices that try to create order through the development of guidelines and procedures constrain the organization's ability to grow and learn:

> An organization needs to learn how to anticipate and stay ahead of change. Rules and procedures can rigidify a system, which channels thinking into the most obvious paths and inhibits creativity. The creation of a learning organization demands a proactive, curious, self-directed learner, able to take the perspective of the entire system to address problems or new initiatives. (p. 23)

Strategic quality, focus and dynamism: the missing links in TQM

Porter (1996) claims that quality improvement programmes usually focus on improving operational effectiveness. This, and the ability to satisfy both customers and stakeholders, is an important factor in the battle for competitive advantage. However, improvements in these areas are not enough to make an organization competitive. Furthermore, 'few companies have competed successfully on the basis of operational effectiveness over an extended period, and staying ahead of rivals gets harder every day' (1996: 63). The reasons for these long-term failures are that 'competitors can quickly imitate management techniques, new technologies, input improvements and superior ways of meeting customer needs' (p. 63). Porter argues that the missing link in quality improvement programmes is strategy. Butz (1995) also takes this view, suggesting that the root cause of many TQM failures is the limited integration of TQM programmes with the fundamental strategies of the business. This view is consistent with other researchers within the TQM field who have also identified the lack of a strategic focus in quality initiatives as a main cause of failures (Foster and Beardon, 1993; Atkinson, 1990; Gallaher, 1991; Erickson, 1992; Dyason and Kaye, 1996).

Self-assessment frameworks (and their associated models) can be key drivers of TQM initiatives, and useful tools for guiding organizations through the process of quality improvement, as they provide a structured approach to developing a philosophy of continuous improvement (Davis *et al.*, 1996). However, issues have been raised about their validity, and their real effectiveness in improving the performance of organizations (Black and Porter, 1996; Wiele *et al.*, 1995). Conti (1997) also expressed concerns regarding their lack of a strategic focus, suggesting that company mission, goals and objectives should be systematically considered more within the frameworks. Quality Management researchers have found that quality initiatives are generally too introspective and internally focused (Foster and Beardon, 1993). Wiele *et al.*'s (1995: 15) own study of self-assessment in European organizations confirms this view, in that the highest ranking reason for starting self-assessment is 'internal issues'.

The above discussion has raised some important issues relating to the lack of strategic and market focus in many TQM initiatives. This lack of strategic and marketing activity in quality improvements provides the key proposition focusing on the notion of strategic quality:

1 *Requirement for Strategic Quality* – i.e. initiatives, quality improvement programmes, product and service developments that are market-led, continually satisfy the requirements and expectations of the external environment, and thus create and sustain a competitive advantage.

A lack of focus, and integration of quality improvement initiatives with an organization's management practices, is another key deficiency of quality efforts aiming to achieve tangible business objectives. If the market does not want or need these improvements, or if no real enhancement to the business can be achieved, then the initiative is not viable (Iacobucci, 1996). Too many quality improvement programmes fail to focus on critical, strategic business processes, which provide a good return on investment (ROI) (Tatikonda and Tatikonda's, 1996; Erickson, 1992). Brown *et al.* (1994) raise questions about the timing and pacing of TQM programmes, suggesting that the prioritizing of critical areas for change is the key to successful implementation. This leads to the second main proposition, that there is a requirement for *prioritized and focused quality initiatives*:

---

2 Prioritized and Focused Quality Initiatives that are focused on areas or processes that add value to:

- the customer, who sees and appreciates this value and is willing to pay for it, over competitors products and services;
- the organization in terms of profit, market share, reputation and position, and to all its stakeholders including the community.

An organization's ability to change continually and learn to innovate in relation to the changing marketplace is also a key issue for TQM programmes. As Hubiak and O'Donnell (1996) claim, the process of developing organizational procedures, guidelines or rules can constrain learning, creativity and innovation. Organizations engaged in quality improvement programmes typically operate in an introspective manner (Foster and Beardon, 1993; Hubiak and O'Donnell, 1996), and non-critical or non-strategic areas are focused on (Tatikonda and Tatikonda, 1996). Hubiak and O'Donnell found that most organizations engaged in quality improvements (including the Malcolm Baldridge National Quality Award (MBNQA) winners) were mainly involved in problem-solving, and product development was generally 'reactive, responding to rather than antici-pating customer demands' (p. 25). This leads to the third and final proposition – that organizations and their programmes must be dynamic:

---

3 *Dynamism:* Organizations and their quality improvement programmes must be dynamic. They must have the ability to drive, respond and anticipate the continually changing forces, requirements and expecta-tions of both the external and internal environment.

These three propositions provide the structure and focus of the chapter. The next section introduces the concept of an intelligent system for addressing the above issues.

The use of intelligent systems to support TQM initiatives

The above discussion and analysis has raised important issues for TQM implementation: (1) it has identified the three issues that are the key strategic factors in the reported failures of TQM programmes; (2) the discussion has highlighted the need for strategic support and guidance during quality improvement programmes; it is important for businesses to know what changes need implementing and why, and what impact they will have on their performance; (3) once a key business area has been identified, how should the organization go about implementing the change – what techniques, methods or resources will it allocate and use? Expert advice or knowledge about the problem domain – *TQM and competitive advantage* would be highly useful to the organization when making such important strategic decisions. Consultants provide expert support in solving difficult problems, and can be cost effective if they are internally sourced and the organization is sufficiently sized and resourced to employ such experts. If, however, an organization is not in this position and seeks outside consultants, the cost incurred could therefore be prohibitive (Bird, 1997).

An alternative solution is to use an intelligent system that stores and uses domain expertise and knowledge required to support the problem-solving or decision-making process. This overcomes the expense of 'buying-in' expertise to support strategic decisions, which is often a short-term solution to the problem. Furthermore, if an organization does employ an internal expert, their knowledge and skills can be stored within an intelligent system. This has the following benefits for the organization (Guida and Tasso, 1995: 119):

- the intelligent system could support decision-making tasks that are more general in nature, thus allowing the expert to deal with more strategic or critical tasks;
- it allows an organization to capture and store their valuable expertise which otherwise could be lost due to employee turnover or retirement;
- it enables an organization to effectively distribute and exploit knowledge throughout the organization, and thus proliferate a consistently high level of expertise across a number of sites;
- it makes knowledge explicit, promoting organizational learning.

The application of intelligent systems technology to the TQM and competitive advantage domains can yield similar 'knowledge-based' benefits for organizations implementing quality improvement programmes. Furthermore, it could store and utilize knowledge and expertise that would both highlight the need for, and provide support for, strategic quality, prioritized and focused quality initiatives and dynamism. There is growing interest in the use of intelligent systems in business, in particular for enhancing financial and marketing activities, improving decision-making procedures at strategic levels, and for supporting TQM initiatives (Mockler and Dologite, 1992; Guida and Tasso, 1995; Edgell and Kochhar, 1992; Bird, 1997). However, the concept of using an intelligent system to encourage a strategic and market-led approach to quality improvement programmes, is novel. The research project proposes the development of an intelligent system called ESAS – Enterprise Strategic Advisory System which is designed to address the domain/research issues identified above. In addition, ESAS has been designed in the spirit of TQM frameworks and models such as ISO 9000, EFQM and MBNQA; in that the system will be generic in nature and designed to provide advice that can be considered useful by most organizations, private and public. The design, development and evaluation of the ESAS prototype essentially represents a feasibility study, which assesses the potential of applying intelligent system technology to the domains of TQM and competitive advantage.

Development of the Enterprise Strategic Advisory System

As discussed earlier, intelligent systems are designed to display the qualities inherent in human intelligent behaviour for a particular task or problem domain, a major component being the simulation of human reasoning (Jackson, 1990). This basically involves an attempt to emulate a human's problem-solving or task performing abilities, which can include: diagnosis, monitoring, control, prediction, design and planning.

The selection of an appropriate method or reasoning paradigm for a system will depend greatly on the application domain (Kolodoner, 1993). Michalski and Littman (1991) state that AI research has two general paradigm options to choose from: the *symbolic paradigm* and the *connectionist paradigm*. The symbolic paradigm focuses attention on the manipulation of symbolic representations to derive inferences. Symbolic representations are essentially; rules, objects, frames, scripts, semantic nets and cases.[3] The connectionist paradigm focuses on the 'non-distributed perspicuous knowledge representations, and their modification through changing weights of their interconnections' such as Neural Networks (NN) (Michalski and Littman, 1991: 66). The latter state that the chosen paradigm not only depends on the characteristics of the application domain, but also on the researcher's own view of human cognition. General techniques currently being used within symbolic and connectionist methodologies are Rule-Based Reasoning (RBR),[4] Model-Based Reasoning (MBR),[5] and Case-Based Reasoning (CBR) (Symbolic) and Neural Networks (NN)[6] (Connectionist). As stated earlier, ESAS is a case-based intelligent system, and thus utilizes CBR as its AI technique. The rationale for this is based on the complexity of the application domain of TQM and the systems requirement for dealing with dynamism and change. The following section discusses in detail the rationale for adopting CBR over other AI techniques such as RBR, MBR and NN.

Case-based reasoning: the appropriate technique?

Case-based reasoning (CBR) is based on the proposition that human experiences are stored in the human brain in the form of *previous cases*, rather than a set of rules (Riesbeck and Schank, 1989). This implies that experts solve problems through the application of their experience, whereas novices solve problems by applying rules (Watson and Abdullah, 1994).

CBR represents knowledge in the form of cases. Each case represents an experience or episode of an event or task within a domain. Problem-solving and reasoning for CBR are therefore a process of remembering a case or experience which is similar to a new situation, and using the solution within this retrieved case to derive a solution for the new situation. Because CBR represents its domain knowledge by a store of cases, it does not require an explicit domain model as in RBR and MBR, so knowledge acquisition simply becomes a task of gathering case histories to build-up a case-library (Watson, 1995).[7]

Dynamism is a key feature of the application domain. Since CBR is not constrained to a model, it allows the addition and subtraction of *new cases* or *experience* as they arise (i.e. from activities or changes in the environment) without the need of complex debugging as in rule-based reasoning (RBR). In addition, researchers studying TQM and its implications for competitive advantage have stated that no empirically proven model or theory exists that can accurately and confidently represent the domain (Black and Porter, 1996; Matter *et al.*, 1986). Therefore it must be assumed that these theories and models are weak, and that AI approaches that require extensive modelling are not appropriate for ESAS. Research carried out by Dreyfus (1982) that examined the human process of knowledge acquisition for business experts concluded that experts have a superior perceptual ability to grasp or understand a problem quickly, compared to novices. This form of knowledge or intuition allows experts to perform a detailed situation assessment of the new problem, and then use past concrete situations as paradigms, which leads them to the relevant part of the problem, without wasting time deliberating over irrelevant options (Benner, 1984). These findings of expert problem-solving substantiate the work carried out by Schank and Abelson (1977), Schank (1982) and Riesbeck and Schank (1989) in *reminding* and problem-solving through cases.

In addition, an initial investigation into the nature of problem-solving in the domain of study has shown that when addressing strategic quality problems and creating strategies for competitive advantage, managers and strategists do so in a case-based way.[8] When asked how they approach strategic quality problems, they stated that they would search for past problems that have been solved for guidance on how to solve the new problem (see footnote 3). This would involve using information about the new situation (i.e. a problem description) to guide the search for similar cases. Depending on the type and nature of the problem, searching would be carried out on either a store of cases on file (e.g. filing system, wordprocessor files, databases, Quality Management systems), or from memory. The 'best match' case will then be retrieved, adapted, evaluated and repaired until it fits the new situation (Figure 1.1).

Asked why a case-based approach was used during strategic quality problems, the interviewees stated that using past cases avoided the need to return to first principles and bypassed options that have or will fail to produce desired outcomes. As one of the interviewees stated, 'we haven't got the time to start solving problems from scratch'. However, CBR does have its drawbacks. By its nature it can only provide approximate, or partial solutions to problems,[9] and when a best-match past case has been retrieved, its solution almost always needs adaptation to fit the new situation (Kolodoner, 1996; Wan, 1996). Adaptation is an important issue for CBR, and can sometimes be a difficult and complex problem depending on the level of automation of the intelligent system.[10] Rule-based systems on the other hand overcome the issue of adaptation, because they provide users with exact matches to problems and their solutions are usually accepted *verbatim*. RBR systems are also well suited to domains that are well understood, because the rule-base can be developed much more quickly, and the domain can be represented more deeply (Althoff *et al.*, 1995; Kolodoner, 1993). The negative side to these attributes is that any problem outside the rule-base will receive no output and thus no guidance.

MBR also overcomes the problems associated with adaptation, because they hold knowledge about the validation and evaluation of solutions. They do not, however, offer any guidance for construction of solutions to problems (Kolodoner, 1993). Adaptation is not an issue for NN, but their solutions and

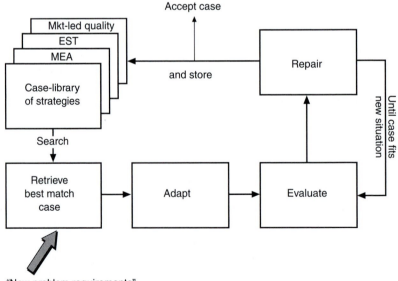

Figure 1.1 CBR process in strategic quality problem-solving.

Source: adapted from Frangou, 1997.

internal workings lack transparency, and the resulting system cannot be easily validated by domain experts (Althoff *et al.*, 1995).

Table 1.2 summarizes the applicability and advantages of using CBR in strategic Quality Management implementation (Frangou, 1997; Frangou *et al.*, 1998; 1999).

ESAS: promoting strategic quality through case-based strategies

The Enterprise Strategic Advisory System is a case-based prototype intelligent system designed to encourage Quality Management specialists to behave more dynamically and strategically with regards to quality improvements. In essence, ESAS acts as a teaching and learning tool, presenting users with case-based strategies that describe both successful and unsuccessful attempts at improving an organization's performance through quality. It is hoped that through this process of case-based consultation, the user is exposed to a broad range of cases from differing industries that emphasize the strategic significance of quality. This heightened strategic awareness, will in turn filter through to quality improvement programmes, where a more innovative approach to quality at a strategic level will be adopted.

The scope and structure of ESAS

ESAS has been implemented on a personal computer (PC) windows platform using a CBR development shell called ReMind™ (Cognitive Systems, 1992). The system has been designed with both public and private sector organizations in mind. ESAS's case-library (case memory) stores over 100 cases that have been collected from a broad range of organizations. Collaborating organizations included those operating in healthcare, manufacturing, higher education, finance and insurance, information systems, and the judicial system. Case data was sourced from senior managers and two directors with specific responsibility for influencing and developing quality policies. Cases were collected through interviews and postal surveys. The case collection process focused on episodical data that described how managers went about addressing strategic quality problems and decision-making. Specific emphasis was placed on the key driving issues raised, i.e. strategic quality, focus and dynamism. From this perspective past case data that described the process of market environmental analysis (MEA) and enterprise strategy (EST), and their importance and impact on quality policy was targeted (Frangou *et al.*, 1999). The scope of ESAS is based around these two business tasks as illustrated in Figure 1.2.

Figure 1.2 illustrates ESAS's system conceptual framework (SCF), which specifies the boundaries of the system and the proportion of the problem domain it covers. The SCF also highlights the type and nature of the cases that need to be stored within the systems case-library. It is the product of a detailed problem domain task analysis that examined the business tasks outlined above, i.e. MEA

Table 1.2 Advantages of using CBR for Strategic Quality Management (SQM)

No explicit domain model exists, and current modelling techniques are inadequate as the market environment is ever changing and so complex. CBR does not require an explicit model, so knowledge elicitation is achieved by acquiring cases (Watson, 1995)

'Strategic planning is heuristic and judgmental in nature with knowledge not being as structured as in the form of production rules' (Arunkumar and Janakiram, 1992). Studies into the nature of business expertise and problem-solving show that it is case-based (Dreyfus, 1982). This suggests that the problem domain is more suited to CBR techniques than MBR or RBR

CBR systems have the ability to grow and learn as new knowledge becomes available. This feature is relevant to the problem domain, because as market changes are experienced, these new cases can be simply inputted into the system. This would not be easy for rule or model base systems, because the updating process would require complex debugging for the inclusion of new knowledge. Therefore CBR systems are easier to maintain (Frangou *et al.*, 1997)

Inexperienced users who lack in-depth domain knowledge, may find CBR more user-friendly since they have the ability to retrieve cases, whether or not the user has inputted *all* the necessary problem situation data (Watson, 1995; Wan, 1996)

CBR systems are less expensive and time consuming to build than model or rule-based systems. It is claimed that RBR systems are around eight times more costly to build than CBR systems (Simoudis and Miller, 1991; Simoudis, 1992). This is because the cost of knowledge acquisition and knowledge-base validation is low

Experts find it difficult to articulate the domain rules involved in their problem-solving, finding it easier to talk about their experiences, or tell stories that describe their experience. CBR is an approach that can support this form of case collection (Slator and Riesbeck, 1992)

In CBR every new problem solved can be stored within the case-library thus enabling it to grow with the user and organization. It can also store both 'successful' and 'unsuccessful' cases which facilitates learning. RBR systems waste problem-solving interactions because there is no way for the experience to be stored (Leake, 1996; Slator and Riesbeck, 1992)

Confidence in the advice given by CBR systems is higher than RBR or NN because the retrieved solutions are based on actual transparent cases. In RBR decisions are based on a chain of rules, which may have no meaning to the user. Also, if a RBR system provides incorrect solutions, it will do so until the chain of rules are corrected. Worst still in NN the solutions lack transparency completely (Riesbeck, 1988)

The quality of solutions from CBR systems is higher than RBR systems because 'cases reflect what really happens in a given set of circumstances' (Leake, 1996). Furthermore, the latest up-to-date evidence or knowledge within a domain can be stored as cases even though it has not been formalized (Hunter, 1986)

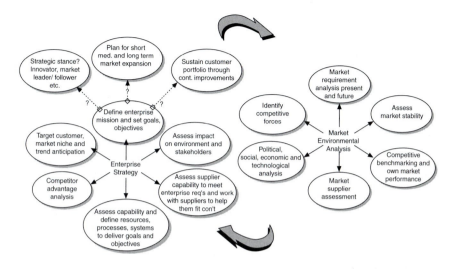

Figure 1.2 ESAS scope and domain coverage – *System Conceptual Framework (SCF)*.
Source: adapted from Frangou, 1997.

and EST within a TQM context (see page 7). The SCF is further underpinned by the Malcolm Baldridge National Quality Award (NIST, 1997), the strategic and marketing concepts and processes as defined by Porter (1982; 1985), Johnson and Scholes (1997), Bhide (1994), Mintzberg (1994), Hamel and Prahalad (1994), and the strategic quality perspective as described by Garvin (1988) and Bounds *et al.* (1994). In addition the SCF was also validated using input from the project's collaborators as referred to earlier.

The structure of ESAS is based around the SCF and is modular in form to aid user consultation. In addition, the modular structure allows greater flexibility when searching for task specific problems. Thus quality improvement efforts can be prioritized and focused. The initial structure of ESAS consisted of two main task modules as described by the SCF. However, initial collaborator feedback highlighted the need to broaden ESAS's appeal by focusing on the *market-led quality* condition alluded to earlier. This enables users to search for specific case examples relating to market-led quality problems, but not to necessitate system redesign; rather selective case collection as directed by the MEA SCF task. In addition, a fourth module has been implemented to assist with general problem-solving sessions associated with novice users. These four domain task modules have been implemented to guide the search process during strategic quality problem-solving and decision-making as illustrated in Figure 1.3.

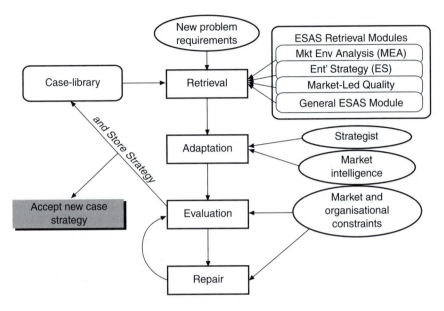

Figure 1.3 ESAS structure.

Source: adapted from Frangou *et al.*, 1999.

Case data analysis

This SCF formed the basis of a case collection questionnaire that was used in both the interview process and the postal surveys. Collected case data was analysed using (1) the case analysis (Patton, 1990) approach as described by Bell and Hardiman (1989), and (2) the guidelines as described by Kolodoner (1993). Kolodoner (1993: 13) states 'a case is a contextualized piece of know-ledge representing an experience that teaches a lesson fundamental to achieving the goals of the reasoner', that has three main parts; a problem description, a solution and an outcome. In the context of this research, a case would have the following components:

- *Problem description:* provides a problem situation assessment by describing the problem at hand – i.e. 'We have experienced a drop in sales through increased competition...',
- *Solution:* describes the strategy taken to solve the problem, i.e. 'To over-come this increase in competition we...',
- *Outcome:* describes the state of the world, after the solution has been imple-mented, i.e. 'Our strategy was successful, we were able to reverse our loss in sales, and recover our market position...'.

The above framework was applied to the case data, to elicit cases suitable for ESAS. An example stored case is presented in Figure 1.4.

Problem description
Competitors have introduced a new product/service that has threatened our current business. We have subsequently lost ground in the market, because it is considered more positively by the market. This is because our competitor's product uses new technology, which is perceived to be far superior to ours. Subsequently, our products are now perceived as 'outdated', the result being that our position in the marketplace has been seriously damaged.

Solution:
Consumers have been attracted to the new product/service, because they perceive it to be 'modern' and thus superior. We embarked on a comparative advertising campaign to highlight the benefit of our product over the competitions. The aim of this campaign was to inform consumers of the benefits of our technology, so that its advantages are understood. Various mediums were used such as TV, trade magazines, newspapers, posters etc to raise the profile of both the product range and company. We were able to change the consumers' perception of products available and their associated technology. Attention was placed on the quality and ease of use of our product in comparison to competitors.

Outcome:
The campaign was successful from a strategic aspect, in that it took our competitor by surprise. We were able to undermine current myths about the technologies used, by educating the consumer of the certain aspects of our product and the service that it delivers. Subsequently our company experienced a 50% increase in sales.

Figure 1.4 Case describing an experience of 'competitor threat' via new product release.
Source: adapted from Frangou, 1997.

Case-library development

CBR falls within the symbolic paradigm of AI, in that it uses symbolic representations to derive inferences, where cases are used to represent domain knowledge in the form described in Figure 1.4. However, case representation within a system requires careful consideration, in that a cases' structure must include the following: (1) some form of symbolic representation for computational purposes (i.e. what the system uses to index, match and retrieve with), and (2) some form of user-orientated representation that is required by the user to reach their decision-making goal. ReMind addresses case representation issues in two ways. (1) for symbolic representation, it allows developers to generate symbol hierarchies which graphically represent the concepts, relations, facts and principles that define the problem domain (Sowa, 1984). This is used to underpin the case representation and operationalize case indexing and retrieval.

Figure 1.5 illustrates the symbol hierarchy which essentially represents generalizations and specializations within the problem domain, and defines issues that can influence the ability of an organization to create a competitive advantage through strategic quality (Frangou *et al.*, 1999).

In all, eleven main symbol classifications have been derived from the case data. These are all related to an organizations structure, capabilities, performance and strategic options for strategic quality improvements, and includes the

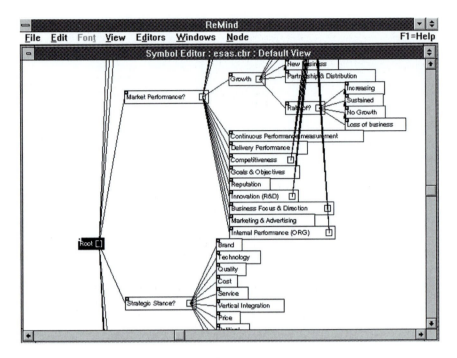

Figure 1.5 Symbol hierarchy within ESAS.

Source: adapted from Frangou *et al.*, 1998.

following: business type, market environment description, measure of market performance, supplier performance, strategic stance, organizational structure, relative strategic time-scales, acceptable risk-level for strategic options, evaluation of strategic option, case source, and ESAS consultation mode (to prioritize case retrieval) (Frangou *et al.*, 1999).

(2) for user-orientated representation ReMind uses a form-like representation consisting of 42 case fields slots that define the various features that make up a case[11] as shown in Figure 1.6.

Case indexing and retrieval

Case indexes are essentially important weightings that are applied to key features so that cases can be stored effectively within the case memory, and so that they can easily be retrieved when required. During *nearest neighbour* (NNR) case retrieval,[12] a numerical evaluation function is used to search and find a best case match between the new problem case and a stored solved case. In practice, the user inputs a new problem case using the form-like case editor shown in Figure 1.6, by describing the case via the defined case features. The consultation process and thus case retrieval involves the assessment of similarity between the

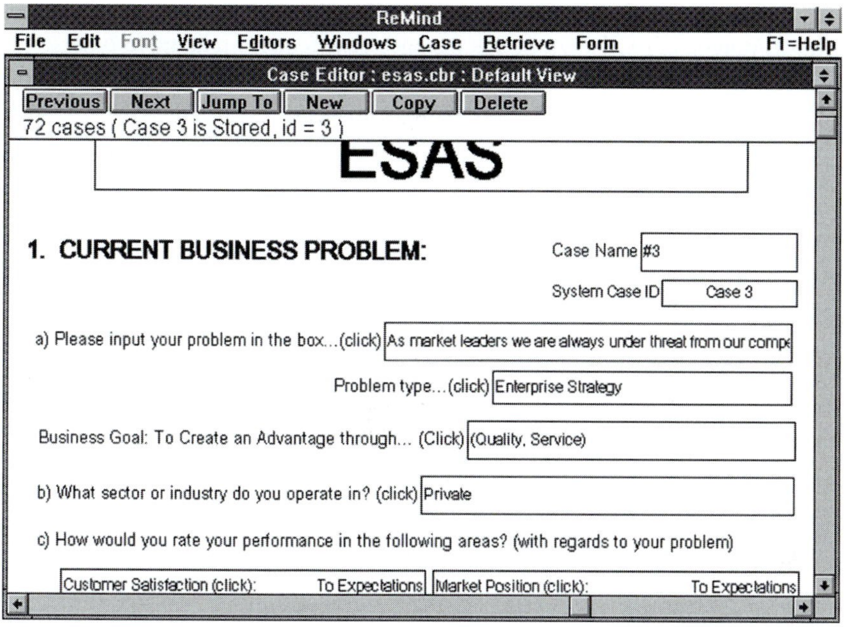

Figure 1.6 Form-like user oriented case representation.
Source: adapted from Frangou, 1997.

new case and stored cases, by comparing the weighted case features in the new case to those of the case-memory, the scale of case match being determined by these weights. The product of retrieval is a presentation of the best matching cases ranked according to their match aggregate score (Frangou *et al.*, 1999).

Case adaptation, evaluation and repair

One of the disadvantages of CBR is that retrieved cases very rarely provide an exact match to the new problem case. Case adaptation is a process which addresses this problem by allowing the user to make the necessary changes to the retrieved case so that it can fit the situation described within the new problem case. In practice, adaptation effects key ESAS case features associated with the business context of each problem. These include features that describe conditions or constraints that are associated with the type of industry in which the problem has arisen, or the range of business goals available or acceptable to the industry. In addition, these changes will also affect a retrieved case's proposed solution and related features. These may include both symbolic or textual features that describe strategies for addressing the problem. For example, if ESAS's response to a pharmaceutical problem relating to an increase in drug development was a retrieved case proposing a rapid product development strategy as in the PC market, some elements of the case may be unacceptable due to industry regulatory forces enforcing lengthy R&D life-cycles and clinical trials (Frangou *et al.*, 1999). In this instance case features relating to time scales and new product testing will require modification.

Case evaluation and repair is an iterative process which governs case adaptation to ensure that changes are legal or acceptable to the industry (see Figure 1.1). In the context of the pharmaceutical example above, *evaluation* will ensure that adaptations to proposed time scales and strategies for market testing are in line with current industry regulation. If they are not, further repairs to the case will be actioned and then evaluated until all the conditions of the new case are met, and the case accepted.

System implementation of case adaptation, evaluation and repair is at present manual. This is due to the complexity of the application domain, the lack of any robust domain model, and the nature of strategic decision-making (which is intuitive and judgmental in nature). Furthermore, as strategic quality planning is a high risk process performed by humans, it is advisable that case adaptation remain a manual process. In addition, leaving adaptation to users will both encourage system utilization and trust, and enhance the interactive problem and learning process that is a key feature of the system (Frangou *et al.*, 1999).

System evaluation

Intelligent systems evaluation has generally taken the *verification* and *validation* (V&V) route. In principle V&V is concerned with system quality from the perspective of design specification and correctness (Sharma and Conrath, 1992). Its emergence as a technique has coincided with the growing complexities of AI systems. In particular V&V techniques are commonly used to determine the *correctness, completeness and consistency* of inference rules that form the chains of reasoning within rule-based systems (Klein and Methlie, 1995). Critics of traditional evaluation techniques argue that V&V is only part of the evaluation equation, as it ignores the function and role of intelligent systems in the decision-making environment (Hollnagel, 1989). Therefore, system quality must be concerned with more than just the quality of the decisions or advice its giving, or whether or not its knowledge-base is a faithful representation of the problem domain.

Sharma and Conrath (1992) propose a social-technical model of system evaluation, in which a holistic view of 'total quality' is a key consideration. This approach provides the foundation for ESAS's evaluation programme. Using a global definition of quality such as the British Standards BS4778 (1991), and the guidelines given by Sharma and Conrath (1992), a holistic approach was taken to identify key system performance criteria. These were described in terms of 'fit' (Curet and Jackson, 1995) and included the following (Frangou *et al.*, 1999):

- *Task-fit:* How well does the system support the task it is designed to support? Does the system provide clear, concise advice on the major task components? Is the system effective?

- *Domain-fit:* Does the systems approach, range of cases in memory, or case vocabulary represent the problem domain effectively?
- *User-fit:* Does the system support the type of decision-making and problem-solving tasks carried out by the target user? System-user interaction is the main focus, effective presentation of case information, ease of use, operational and interface problems and issues etc.
- *Organizational-fit:* How well does ESAS fit the target implementation environment? What about the technology's acceptance, and confidence between its users and sponsors? What impact will the system have on training and overall firm performance?

ESAS was evaluated by senior managers from a variety of organizations representing healthcare, manufacturing, education, IT, and the judicial system. The above four evaluation criteria were used to generate a questionnaire that provided the basis of the test. The system evaluation procedure followed a 'hands-on' approach in an interactive interview setting using five evaluators[13] (Frangou *et al.*, 1999). The first stage of the evaluation centred mainly on the system's ability to retrieve a 'good' or match cases given a randomly selected set of test cases. This test was based on Goodman's (1989) 10/90 test that uses 10 per cent of the case-libraries as test cases. System performance was categorized as hits, misses or not-sure by evaluators. The systems ability to provide advice for a real world problem was also assessed using a known marketing strategy case-study.[14]

Analysis of the evaluation results

The results of the systems evaluation for the four main criteria are displayed in Table 1.3. In addition, ESAS achieved the scores in Table 1.3 which represent critical measures for the following:

Table 1.3 Evaluation results for ESAS

Main test criteria	Percentage score (per cent)
Task-fit	72.2
Domain-fit	79.8
Organizational-fit	67
User-fit	70.2

Sub-test criteria	Percentage score (per cent)
10/90 test	60.3
Case-study test	76
Problem-solving capability	68.6
Teaching and learning capability	86.3

Total system performance score 71.4 per cent

- 10/90 and real world case-study retrieval tests, part of the task-fit criteria;
- systems problem-solving and teaching and learning capabilities rating, part of the organizational-fit;
- the systems ability to satisfy its main objectives and its potential business goals;
- overall system performance.

In general, feedback from evaluators indicated that the system's case retrieval modules were performing well in the tests. However, the 10/90 score of 60.3 per cent indicates only an above average performance for case retrieval. Further analysis showed that evaluators had difficulty in assessing the degree of match in some cases, where 7.7 per cent of retrieved cases were categorized as 'not-sure'. This was due to some cases lacking sufficient detail to make a full assessment.[15] ESAS faired better in the real world case-study test scoring 76 per cent.

The reason for this improvement in performance was the addition of company specific information in the test case, which made assessment of case match easier.

As a tool designed to support both problem-solving and teaching and learning within organizations, ESAS scored 68.6 per cent and 86.3 per cent respectively. This result in one respect substantiates the view that a system designed to promote 'good practice' or encourage a change in behaviour is more acceptable than a system that prescribes finite solutions (see earlier).

Conclusion and future research possibilities

This chapter has attempted to highlight the potential of intelligent systems technology, notably case-based reasoning (CBR) in relation to business and strategic quality applications. By reviewing the concept of case-based intelligent systems, and discussing the major development and evaluation issues in building ESAS, it is hoped that managers will be encouraged to consider the potential of such systems for supporting strategic business processes.

ESAS's principal aim is to challenge how organizations go about implementing quality improvements, by emphasizing the strategic significance of quality for competitive advantage. The system achieves this by engaging the user in a case-based consultation process, where they are presented with a range of real-world strategies that describe how a broad range of organizations have attempted to create an advantage through quality. This generic capability is crucial to the proactive and lateral approach prescribed by the ESAS concept. An example of this is the initial reluctance of one senior manager, who could not see the benefit of using case-based quality strategies originating from a different industry. However, through the consultation process, this evaluator was presented with a case solution from a different industry that provided a good match to a current strategic quality problem in his/her organization. In addition, ESAS also stores both good and bad examples of practice (Frangou *et al.*, 1999). This is an essential teaching and learning feature that benefits users in terms of professional and skill-base growth. Furthermore, in terms of organizational learning and knowledge management issues, case-based systems such as ESAS can help to ensure that valuable expertise is not lost, and is used effectively and efficiently company-wide for competitive leverage.

In terms of performance, ESAS has produced positive results. Most evaluators found the system easy to use and efficient, and practical in its approach in supporting problem-solving and decision-making processes. But most of all, ESAS was able to encourage lateral thinking in problem-solving and decision-making, which is a fundamental objective of the system. Weaknesses were raised about the system's interface, which is outdated and sometimes hindered case presentation and system navigation. Also, in some instances stored cases lacked enough depth to provide detailed advice on certain problems. Evaluators also pointed out that the generic capabilities of the system, may cause some inexperienced users problems in terms of industry terminology – here a glossary of terms would help.

Current efforts are being made to address the limitations highlighted by ESAS's evaluation. Various CBR development shells such as KATE, ESTEEM, ART*Enterprise and KnowMan are readily available that enable both graphical user interface construction and multimedia integration. Redeveloping ESAS around these tools will go some way to rectify its current interface limitations, and improve its teaching and learning capabilities through the use of interactive multimedia. Efforts are also being made at increasing the depth of advice that cases provide. This includes storing more cases from the public domain, and the addition of more company/industry specific data.

An emerging key theme from this research is the apparent lack of case-based intelligent systems applications in business and management. This is a point clearly made by ESAS's evaluators, and in particular the potential of developing case-based intelligent systems for supporting a range of business processes. Such applications present great extensive opportunities for business and academia, both in terms of competitive enhancement and contribution to knowledge (Frangou *et al.*, 1999).

Notes

1 A case-based intelligent system emulates human problem-solving via the uses of past case examples of problem-solving. The associated technology will be explained in detail later on in the chapter.

2 In terms of a reduction in customer complaints and increase in new customer orders.

3 These representations are symbolic in nature for computational purposes. Symbol and symbol structures can be construed as standing for various concepts and relationships within the problem domain (Jackson, 1990).

4 In *rule-based reasoning* (RBR) systems, knowledge is represented as a *production system* or a set of production rules. These rules take the form of condition-action pairs: 'IF this condition occurs, THEN ... will occur' (Turban, 1993). RBR is AI's traditional view of human cognition, which suggests that intelligent behaviour is generally rule-governed (Jackson, 1990) and is founded on Newell and Simon's (1972) model of human cognition.

5 *Model-based reasoning* (MBR) is similar to CBR in that both techniques use large

chunks of knowledge to base decisions on, rather than reasoning from scratch as in RBR. They differ in the type of knowledge used during reasoning – in MBR casual models represent general domain knowledge, whereas CBR uses cases that represent specific knowledge (Kolodoner, 1993: 97).

6   *Neural networks* (NN) are based on a 'connectionist' theory which suggests a model of human behaviour based on the structure of the human brain (Kluytmans *et al.*, 1993). A NN is a network of highly interconnected parallel processing elements called artificial neurons (or nodes), which simulate the neurons in the human brain (Mockler and Dologite, 1992; Freeman and Skapura, 1991).

7   This has obvious benefits for the knowledge engineer (KE) in that CBR overcomes the disadvantages associated with traditional knowledge acquisition such as the 'the bottleneck' of AI systems development which includes: the formulizing of rules within weak-theory domains, the difficulty of experts articulating rules governing problem-solving, validation and verification of the rule-base, and human expert time and access constraints.

8   A pilot survey of senior managers and specialists responsible for strategic quality who represented IT, process, manufacturing, computer, healthcare, finance, insurance, judicial and HE sectors was conducted to assess the suitability of a CBR approach.

9   However, this gap is minimized through adaptation.

10 In order for adaptation to work efficiently adaptation methods that are consistent with the domain have to be implemented. Both heuristics and commonsense techniques can be used for adaptation depending on the system being built. These issues will be explored further later.

11 To derive associated case features and domain symbols a combination of conceptual analysis (Sowa, 1984) and case analysis (Patton, 1990) was used.

12 Inductive retrieval (IR) is another technique that can be used within CBR. It involves the clustering of cases according to specified indexes. Clustering creates a hierarchical structure in the form of a discrimination network. Cases that are similar to one another are clustered together to form a tree. Case retrieval is achieved by traversing across the tree and comparing the new case against those stored in the tree. This speeds up retrieval because unlike NNM, only those cases stored in the tree are matched against. IR is best suited to applications that use very large case-libraries and speed. However, because IR does not search the whole library important cases could be missed. This, together with the fact that speed is not an issue for ESAS, means that NNM is the most suitable technique.

13 Five evaluators were involved in the system testing – these specialists represented the following sectors: Judicial System, IT, NHS, Manufacturing and Higher Education.

14 A test case describing a real world situation was used to test ESAS's ability to solve a strategic problem. This test case focused on a competitive battle between two companies producing bulldozers – Caterpillar and Komatsu, and the loss of competitive advantage.

15 To maintain confidentiality among case data sources, company names were not included in each case.

References

Althoff, K-D., Auriol, E., Barletta, R. and Manago, M. (1995) *A Review of Industrial Case-Based Reasoning Tools*. Oxford: AI Intelligence.

American Quality Foundation and Ernst & Young (1991) *International Quality Study: The Definitive Study of the Best International Quality Management Practices*. Cleveland, OH: Ernst & Young.

Atkinson, P. (1990) *Creating Culture Change: The Key to Successful Total Quality Management*. Bedford: IFS Publications.

Bell, J. and Hardiman, R.J. (1989) The third role – the naturalistic knowledge engineer. In D. Diaper (ed.), *Knowledge Elicitation – Principles, Techniques and Applications.* Chichester: Ellis Horwood, 49–85.

Benner, P.E. (1984) *From Novice to Expert: Excellence and Power in Clinical Nursing Practice.* Menlo Park, California; London: Addison-Wesley.

Bhide, A. (1994) How entrepreneurs craft strategies that work, *Harvard Business Review*, March–April, 150–61.

Bird, J. (1997) Strategy in a box, *Management Today*, May, 77–83.

Black, S.A. and Porter, L.J. (1996) Identification of critical factors of TQM, *Decision Sciences* **27**(1), Winter, 1–21.

Bounds, G., Yorks, L., Adams, M. and Ranney, G. (1994) *Beyond Total Quality Management: Toward the Emerging Paradigm.* New York; London; McGraw-Hill.

Boyce, G. (1992) Why quality programs aren't and how they could be, *Business Quarterly*, Autumn, 57–64.

Brelin, H., Davenport, K., Jennings, L. and Murphy, P. (1996) Bringing quality into focus, *Security Management* **40**(2), February, 23–4.

Brown, M.G., Hitchcock, D.E. and Willard, M.L. (1994) *Why TQM Fails and What To Do About It.* Illinois: Irwin Professional Publishing.

Brown, S. (1996) *Strategic Manufacturing for Competitive Advantage: Transforming Operations from Shop Floor to Strategy.* London: Prentice-Hall.

BS 4778 (1991) *Quality Vocabulary: Part 2. Quality Concepts and Related Definitions.* British Standards Institute, 389 Chiswick High Road, London W4 4AL.

Butz, H.E. (1995) Strategic planning: the missing link in TQM, *Quality Progress*, May, 105–8.

Buzzell, R.D. and Gale, B.T. (1987) *The PIMS Principles: Linking Strategies to Performance.* New York: Free Press.

Candlin, D.B. and Day, P.J. (1993) Introducing TQM in a service industry, *Quality Forum* **19**(3), 133–42.

Capon, N., Farley, J.V. and Hoening, S. (1990) Determinants of financial performance: a meta-analysis, *Management Science* **36**(10), 1143–59.

Cognitive Systems Inc. (1992) *Remind Development Shell: Developers Reference Manual.* Boston: Cognitive Systems Inc.

Conti, T. (1997) Optimizing self-assessment. In *Total Quality Management Special Issue: Proceedings of the 2nd World Congress for Total Quality Management – The Quality Journey*, Sheffield, July, S5–S15.

Cottrell, J. (1992) Favourable recipe. *TQM Journal,* February, 17–20.

Curet, O. and Jackson, M. (1995) Tackling cognitive biases in the detection of top management fraud with the use of case-based reasoning. In *Proceedings of Expert Systems the 15th Annual Technical Conference of the BCSSG on ES*, December, Cambridge, 223–36.

Curry, D.J. (1985) Measuring price and quality competition, *Journal of Marketing* **49**, April, 106–17.

Davis, T.R.V. (1992) Conference report – Baldridge winners link quality, strategy, and financial management, *Planning Review*, Nov/Dec, 36–40.

Davis, J., Khodabocus, F. and Obray, C. (1996) Self-assessment: a path to business excellence, *Quality World: Technical Supplement*, March, 4–11.

Dreyfus, S.E. (1982) Formal models vs. human situational understanding: inherent limitations on the modelling of business expertise, *Office: Technology & People* **1**, 133–65.

Dyason, M. and Kaye, M.M. (1996) Achieving a competitive edge through strategic measurement, *Proceedings of the 1996 Learning Edge Conference,* European Foundation for Quality Management, 379–90.

Edgell, N. and Kochhar, A. (1992) BS 5750 quality assurance system – a knowledge based approach to system audit and implementation, *3rd International Conference on Factory 2000. Competitive Performance through advanced Technology,* 27–29 July 1992, 87–94.

Erickson, T.J. (1992) Beyond TQM: creating the high performance business, *Management Review,* 58–61.

Foster, M. and Whittle, S, (1989) The Quality Management maze. *TQM Journal,* May, 143–8.

Foster, M. and Beardon, S. (1993) Caring for more than health, *Managing Service Quality,* May, 143–8.

Frangou, A.J. (1997) *ESAS: Towards a Case-Based Intelligent System for Competitive Advantage.* Ph.D. Thesis, University of Portsmouth: UK, November.

Frangou, A.J., Yan, W., Antony, J. and Kaye, M.M. (1998) ESAS: A case-based approach to business planning and monitoring, *Expert Systems: The International Journal of Knowledge Engineering and Neural networks* **15**(3), 182–96.

Frangou, A.J., Antony, J. Kaye, M.M. and Wan, Y. (1999) Towards a case-based intelligent system for competitive advantage, accepted for publication in *The New Review of Applied Expert Systems,* Vol. 5.

Freeman, J.A. and Skapura, D.M. (1991) *Neural Networks: Algorithms, Applications and Programming Techniques.* Reading, Mass: Addison-Wesley.

GAO (1991) *Management Practices: U.S. Companies Improve Performance through Quality Efforts.* Washington D.C., General Accounting Office, GAO/NSIAD-91-190.

Gallaher, H. (1991) Avoiding the pitfalls, *Total Quality Management,* June, 157–60.

Goodman, M. (1989) CBR in battle planning. In *Proceedings: Workshop on Case-based Reasoning (DARPA), Pensacola Beach, Florida.* San Mateo, CA: Morgan Kaufmann, 264–9.

Guida, G. and Tasso, C. (1995) *Design and Development of Knowledge-Based Systems: From Life-Cycle to Methodology.* Chichester: John Wiley & Sons.

Hamel, G. and Prahalad, C.K. (1993) Strategy as stretch and leverage, *Harvard Business View,* Mar.–Apr., 75–84.

Hollnagel, E. (1989) Evaluation of expert systems. In G. Guida and C. Tassos (eds), *Topics in Expert Systems Design Methodologies and Tools.* Amsterdam: Elsevier/North-Holland.

Hubiak, W.A. and O'Donnell, S.J. (1996) Do Americans have their minds set against TQM? *National Productivity Review,* Summer, 19–32.

Hunter, L. (1986) There was this guy: anecdotes in medicine, *Biology in Medicine* **29**, 619–30.

Iacobucci, D. (1996) The quality improvement customers didn't want, *Harvard Business Review,* Jan.–Feb., 20–36.

Jackson, P. (1990) *Introduction to Expert Systems* (2nd edn). Wokingham: Addison-Wesley.

Jacobson, R. and Aaker, D.A. (1987) The strategic role of product quality, *Journal of Marketing* **51** Oct., 31–44.

Johnson, G. and Scholes, K. (1997) *Exploring corporate strategy: text and cases,* 4th ed. – London: Prentice Hall.

Johnson, H. (1993) 'There's no more "doubting" Thomases here', *Journal for Quality and Participation,* June, 10–16.

Klein, M.R. and Methlie, L.B. (1995) *Knowledge-based Decision Support Systems* (2nd edn). Chichester: John Wiley & Sons.

Kluytmans, J., Wierenga, B. and Spigt, M. (1993) Developing a neural network for selection of sales promotion instruments in different market situations, *Proceedings of The Second Annual International Conference on Artificial Applications on Wall Street: Tactical & Strategic Technologies*, 19–22 April, New York, Software Engineering Press, 160–4.

Knights, D. and McCabe, D. (1997) How would you measure something like that? *Journal of Management Studies* **34**(3), 371–88.

Kolodoner, J. (1993) *Case-based Reasoning*. Morgan Kaufmann.

Kolodoner, J. (1996) Clarifying the principles of CBR. In D. Leake, *Case Based Reasoning: Experiences, Lessons & Future Directions*, California: The MIT Press, 349–70.

Lakhe, R.R. and Mohanty, R.P. (1994) Understanding TQM, *Production Planning and Control* **5**, 426–41.

Law, P. and Cousins, L. (1991) Is quality market-led? *Proceedings of the British Academy of Management Conference 1991*, Bath: BAM.

Leake, D.B. (1996) CBR in context: the present and future. In D. Leake *Case Based Reasoning: Experiences, Lessons & Future Directions*, California: The MIT Press, 3–30.

Leonard, F.S. and Sasser, W.E. (1982) The incline of quality, *Harvard Business Review*, Sept.–Oct., 163–71.

Matter, K., Davis, J., Mayer, R. and Conlon, E. (1996) Research questions on the implementation of TQM, *Total Quality Management* **7**(1), 39–49.

Michalski, R.S. and Littman, D.C. (1991) Future directions of artificial intelligence in a resource-limited environment. In P.A. Flach and R.A. Meersman (eds), *Future Directions in Artificial Intelligence*, IFIP TC12 Founding Workshop Collected Papers, Amsterdam, North-Holland, 63–9.

Mintzberg, H. (1994) *The Rise and Fall of Strategic Planning*. New York; London: Prentice-Hall.

Mockler, R.J. and Dologite, D.G. (1992) *Knowledge based systems: An Introduction to Expert Systems* (2nd edn). New York: Macmillan.

Morgan, N.A. and Piercy, N.F. (1996) Competitive advantage, quality strategy and the role of marketing, *British Journal of Management* **7**, 231–45.

Morgan, G. (1992) Proactive management. In D. Mercers (ed.), *Managing the External Environment*. London: The Open University and Sage, 24–37.

Newell, A. and Simon, H.A. (1972) *Human Problem Solving*. Englewood Cliffs, NJ: Prentice-Hall.

NIST, The National Institute of Standards and Technology (1997) *The Malcolm Baldridge Quality Award 1997: Criteria for Performance Excellence*, Gaithersburg, MD 20899-0001, USA, NIST.

O'Neal, C.R. and Lafief, W.C. (1992) Marketing's lead role in total quality, *Industrial Marketing Management* **21**, 133–43.

Patton, M.Q. (1990) *Qualitative Evaluation and Research Methods* (2nd edn). London: Sage.

Porter, M.E. (1985) *Competitive Advantage: Creating and Sustaining Superior Performance*. New York: The Free Press.

Porter, M.E. (1982) *Competitive Strategy: Techniques for Analysing Industries and Competitors*. New York: The Free Press.

Porter, M.E. (1996) What is Strategy?, *Harvard Business Review*, Nov.–Dec., 61–78.

Powell, T.C. (1995) Total Quality Management as competitive advantage: a review and empirical study, *Strategic Management Journal* **16**, 15–37.

Reed, R., Lemark, D.J. and Montgomery, J.C. (1996) Beyond process: TQM content and firm performance, *Academy of Management Review* **21**(1), 173–202.

Riesbeck, C. (1988) An interface for case-based knowledge acquisition. In J. Kolodoner (ed.), *Proceedings of the DARPA Case-Based Reasoning Workshop*, Morgan Kaufmann, 312–26.

Riesbeck, C.K. and Schank, R.C. (1989) *Inside Case-Based Reasoning*. Hillsdale: Lawrence Erlbaum Associates.

Schaffer, R.H. and Thomson, H. (1992) Successful change programmes begin with results, *Harvard Business Review*, Jan.–Feb., 80–9.

Schank, R.C. (1982) *Dynamic Memory: A Theory of Learning in Computers and People*. New York: Cambridge University Press.

Schank, R.C. (1990) What is AI anyway? In D. Partridge and Y. Wilks (eds), *The Foundation of Artificial Intelligence: A Sourcebook*. Cambridge, Cambridge University Press, 3–13.

Schank, R.C. and Abelson, R.P. (1977) *Scripts, Plans and Understanding*. Hillsdale, NJ: Lawrence Erlbaum Associates.

Schmalensee, D.H. (1991) Marketers must lead quality improvements or risk becoming irrelevant, *Services Marketing Newsletter* **7**(1), 1–3.

Seddon, J. (1992) A successful attitude, *Managing Service Quality*, July, 81–4.

Sharma, R.S. and Conrath, D.W. (1992) Evaluating expert systems: the social-technical dimensions of quality, *Expert Systems* **9**(3), August, 125–37.

Simoudis, E. (1992) Knowledge acquisition in validated retrieval, *International Journal of Expert Systems* **4**(3), 299–315.

Simoudis, E. and Miller, J. (1991) The application of CBR to help-desk applications. In R. Bareiss (ed.), *Proceedings of the DARPA Case-based Reasoning Workshop*, Morgan Kaufmann, 25–36.

Sowa, J.F. (1984) *Conceptual Structures: Information Processing in Mind and Machine*. Addison-Wesley.

Tatikonda, L.U. and Tatikonda, R.J. (1996) Measuring and reporting the cost of quality, *Production and Inventory Management Journal*, 2nd Quarter, 1–7.

Tilson, D. (1989) Making progress. In PA Consulting Group, *Quality in Financial Services-European Retail Finance for the 1990's*. London: Economist Publications.

Turban, E. (1993) *Decision Support and Expert Systems: Management Support Systems* (3rd edn). New York: Macmillan.

Walker, T. (1992) Creating total quality improvements that last, *National Productivity Review*, Autumn, 473–8.

Wan, Y. (1996) *Cost Estimation of Sewage Treatment Systems Using Artificial Intelligence*, PhD thesis, University of Portsmouth, UK, March.

Watson, I. (1995) An introduction to case-based reasoning. In *Proceedings of the 1st UK CBR Workshop*, The BCS Specialist Group on ES, University of Salford, 12 Jan.

Watson, I. and Abdullah, S. (1994) Developing case-based reasoning systems: a case study in diagnosing building defects, *Colloquium on Case Based Reasoning: Prospects for Applications*, London, Thursday, 3 March, IEE.

Wiele der, T.V., Dale, B., Williams, R., Kolb, F., Luzon, D.M., Schmidt, A. and Wallace, M. (1995) State-of-the-art study on self-assessment, *The TQM Magazine* **7**(4), 13–17.

Wilkinson, A. and Willmott, H. (1995) Introduction. In A. Wilkinson and H. Willmott (eds), *Making Quality Critical: New Perspectives on Organizational Change*. London: Routledge, 1–32.

Wilkinson, A.W., McCabe, D. and Knights, D. (1996) Looking for quality: a survey of quality initiatives in the financial services sector, *Total Quality Management* **7**(1), 67–78.

Wisner, J.D. and Eakins, S.G. (1994) A performance assessment of the U.S. Baldridge quality award winners, *International Journal of Quality and Reliability Management* **11**(2), 8–25.

2 Self-assessment frameworks for business organizations

Ashok Kumar and Ceasar Douglas

Introduction

Business organizations have engaged in periodic assessment of their performance since the beginning of the industrial era. However, until the early 1980s, the process of self-assessment was largely an individual undertaking. Each business carved out its own design of the assessment process that suited its needs and environment. Such customized assessments, and the resulting course corrections, however, turned out to be grossly inadequate in terms of providing the strategic advantage that was expected from the self-assessment. The early 1980s witnessed Japanese industries strategically assaulting American and European companies with unprecedented ferocity and taking large chunks of market share, particularly in automobile and electronic industry. Several studies by westerners ascribed the substantial Japanese gains in competitive grounds primarily to 'a triumph of sheer manufacturing virtuosity' (Hayes and Pisano, 1996). There is wide agreement about what caused the mass market movement towards Japanese products during the 1970s and 1980s. It was not the relatively low cost of their products or protection available from Japanese government, as had been conveniently conjectured by many industrial experts, instead, it was the sizeably low incidence of defects, high reliability, and durability of their products that triggered the momentum in favour of the Japanese companies (ibid.).

The loss of significant competitive turf on part of American manufacturing companies triggered several actions. First, American and Western European business strategists uniformly converged upon the conclusion that they could no longer divorce a well thought out, conscious, deliberate operations strategy from their parent corporate strategy formulations. Secondly, operations strategists found themselves looking for new paradigms of operations strategy that duly factored in quality and other dimensions of competition, e.g., flexibility and delivery, in addition to price, in formulating their overall strategies. Thirdly, businesses began to recognize the fatal flaws that plagued their individualized assessment processes and craved for an 'ideal' or 'model' business framework that could serve as an absolute benchmark. Finally, in the USA, an alarmed congress legislated a national productivity study in October 1982, which led to the recognition of the need for a national quality and productivity award. In response, the Malcolm Baldridge National Quality Award (MBNQA) was born on 20 October 1987, named after the contemporaneous commerce secretary, whose goal was to provide a 'model' or 'ideal' business framework for businesses to assess themselves against, and promote quality practices in American industries.

MBNQA has since served as an instrument of choice for self-assessment of businesses that aspire to achieve business excellence. Not surprisingly, since the institutionalization of MBNQA, there has been an unprecedented growth in self-assessment activity throughout the world. This is reflected in several distinct trends: (1) A growing number of companies in the countries of US, Europe, Australia, and Asia are seeking to engage in self-assessment, (2) a growing number of journals are seeking and encouraging self-assessment related articles (Madu, 1998) that use empirical analysis as a primary vehicle of research, and (3) new journals dedicated to the cause of self-assessment by businesses are being launched in quick succession (Van der Wiele *et al.*, 1995). The heightened interest in self-assessment activity in European countries has surfaced with much greater visibility since 1988. The evidence of this is seen in the evolution of the European Foundation for Quality Management (EFQM) in 1988, institution of European Quality Award (EQA) in 1991, promulgation of the EFQM's non-prescriptive business excellence mode (EFQM Self-Assessment Guidelines, 1995, 1997, 2000), and a plethora of journal publications bear testimony to this claim. Outside the US and Europe, too, there is growing evidence that self-assessment activity is picking up speed in a substantive manner (Voss *et al.*, 1994; Zink and Schmidt, 1998).

This significant spurt in the self-assessment activity is expected to continue into the future as the economies in the US and Europe continue to prosper. Indeed, we surmise that another paradigm shift in self-assessment frameworks is lurking on the horizon. The incidence of information revolution, globalization of markets at a blistering pace, and a near vertical growth of e-commerce in recent years have created a need for a paradigm shift in operations and marketing strategies. The new functional strategies – marketing as well as operations – would have to change to accommodate the increase of a company's agility and flexibility dimensions. Clearly, such significant changes in strategic paradigms will cause self-assessment frameworks to follow suit.

TQM vs organization-based self-assessment frameworks

Before we proceed to discuss various aspects of self-assessment process, it is worth pointing out that organization-based self-assessment processes and TQM-based self-assessment processes are fundamentally the same. Most self-assessments originate in quality departments (Tamimi, 1998) and are channelled through the company's Total Quality Management infrastructure, even though the scope of the process of self-assessment covers the entire organization. This is quite understandable since Total Quality Management is not limited to a single department or area of the organization and its goals are consistent with the broader strategic goals of the organization. Shergold and Reed (1996) observe that '[TQM] is a convergence of ideas initially developed with the post war renaissance of Japanese industry, supported by Deming (1985); Juran (Juran and Gryna, 1980); and Ishikawa (1985) etc., which gradually moved from emphasis on quality control to a broader concept based on organization-wide principles of the ideal organizational culture (Tamimi, 1998)'. Indeed, TQM is an all pervasive philosophy that aims to improve every part of system on a continual basis using teamwork as the main vehicle of progress. Van der Wiele, Dale, and Williams (1997) support this notion when they state 'TQM aims to improve all activities and eliminate wastage on a continuous basis, reorient all activities and employees to focus on the customer (external and internal) by understanding and meeting the requirements, and to involve and develop the members of the organization'. Due to the all-encompassing scope of TQM that pervades all areas of business, the TQM-based self-assessment tools also serve the organization-based self-assessment needs. As such, in this chapter we do not make any distinction between the self-assessment models that are based on TQM practices or other performance measures; the difference basically remains semantic in its import.

Self-assessment in the context of TQM

The goal of self-assessment is to locate the bearings of an organization with respect to an 'excellent' business model and identify the gaps that need to be bridged. The goal of TQM is to lead an organization systematically to a position of business 'excellence' through continuous improvement. It is easy to see that these two are integrally wedded to the same goal and while assessment provides the starting point, TQM provides the vehicle to reach there. In this section we look at some of the salient research trends in TQM frameworks as they relate to or overlap with self-assessment.

The evolution of quality has occurred through four rather distinct phases (Bounds *et al.*, 1994): Inspection, Statistical Quality Control (SQC), Quality Assurance (QA), and Strategic Quality Management (SQM). The first three phases were essentially inward-looking and represented the thinking that quality was a domain of operations/production manager and that it was treated as a narrow concept that began and ended at the product/service quality. However, the fourth phase, that started around 1980, saw a major paradigm shift in how quality was viewed, perceived, and managed. It became 'CWQC' or company-wide quality control in Japan and TQM in USA and Europe. Its domain expanded to beyond production to include every activity in which an organization engaged. The external connotations of quality changed as well to reflect its indispensable role in corporate strategy formulations. It was seen, for the first time, as a formidable competitive weapon, that with appropriate focusing on customer satisfaction, could make or break organizations. Kay and Anderson (1999) observe that the SQM approach needs further course correction. In the decade of the 1990s, and in the next century, organizations will need to move into the fifth phase – the phase of continuous improvement – so that they are 'flexible, responsive, and able to adapt quickly to changes needed in strategy in the light of the feedback from customers and from benchmarking competitors'.

Over the years, there has been a vast array of definitions for TQM, all of which seem to stress the importance of a number of factors: customer focus, continuous improvement, teamwork, leadership, empowerment, organization culture, and strategic focus. Olian and Rynes (1991) see TQM as an approach to management of changes in organizational process, strategic priorities, individual beliefs, individual attitudes, and individual behaviours while Dean and Bowen (1994) link TQM to three basic principles, customer focus, continuous improvement, and teamwork. An even broader view is taken by Reed, Lemak, and Montgomery (1996) where they see TQM as a business-level strategy consisting of a number of necessary but not sufficient factors. Flynn, Schroeder, and Sakakibara define TQM as 'an integrated approach to achieving and sustaining high quality output' (Flynn *et al.*, 1994). For many, TQM is a philosophy aimed at eliminating waste and accomplishing business mission through continuous improvement.

However, there have been only a few studies dedicated to the development of TQM/business frameworks (Anderson *et al.*, 1994; Black and Porter, 1996; Reed *et al.*, 1996; Benson *et al.*, 1991; Bossink, *et al.*, 1992; Flynn *et al.*, 1994; Shergold and Reed, 1996; Van der Wiele *et al.*, 1997; Wisner and Eakins, 1994; Van der Wiele and Brown, 1999; Zink and Schmidt, 1998 and Van der Wiele *et al.*, 1995). Most of these studies start with a predetermined model such as MBNQA and proceed to test the validity of the factors that comprise the model. However, they do not present convincing methodologies that link the descriptive models of TQM to emerging prescriptive models (Grandzol and Gershon, 1998).

Recently, some authors have tried to answer the question: is there a core set of TQM factors or components that have a significant bearing on business performance?

Saraph, Benson, and Schroeder (1989) were among the earliest to address this question. Based on a small number of assessors, they identified leadership, quality data and reporting, process management, product/service design, training, supplier Quality Management, role of quality department, and employee relations as critical factors of TQM that affect business performance. Hackman and Wagerman (1995) and Black and Porter (1996) provide different but informative perspectives on TQM related factors. Based on the Conference Board (1991) survey, Hackman and Wagerman list the top seven practices associated with TQM programmes. The reported practices were, short-term problem solving, employee training, top-down implementation, developing supplier relationships, obtaining customer information, competitive benchmarking, and employee involvement. Black and Porter used MBNQA criteria as possible TQM factors and added those factors that were present in TQM literature but not in MBNQA criteria. The study results suggest that TQM programmes contain the following ten factors: corporate quality culture, strategic Quality Management, quality improvement measurement systems, people and customer management, operational quality planning, external interface management, supplier partnerships, and teamwork. There are a few other works (Adebanjo and Kehoe,

1998; Grandzol and Gershon, 1998; Kay and Anderson, 1999; Voss *et al.*, 1994; Wisner and Eakins, 1994) that have engaged in rigorous empirical research to determine what TQM framework or factors can best project a firm's business performance. Significant overlap in findings across these studies lends content validity to TQM as an overall framework that can justifiably be used for self-assessment as well as performance improvement. The financial studies mentioned earlier that support the notion that TQM helps improve financial improvement (Helton, 1995; Wisner and Eakins, 1994) further supports this conjecture. A recent, large-sample study (Anderson *et al.*, 1994) (1289 respondents) identified with high reliability a nine-manufacturing-management-practice construct that was significantly and positively correlated with each other and showed a significant influence on business performance. These practices are: workforce commitment, shared vision, customer focus, use of teams, personnel training, co-operative supplier relations, use of benchmarking, advanced manufacturing system, product quality.

Based on the above, it can be concluded that certain practices impact the organizational performance in a positive way and as such could be used as levers to improve performance after self-assessment has been conducted. While the debate on what factors constitute TQM is converging, there are still varying school of thoughts in what constitute product quality outcomes. Reliable research is needed in this direction.

Implementation of self-assessment process

A rather loose definition of self-assessment is provided by Hillman (1994): it is the process of evaluating an organization against a model for continuous improvement, in order to highlight what has been archived and what needs improving. A more formal definition is provided in European Foundation for Quality Management (EFQM) as follows:

> . . . a comprehensive, systematic, and regular review of an organization's activities and results referenced against a model of business excellence culminating in planned improvements.

The models of business excellence could be one of the award frameworks, such as MBNQA, EFQM, European Quality Award (EQA), Australian Quality Award (AQA), and BEM (Business Excellence model). Or it could be any of the other frameworks that fit the organizational need and pass the validity test to confirm that the model does indeed accomplish what it was designed to. Irrespective of the business model used for benchmarking, a self-assessment process comprises three salient phases:

- identifying strengths and weaknesses of an organization with respect to its business performance and culture with respect to an 'excellent' or 'ideal' business;

- mapping out a course of action that will bring about necessary improvements in the organizational performance and culture to achieve sustained strategic advantage; and
- implementing and monitoring the actions determined above.

Implementation of self-assessment process

Initiation, sustenance, and conclusion of the self-assessment process is more of an art than a science. It needs a significant amount of planning and creation of appropriate environment before the self-assessment process can be started. There is enough empirical evidence and research to support the fact that 'improper self-assessment can cause organizations to be pushed along blind alleys and take initiatives that are not suited to their current state of TQM development' (Ramirez and Loney, 1993). Both optimistic and pessimistic assessments have their downsides; optimistic assessments would result in rosy evaluations leading to inaction where action would have been warranted, and, on the flip side, pessimistic assessments may cause avoidable loss of morale and redundancy of effort in areas where such an effort was not warranted in the first place. Also, many external assessors may not be sufficiently well-versed in the internal workings of the system under study and may cause erroneous evaluations leading to erroneous corrective actions. On the other hand, internal assessment processes may be subject to bias and individual whims. In what follows, we present a general methodology for implementation of self-assessment. Appropriate tailoring will be needed for custom applications.

All new programmes or projects need a conducive environment and some preparatory work prior to implementation. Self-assessment is no exception. Here is what is needed before self-assessment process can begin.

Preconditions for self-assessment

- An existing corporate policy with visions, mission, and strategic goals.
- Top management's commitment to participate in design and development of the assessment instrument.
- Involvement of company's relevant functional areas in design and development of the assessment instrument.
- Top management's commitment to provide resources for implementation of the tool (time, personnel, assessors, finances for external consultants).
- Training and educating all managers involved in the assessment process.
- Informing people about targets, execution, and consequences of the self-assessment.
- Regular additional third party assessments to gain additional ideas.
- A procedure to constantly monitor and adjust the assessment instrument in response to evolving information.

Implementation process

Based on the literature and our practical experience, the following 11-step process is suggested:

Step 1: *Constitute a steering committee*

Constitute a steering committee comprised of high level personnel that has:

- direct access to CEO,
- authority to influence decisions at strategic level and
- authority to appropriate the wherewithal necessary for the self-assessment process and the follow-up actions.

The following steps are recommended for the steering committee to be carried out in consonance with CEO and other appropriate personnel.

Step 2: *Mission statement*

Review the mission statement of the company. If one is not in place, create one. The mission statement represents an organization's vision as to where it wants to be in 5–10 years' time. The mission statement should:

- be rooted in high value for customer (e.g. quality, flexibility, agility, after sales service, user-friendliness etc.);
- appeal to the customers/users;
- set directions rather than metrics;
- be short.

Step 3: *Set strategic goals*

Set strategic goals with due consideration for:

- the company's mission and competitive priorities;
- customers' needs and preferences;
- the state of competition;
- the company's distinctive competency;
- the company's weaknesses;
- environmental scanning: opportunities;
- environmental scanning: threats;
- entry and exit barriers;
- existing and potential future markets' characteristics: order winners, order qualifiers, and order losing criteria;
- existing and potential products;
- existing and available processes and technologies.

Step 4: *Choose a business excellence model*

The steering committee should decide on a business excellence model that best serves the specific company's vision of excellence. The choices are: MBQNA, EFQM-EM, SACIM, SAMS, and QCIM, which are described in the next section, or any hybrid of these models. If none of these models is deemed appropriate enough to serve the strategic goals of the organization, a new one may be created, drawing from the criteria contained in these models, and augmenting the ones not contained in the integrated model.

Step 5: *Training and education*

All personnel likely to be involved in the assessment process or implementation of excellence-seeking measures later must be trained and/or educated in the following:

- understanding the strategic role of assessment;
- costs and benefits of the assessment process;
- where the business wants/needs to be: the excellence model, performance goals and strategic implications;
- evaluate the status quo in their specific areas of assignment/control with respect to the criteria set forth in the excellence model;
- identify the gaps between the ideal performance being sought by the excellence model and the current status of the organization in the area of assignment/control;
- develop measures for bridging the gaps identified above;
- consequences associated with failure to take action.

Step 6: *Assign responsibility for assessment of individual criteria*

For a meaningful assessment, each criteria and its sub-criteria must be assessed by a competent and unbiased individual or a dedicated team of experts who possess the requisite knowledge, expertise, tools, wherewithal and time to do an honest job. If the assessors are external, as may well be the case, it is incumbent on the steering committee to allow him/her access to all the information needed to conduct the assessment properly and exhaustively. An internal assessor, however, needs to be careful about his/her preconceived notions. The responsibility assignment should be consistent with the person's expertise, area of work, and should be within the timeframe allowed by the overall assessment timeframe.

Step 7: *Collect data/information necessary for self-assessment*

All persons identified in Step 6 should develop a list of the data/information needed for assessment of their specific criterion/sub-criterion, using such tools as brainstorming, flowcharts, vicinity diagram and the like. Vicinity diagram is essentially developed using experts to cluster together similar things. This will need a clear vision of the strategic goals of the organization, level of excellence being sought, how the information would impact upon strategic goals, and how the requisite changes will eventually be brought about. The following are some of the sources that can be tapped for data/information:

- customer surveys, complaints statistics, marketing strategies, Kano model (Matzler, 1998) type analyses, customer needs, wants, preferences, and fashion trends;
- employees surveys, work safety statistics, illness rates, absenteeism, human resource development plans;
- processes – processing times, projects, improvement methods, sequences, yields, scraps, reworks, salvage decisions, quality costs, variances, methods;
- products: defect rates, life duration, and failure rates, failure costs;
- financial data, e.g. profits, income, sales, volume, ROI (Return on Investment), RONA (Return on Net Assets).

Step 8: *Carry out comparison with the excellence model chosen*

In this step, comparison of actual and ideal performance on each criterion and sub criterion must be carried out by individual/team earmarked previously (Step 6) for that criterion. The difference yields the gap/variance that needs to be addressed.

Step 9: *Development of a corrective and preventive action plan*

After the performance and cultural gaps with respect to the excellence model have been identified for each criterion/subcriterion, an appropriate and exhaustive plan should be developed to bridge the gaps. The plan should be developed starting from the variances identified in each criterion/subcriterion then working towards extinction of gaps/variances.

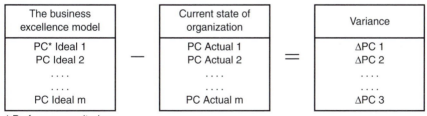

The business excellence model		Current state of organization		Variance
PC* Ideal 1		PC Actual 1		ΔPC 1
PC Ideal 2	−	PC Actual 2	=	ΔPC 2
. . . .		. . . .		. . . .
. . . .		. . . .		. . . .
PC Ideal m		PC Actual m		ΔPC 3

* Performance criterion

Figure 2.1 Determination of variance/gaps between the business excellence and existing model.

- *Gaps/variances with the excellence model:* Clearly establish the current level of performance for each criterion/subcriterion, and the ideal level being sought. To accomplish absolute clarity, numeric goals should be set to the extent possible. For instance: The automated process of producing rubber gaskets currently performing at 0.1 per cent defect rate should be a six-sigma process by June 2001.
- *Assign responsibility:* Consistent with the assignments in Step 6, responsibility should be assigned by name to people who will develop plans and execute them to extinguish the variances identified above.
- *Assign time-windows:* For each variance criterion/subcriterion, assign time windows within which the corrective/preventive action must be initiated and completed. This should be consistent with the overall assessment plan.
- *Total plan:* An overall plan should then be created that integrates the schedules and responsibilities established for each criterion/subcriterion. Effort should be made to run as many activities in parallel as possible. The steering committee is responsible for orderly and timely creation of such a plan.

Step 10: *Monitoring the assessment plan*

The steering committee should develop a monitoring scheme and superimpose its schedule over the corrective action plan for assessment. The checks envisaged in monitoring should be documented in detail and communicated to all concerned.

Step 11: *Authority to proceed for self-assessment plan*

The steering committee, CEO/chairman, and top management should finally meet, review, and issue a final seal of approval to the plan which signifies their commitment for implementation of the plan both in words and deeds. Plan should thereafter be monitored for satisfactory implementation and review at the check points established in Step 10.

Having outlined a general procedure, we now outline a few frameworks for self-assessment that have appeared in literature. It needs to be stated that this list is by no means exhaustive. However, the authors applied their judgment to include these based on the one or more of the following criteria: (1) completeness and exhaustiveness of factors considered as contributory to performance; (2) all factors subjected to a rigorous validation through statistical analyses; (3) reliability of data and sample size; (4) consistency with existing literature.

Self-assessment frameworks

Self-assessment provides a basis for performance improvement. The entire self-assessment literature could be classified under four distinctive streams (see Figure 2.2 below for taxonomy). First of these streams are the models proposed

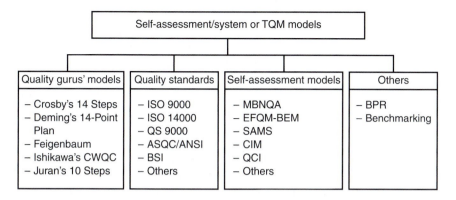

Figure 2.2 Self-assessment/TQM models for organizational performance improvement.

by quality gurus such as Crosby, Deming, Juran, Feigenbaum and Ishikawa. These models are essentially an extraction of the individual guru's wisdom and experience. Implementation of such models needs significant adaptation and requires high degree of expertise. Deming's 14-steps plan (Deming, 1985), Juran's 10-steps (Pun, 1998), Crosby's 10 steps (Deming, 1986), and Ishikawa's CWQC (Ishikawa, 1985) are examples of such models.

The next stream is that of highly structured, rigid-requirement models set forth in international/national standards such as ISO 9000 (ISO, 1994), QS 9000, ISO 14000 (ISO, 1996) and ANSI-90. Due to the uniformity of quality systems these standards prescribe, they are in high demand within and across trading countries throughout the world. As such they have assumed a strategic role as an order winner in the market place.

The third stream comprises highly structured models that envision an organization's overall performance as a weighted sum of its performance on several criteria and sub-criteria. Due to the quantitative approach of these models, they lend themselves to a well-defined, rigorous implementation methodology. For these reasons, such models are popular and perceived to be more useful than their counterparts. Five of these models (MBQNA, Business Excellence model of European Foundation of Quality Management, Self-assessment Model for continuous improvement, Standard Quality Management Systems, and Quality Competitiveness Index based Self-Assessment Systems) are the focus of discussion in the next section. The fourth and the last stream contains general tools or techniques such as: Business Process Reengineering and internal and external benchmarking, which have been extensively used by businesses as instruments of organizational improvement.

The applicability of some of these models depends on the degree of quality maturity an organization has. For instance, ISO/standards models work well when an organization is at the early stages of its quality improvement efforts and is primarily seeking to improve housekeeping and documentation. In an overall journey to excellence, these models provide the *satisfying* aspects of the total effort. However, as the organization matures, the third stream models become more appropriate.

Self-assessment frameworks and models

In this section, we describe five salient self-assessment frameworks/models introduced as the third stream models in the previous section at some length.

Malcolm Baldridge National Quality Award (MBNQA)[1]

MBNQA, one of the pioneering efforts in the development of business self-assessment models, and the most notable thus far, was instituted in August 1987 in the face of Japanese strategic onslaught. The objective of the award was to create 'awareness of performance excellence as an increasingly important element in competitiveness (N.I.S.T, 1987, 1992, 1995, 1998, 2000)'. Several studies have shown that MBNQA winners have consistently outperformed the stock markets (Helton, 1995; Zhao *et al.*, 1995) establishing a clear relationship between quality improvement and financial performance. MBNQA-2000 encompasses five industries: manufacturing, service, small business, healthcare and education, with up to two awards per year per industry.

The MBNQA assessment model is an exhaustive one. It comprises of seven criteria, each having several sub-criteria. Each criterion/sub-criterion is assigned a score that reflects its importance on a scale of 1000. While the fundamental assessment criteria have endured since they were first promulgated in 1987, their categorization and weights have constantly evolved over the years to suit the need of the times. Table 2.1 shows the assessment criteria. Table 2.2 shows how the actual scoring occurs based on the participant's actual performance. Figure 2.3 shows inter-relationships between MBNQA criteria.

The revised MBNQA framework places greater emphasis on business results as they reflect the influence of strategy-driven performance, addresses needs of all stakeholders (employees, customers, shareholders) and lays greater emphasis on the alignment of company strategy, customer/market knowledge, high performance workforce, key company processes, and business results. In addition there is increased focus on all aspects of organizational and employee learning. A score card outlining the scale for scoring various criteria for MBNQA is placed at Table 2.2.

EFQM excellence model (EFQM-BEM)[2]

The European Foundation on Quality Management, established in 1988, developed the Business Excellence model, also known as the EFQM excellence model. EFQM instituted the European Quality Award (EQA) in 1991 to recognize organizations that 'demonstrate excellence in the management of quality as their fundamental process for continuous improvement'. The organizations that

Table 2.1 Malcolm Baldridge National Quality Award (2000) criteria for performance excellence*

2000 Categories/Items		Point values
1	**Leadership**	**125**
	1.1 Organizational leadership	85
	1.2 Public responsibility and citizenship	40
2	**Strategic planning**	**85**
	2.1 Strategy development	40
	2.2 Strategy deployment	45
3	**Customer and market focus**	**85**
	3.1 Customer and market knowledge	40
	3.2 Customer satisfaction and relationships	45
4	**Information and analysis**	**85**
	4.1 Measurement of organizational performance	40
	4.2 Analysis of organizational performance	45
5	**Human resource focus**	**85**
	5.1 Work systems	35
	5.2 Employee education, training, and development	25
	5.3 Employee well-being and satisfaction	25
6	**Process management**	**85**
	6.1 Product and service processes	55
	6.2 Support processes	15
	6.3 Supplier and partnering processes	15
7	**Business results**	**450**
	7.1 Customer focused results	115
	7.2 Financial and market results	115
	7.3 Human resource results	80
	7.4 Supplier and partner results	25
	7.5 Organizational effectiveness results	115
TOTAL POINTS		**1000**

can compete for the EQA are: (1) companies, (2) operational units of companies, (3) public sector organizations, and (4) small and medium enterprises. The assessment framework used by EFQM for evaluation of the organizations is known as BEM, which has evolved from the initial EQA assessment framework. The EQA assessment model, in turn, was derived largely from the MBNQA framework.

The EFQM excellence model is a practical, non-prescriptive framework that assesses organizations' performance through: (1) measurement of where they are on the path to *excellence*, (2) helping them understand the gaps, and (3) stimulating solutions to bridge the gap. A schematic of its assessment framework is provided in Figure 2.4.

The EFQM excellence model is based on eight fundamental concepts of good performance (EFQM; 1995, 1997, 2000).

Table 2.2 Malcolm Baldridge National Quality Award: criteria score sheet

Score	Results
0%	• No results or poor results in areas reported
10–20%	• Some improvements *and/or* early good performance levels in a few areas • Results not reported for many to most areas of importance to the organization's key business requirements
30–40%	• Improvements *and/or* good performance levels in many areas of importance to the organization's key business requirements • Early stages of developing trends and obtaining comparative information • Results reported for many to most areas of importance to the organization's key business requirements
50–60%	• Improvement trends *and/or* good performance levels reported for most areas of importance to the organization's key business requirements • No pattern of adverse trends and no poor performance levels in areas of importance to the organization's key business requirements • Some trends *and/or* current performance levels – evaluated against relevant comparisons *and/or* benchmarks – show areas of strength *and/or* good to very good relative performance levels • Business results address most key customer, market, and process requirements
70–80%	• Current performance is good to excellent in areas of importance to the organization's key business requirements • Most improvement trends *and/or* current performance levels are sustained • Many to most trends *and/or* current performance levels – evaluated against relevant comparisons *and/or* benchmarks – show areas of leadership and very good relative performance levels • Business results address most key customer, market, process, and action plan requirements
90–100%	• Current performance is excellent in most areas of importance to the organization's key business requirements • Excellent improvement trends *and/or* sustained excellent performance levels in most areas • Evidence of industry and benchmark leadership demonstrated in many areas • Business results fully address key customer, market, process, and action plan requirements

- *Results orientation:* Excellence is dependent upon balancing and satisfying the needs of all relevant stakeholders (this includes the people employed, customers, suppliers and society in general as well as those with financial interests in the organization).
- *Customer focus:* The customer is the final arbiter of product and service quality and customer loyalty, retention and market share gain are best optimized through a clear focus on the needs of current and potential customers.

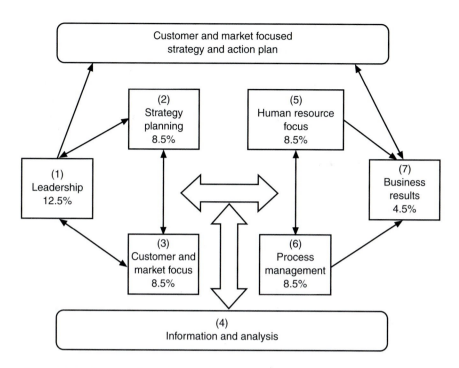

Figure 2.3 Malcolm Baldridge Award criteria and their interrelationship.
Source: NIST (1997).

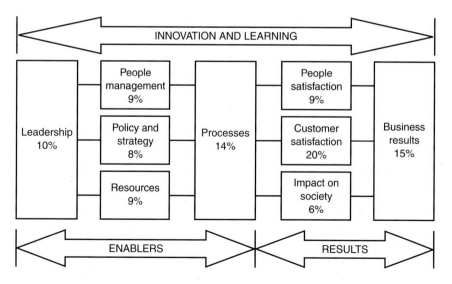

Figure 2.4 European Foundation of Quality Management: Business Excellence model.
Source: EFQM (1995, 1997, 2000), www.efqm.org/

- *Leadership and constancy of purpose:* The behaviour of an organization's leaders creates a clarity and unity of purpose within the organization and an environment in which the organization and its people can excel.
- *Management by processes and facts:* Organizations perform more effectively when all inter-related activities are understood and systematically managed and decisions concerning current operations are planned. Improvements are made using reliable information that includes stakeholder perceptions.
- *People development and involvement:* The full potential of an organization's people is best released through shared values and a culture of trust and empowerment, which encourages the involvement of everyone.
- *Continuous learning, innovation and improvement:* Organizational performance is maximized when it is based on the management and sharing of knowledge within a culture of continuous learning, innovation and improvement.
- *Partnership development:* An organization works more effectively when it has mutually beneficial relationships, built on trust, sharing of knowledge and integration, with its partners.
- *Public responsibility:* The long-term interest of the organization and its people are best served by adopting an ethical approach and exceeding the expectations and regulations of the community at large.

Elements of EFQM-BEM model

The model is equally split between enablers and results criteria, each carrying a total of 50 per cent of the weight. The enablers are those set of factors that 'enable' an organization to accomplish model performance. Results are essentially what an organization actually accomplishes with respect to the criteria set forth in the results category. Both criteria are shown in Figure 2.4 and described next.

- *Leadership:* Relates to the behaviour of managers inasmuch as how they inspire, drive and reflect total quality as the fundamental process for improvement.
- *Policy and strategy:* Reviews the organization's mission, values, vision and strategic directions. How the principles of total quality are embodied in policy and strategy decisions.
- *People management:* Studies the management of the organization's people to see how the organization releases and utilizes people's full potential to obtain better business performance.
- *Resources:* Investigates how the organization's resources are deployed in support of policy and strategy.
- *Processes:* Studies how the processes are reviewed and revised to ensure that they add value consistent with the principles of continuous improvement.
- *Customer satisfaction:* Examines the degree to which the organization satisfies its customers.

- *People satisfaction:* Examines the degree to which the organization satisfies its people (primarily, employees).
- *Impact on society:* Probes what organization is achieving in terms of the needs and expectations of the community it serves.
- *Business results:* Reviews what the organization is achieving in relation to its planned business and/or service objective and in satisfying the needs and expectations of everyone who has a stake (customers, employees, stock holders) in the organization.

The scoring criterion for EFQM-BEM is provided in Table 2.3.

A Self-Assessment Model for Continuous Improvement (SACIM)

While MNQBA and EFQM-BEM have been used extensively (MNQBA in the US and EFQM in Western Europe), their frameworks seem to lack a dynamic emphasis on performance (Dyason and Kaye, 1995). This means that while these frameworks provide an excellent snapshot of strengths and weaknesses of an organization at the time they are assessed, they do not have a built-in structure that will create or sustain a improvement momentum. Dyason and Kaye (1995) identify a set of three factors – organizational mission, critical success factors, and aims – that would be helpful in sustaining a momentum for continuous improvement of an organization created after self-assessment. The primary role of such factors, called *drivers*, is to provide continued vision and direction to an organization in a dynamic environment. See Figure 2.5.

Table 2.3 Scoring criteria for EFQM Business Excellence model

Enablers		
Approach	*Score*	*Deployment*
Anecdotal	0	Little usage
Soundly base systematic preventive	25	About a quarter of the potential
Integrated reviewed	50	About half the potential
Refinement	75	About three-fourth the potential
Role model	100	About full potential
Results		
Approach	*Score*	*Deployment*
Anecdotal	0	Few/relevant areas
Positive trends	25	Some
Comparison: targets Comparison: external	50	Many
Sustenance and excellence	75	Most
Role model	100	All

Motivated by, and consistent with, the mission, the leadership chalks out policies and strategies that determine the shape and genre of peoples management and resource deployment. The satisfaction derived by people (e.g. employees) and customers as well as the impact on community determines how well the drivers used the enablers to yield results. A feedback loop from results to drivers and enablers creates new opportunities for continuous improvement on a dynamic basis.

Self-assessed Quality Management System

The models of self-assessment presented thus far would serve well those companies that are quite advanced in the pursuit of Total Quality Management and are looking for tuning up their systems for the best performance. However, companies that are in the earlier stages of TQM implementation and are looking for compliance with ISO 9000, QS 9000, and ISO 14000, with an eventual eye to winning awards, will benefit more by using assessment models that integrate the requirements in these standards and MBNQA/EFQM-BEM. One such model is Self-assessed Quality Management System (SQMS) developed by Pun, Chin and Lau (1999).

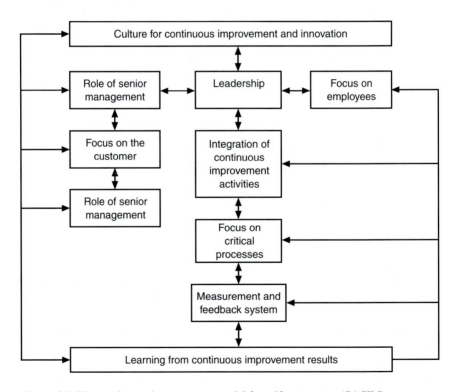

Figure 2.5 The continuous improvement model for self-assessment (SACIM).

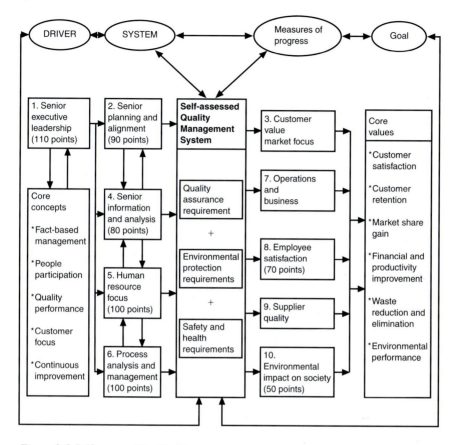

Figure 2.6 Self-assessed Quality Management systems.

SQMS adopts seven evaluation criteria embodied in the framework of MBNQA (Brown, 1996; Shergold and Reed, 1996) (see Figure 2.6). However, in order to integrate the principles of TQM set forth in ISO 9000, the evaluation criteria are extended from 7 to 10. These are: employee satisfaction, supplier quality and relationships, and environmental impact on society. Some of the scope of these criteria overlaps with that of the MBNQA criteria. The net effect of these changes is inclusion of the following criteria (Ramirez and Loney, 1993): employee satisfaction (sub-criteria: human resource results, recognition and measurement, involvement well-being and morale, safety and hygiene), supplier quality and relationship (sub-criteria: supplier and partner results, supplier relationship enhancement, supplier service standards), environmental impact on society (sub-criteria: public and social responsibilities, environmental protection and conservation).

The Quality Competitiveness Index Model (QCIM) (Kumar et al., *1999)*

Finally, we describe the QCIM model that can be used for self-assessment and to improve business performance on a static as well as dynamic basis. In addition, this model creates a unique opportunity for internal and external benchmarking. The model integrates the findings from several works related to the area of self-assessment (Ahire *et al.*, 1995); Black and Porter, 1996; Flynn *et al.*, 1994; Gadd, 1995; Shergold and Reed; 1996; Voss *et al.*, 1994, Wisner and Eakins, 1994) and concepts and principles propounded by quality gurus such as Crosby (Crosby, 1979), Deming (Deming, 1986), Ishikawa (Ishikawa, 1985), and Juran (Juran and Gryna, 1980), and certain evaluation criteria used in MBNQA (NIST, 1995, 2000) and EFQM-BEM (EFQM, 1997 and 2000).

A unique strength of this model is that it considers functional units and the state of quality awareness associated with those units as independent variables that impact upon the degree of competitiveness contributed by a given TQM practice or factor. Thus, the model explicitly allows for the fact that implementing SPC in production area would have much more salutary effect on a company's quality of conformance and, thereby on its competitiveness, as opposed to when SPC is implemented in an accounting or human resource department. Furthermore, the degree of awareness of quality in general, and SPC in particular, in that unit would determine the marginal competitiveness resulting from SPC effort in that unit.

The set of factors/techniques which impact on a company's performance were developed by creating an intelligent superset of factors/sub-factors that were used in the references indicated above, and then deleting the redundant ones and those that were generally not considered effective in influencing business performance. The states of awareness were taken from the five-point grid suggested by Crosby (1979). These are: Uncertainty, Awakening, Enlightenment, Wisdom and Certainty.

The QCI for a company comprises additive cellular combinations from each sub-factor-department-awareness cell. In that sense it provides microscopic information that will be helpful in fine-tuning the areas that need the most attention. The process of generating desired matrices also facilitates benchmarking. Five steps involved in determination of the QCI are reproduced below. The actual computation is detailed and involved and readers are advised to refer to the original reference for this model (Kumar *et al.*, 1999).

Step 1   Create a department-consciousness matrix.
Step 2   Compute the weighted quality consciousness level.
Step 3   Create a quality competitiveness matrix.
Step 4   Compute the quality competitiveness index of each element of the factor-awareness-department combination.
Step 5   Compute the quality competitiveness index of the company.

A comparative study of five self-assessment frameworks

Each of the five models studied have different strengths and weaknesses. However, based on our experience, the QCI model presents certain advantages over other models. It allows the organization to generate its own assessment instrument based on its competitive priorities and market environment. Furthermore, it allows flexibility of assigning weights and allows opportunities to customize to the maximum extent possible. Finally, it can be used for internal as well as external benchmarking purposes. In terms of overall flexibility, this model appears to stand out over its counterparts. A comparative evaluation of these frameworks is placed in Table 2.4.

Concluding remarks

The self-assessment process is rooted in strategic transformation of an organization. As the Japanese companies began to make significant inroads into American and western markets, organizations scrambled to find what was wrong with their existing strategic formulations, business practices, behavioural cultures, and performance evaluations. Studies revealed, among other things, that there was a significant gap between the quality and reliability of American and Western European products as compared to their Japanese counterparts. This set in motion, apart from restructuring of the formulations of business strategy, a search for a well-structured, meaningful self-assessment framework that brings out the weaknesses and strengths of an organization in a holistic manner. The first such known framework is the Malcolm Baldridge National Quality Award promulgated by the US government in 1987. Inception of MBNQA had a profoundly positive effect on the quality of US products and triggered parallel action worldwide, especially in Western Europe. Several frameworks and awards have since surfaced in Europe, Australia, Asia and elsewhere, with the same undergirding – to achieve excellence in business performance to attain higher levels of competitiveness. We presented five salient models of self-assessment in some detail: MBNQA, EQFM-BEM, SACIM, SAQM, and QCIM that would serve the purpose of identifying the gaps in performance and culture of a given business with respect to an 'excellent' business. These models would be appropriate at different stages of quality awareness of a company. In addition a general framework for the assessment process was presented, called the QCI model, which would apply in vast majority of situations with appropriate amount of tailoring. A comparative chart is provided in Table 2.4 which underscores the strengths and weaknesses of five frameworks presented here.

It should be stated that this chapter by no means presents the material and models related to self-assessment with total exhaustiveness. It is our hope, however, that the chapter would serve as a significant background and reference to the readers interested in designing and implementing a process of self-assessment that applies to a vast majority of organizations.

Table 2.4 Comparison of self-assessment models

Characteristic	MBNQA	EFQM-BEM
Primary reference	http://www.mbnqa.org	http://www.efqm.org
Dynamic capability (continuous Improvement, self learning)	Static/snapshot	Static/snapshot
Industry suitability	Manufacturing/service	Service/service
Factor(s) most emphasized	Business results (customer focus, leadership)	Processes, customer satisfaction
Purpose/objective	Evaluate firms for National (US) Quality Award	Evaluate firms for Regional (European) Quality Award
Evaluation mechanism	Weighted linear sum of performance measures	Weighted linear sum of performance measures
Validation status	Some measures are validated, others are not	Some measures are validated, others are not
Flexibility	Prescriptive model, no flexibility to change factors or weights	Recommended model, no flexibility to change factors or weights
Number of factors/criteria	7 criteria, 9 factors	9 factors based on 10 fundamental concepts
Benchmarking capability	External benchmarking only administrator dependent	External benchmarking only administrator dependent
Identification of competitive strengths and weakness	Yes	Yes

Notes

1   http://www.quality.nist.gov/
2   http://www.efqm.org/

References

Adebanjo, D. and Kehoe, D. (1998) An evaluation of quality culture problems in UK companies, *International Journal of Quality Science* **3**(3), 275–86.

Ahire, S.L., Landeros, R. and Golhar, Y. (1995) Total Quality Management: a literature review and an agenda for future research, *Production and Operations Management* **4**(3), 288–306.

Anderson, J., Rungtusanatham, B. and Schroder, M. (1994) A theory of Quality Management underlying the Deming management method. *Academy of Management Review* **19**, 419–45.

Benson, P.G., Saraph J.V. and Schroder, R.G. (1991) The effects of organizational context on Quality Management, *Management Science* **37**(9), 1107–24.

SACIM	SAQMS	QCIM
Kaye and Anderson (1999)	Pun Chin, and Lau (1999)	Kumar, Motwani, and Stecke (2000)
Capable through drivers	Static/snapshot	Capable through implementation actions
Service/service	Service/service	Service/service
Continuous improvement top management	Strategic/system planning leadership	Competitiveness
Performance evaluation with continuous drive for improvement	Performance evaluation for integrated MBNQA-ISO 9000- ISO 14000 Compliant system	Performance evaluation for competitiveness capability of quality activities
Combining mechanism across factors not available	Combining mechanism across factors not available	Sequential, matrix-based weighted sum of performance measures
All factors validated through statistical analysis	All factors validated through statistical analysis	Methodology validated Not all factors validated
Predetermined set of factors Weights not specified	Predetermined set of factors Weights not specified	Allows choice of factors and specification of arbitrary weights
10 criteria, 56 factors	10 criteria, 33 factors	9 broad criteria, 57 factors
None	None	External and internal organization dependent
None	None	Yes, especially designed for this purpose

Black, A.S. and Porter, J.L. (1996). Identification of the critical factors of TQM, *Decision Sciences* 27(1), 1–21.

Bossink, B., Gieskes, J. and Pas, T. (1992) Diagnosing total Quality Management – Part 2, *Total Quality Management, 1992* **4**(l), 5–12.

Bounds, G., Yorks, L., Adams, M. and Ranney, G. (1994) *Beyond Total Quality Management Toward the Emerging Paradigm*. New York: McGraw Hill.

Brown, M.G. (1996) *Baldridge Award Winning Quality*. Quality Resources/ASQC Press, Milwaukee Wisconsin, USA.

Conference Board (1991) Employee Buy-in to Total Quality. Conference Board, New York.

Crosby, P.B. (1979) *Quality is Free*. New York: McGraw-Hill.

Dean, J.W. and Bowen, D.E. (1994) Management theory and total quality: improving research and practice through theory development. *Academy of Management Review* **19**, 392–418.

Deming, W.E. (1985) *Out of Crises*. Cambridge, MA: MIT Press.

Deming, W.E. (1986) *Out of the Crisis Quality Productivity and Competitive Position*. Cambridge, MA: Cambridge University Press.

Dyason, M.D. and Kaye, M.M. (1995) Is there life after total Quality Management? (II), *Quality World*, January.

EFQM Self-Assessment Guidelines (1995) European Foundation for Quality Management, Brussels.

EFQM Self-Assessment Guidelines (1997) European Foundation for Quality Management, Brussels.

EFQM Self-Assessment Guidelines (2000) European Foundation for Quality Management, Brussels; http:/www.EFOM.org

Flynn, B.B., Schroeder, R.G. and Sakakibara, S. (1994) A framework of Quality Management research and an associated measurement instrument, *Journal of Operations Management* **11**, 339–66.

Gadd, K.W. (1995). Business of self-assessment: a strategic tool for building process robustness and achieving integrated management, *Business Process Reengineering and Management Journal* **1**(3), 66–85.

Grandzol, J.R. and Gershon, M. (1998) A survey instrument for standardizing TQM modeling research, *International Journal of Quality Sciences* **3**(1), 80–105.

Hackman, J.R. and Wagerman, R. (1995) Total Quality Management: Empirical, conceptual and practical issues, *Administrative Science Quarterly* **40**, 309–42.

Hayes, R. and Pisano, G.P. (1996) Manufacturing strategy at the intersection of two paradigm shifts, *Production and Operations Management* **5**(1), 25–41.

Helton, R.B. (1995) Baldie play, *Quality Progress* **28**(2), 43–5.

Hill, T. (2000) *Manufacturing Strategy: Text and Cases.* New York: McGraw Hill.

Hillman, G.P. (1994) Making self-assessment successful, *The TQM Magazine* **6**(3), 29–31.

Ishikawa, K. (1985) *What Was Total Quality Control? The Japanese Way.* Englewood Cliffs, NJ: Prentice Hall.

ISO (1994) EN/ISO9001-1 *Quality Management and Quality Assurance standards, Part 1: Guidelines for Selection and Use*, International Organization for Standardization.

ISO (1996) EN/ISO 14001, *Environmental Management Systems: Specification with Guidance for Use*, International Organization for Standardization.

Juran, J.M. and Gryna, F.M. (1980) *Quality Planning and Analysis.* New York: McGraw Hill.

Kay M. and Anderson, R. (1999). Continuous improvement: the ten essential criteria, *International Journal of Quality and Reliability Management* **16**(5), 485–506.

Kumar, A., Motwani, J. and Stecke, K.E. (1999) A quantitative approach to measure quality-based competitiveness of an organization. University of Michigan Business School Working Paper # 99001, University of Michigan, Ann Arbor, MI, USA.

Madu, C.N. (1998) An empirical assessment of quality: research considerations, *International Journal of Quality Sciences* **3**(4), 348–55.

Matzler, K. (1998) How to make product development projects more successful by integrating Kano's model of customer satisfaction into quality function deployment, *Technovation* **18**(1), 25–38.

NIST (1987) *Malcolm Baldridge National Quality Award Criteria*, US Department of Commerce, National Institute of Standards and Technology, Washington DC.

NIST (1992) *Malcolm Baldridge National Quality Award Criteria*, US Department of Commerce, National Institute of Standards and Technology, Washington DC.

NIST (1995) *Malcolm Baldridge National Quality Award Criteria*, US Department of Commerce, National Institute of Standards and Technology, Washington DC.

NIST (1998) *Malcolm Baldridge National Quality Award Criteria*, US Department of Commerce, National Institute of Standards and Technology, Washington DC.

NIST (2000) *Malcolm Baldridge National Quality Award Criteria*, US Department of

Commerce, National Institute of Standards and Technology, Washington DC. Web address: www.nist.gov

OAO (1991) *Management Practices: U.S. Companies Improve Performance Through Quality Efforts.* GAO/NSIAD91-190, General Accounting Office, Washington DC.

Olian, J.D. and Rynes, S.L. (1991) Making total quality work: aligning organizations, performance measures, and stakeholders, *Human Resource Management* **30**, 303–33.

Pun, K.F. (1998) Implementing an integrated Quality Management system, *Proceedings of the 52nd Annual Quality Congress*, 356–62, Philadelphia, PA.

Pun, K.F., Chin, K.S. and Lau, H. (1999). A self assessed Quality Management system based on integration of MBNQA/ISO 14000, *International Journal of Quality and Reliability Management* **16**(6), 606–29.

Ramirez, C. and Loney, T. (1993) Baldridge Award winners identify the essentials of a successful quality process, *Quality Digest*, January, 38–40.

Reed, R., Lemak, D.J. and Montgomery, J. (1996) Beyond process: TQM content and firm performance, *Academy of Management Review* **21**(1), 173–94.

Saraph, J.V., Benson, P.C. and Schroeder, R.G. (1989) An instrument for measuring the critical factors of Quality Management, *Decision Sciences* **20**(4), 457–78.

Shergold K. and Reed, D.M. (1996). Striving for excellence: how self-assessment using the business excellence model can result in step improvements in all areas of business activities, *The TQM Magazine* **8**(8), 48–52.

Tamimi, N. (1998) A second order factor analysis of critical TQM factors, *International Journal of Quality Science* **3**(1), 71–9.

Van der Wiele, T. and Brown, A. (1999) Self-assessment practices in Europe and Australia, *International Journal of Quality and Reliability Management*, **16**(3), 238–51.

Van der Wiele, T., Dale, B.G. and Williams, A.R.T. (1997) ISO 9000 series registration to total Quality Management: the transformation journey, *International Journal of Quality Sciences*, **2**(4), 236–52.

Van der Wiele, T., Dale, B.G., Williams, A.R.T., Kolb, F., Luzon, D.M., Schmidt, A. and Wallace, M. (1995). State-of-the-art study on self-assessment, *The TQM magazine* **7**(4), 13–17.

Van der Wiele, T., Williams, A.R.T., Dale, B.G., Carter, G., Kolb, F., Luzon, D.M., Schmidt, A. and Wallace, M. (1996). Self-assessment: a study in progress in Europe's leading organizations in Quality Management practices, *International Journal of Quality and Reliability Management* **13**(1), 84–104.

Voss, C.A., Chiesa, V. and Caughlan, P. (1994) Developing and testing benchmarking and self-assessment frameworks in manufacturing, *International Journal of Operations and Production Management* **14**(3), 83–100.

Wisner, J.D. and Eakins, S.G. (1994) A performance assessment of the U.S. Baldridge quality award winners, *International Journal of Quality and Reliability Management* **11**(2), 8–25.

Zhao, X., Maheshwari, S.K. and Zhang, J. (1995) Benchmarking quality practices in India, China, and Mexico, *Benchmarking for Quality Management and Technology* **2**(3), 20–40.

Zink, K.J. and Schmidt, A. (1998). Practice and implementation of self-assessment, *International Journal of Quality Sciences* **3**(2), 147–70.

Part II

Quality improvement tools and techniques for the twenty-first century

3 QFD

Customer driven design of products and services

Graeme Knowles

Introduction

Customer satisfaction lies at the heart of all modern thinking on quality and business management. Many corporate mission statements set customers as the focus of an organization's business activities, and key thinkers have defined the quality of goods and services with reference to how well they satisfy needs and expectations of the customer base (Deming, 1990; Juran, 1989). When the Boston Consulting Group and Product Development Consulting Inc. (1993) looked at competitive advantage in 600 European, Japanese and US manufacturers, they discovered that features such as product development speed, innovation in products and feel for market changes all had significant impact on market share growth. Worryingly, Cooper (1993) estimated that 46 per cent of product development resources are invested in products that either don't get made or are not profitable in the market place.

In the past, product or service design and development has been focused on the – often erroneous – company view of customer requirements. It has been largely concerned with specification and, while honest attempts have been made to link the design activity and specifications to the final customer, these have not always been successful due to the complex nature of the process of designing and producing products and services. In many cases the true customer requirements have become lost in the technical debate over historical precedent, producibility and technological capability.

The new economic era (Deming, 1993), where customers have much more choice than in the past, and where they are far more likely to exercise it, has made it an imperative for organizations to become much more customer focused. Many tools, techniques and philosophies have been developed to support this shift in focus from internal to external. Quality Function Deployment (QFD) is, perhaps, the most complete technique available for supporting this highly desirable cultural change.

Definition of QFD

QFD theory was first defined by Yoji Akao in 1966 and its initial application was at the Kobe shipyard of Mitsubishi in 1972 (Ungvari, 1991) when they began to use a matrix that put customer demands on the vertical axis and the methods by which they would be met on the horizontal axis.

The system has developed from this simple basis to encompass the broad range of activities within most manufacturing and service organizations; the comprehensive application of the technique has been defined thus:

> A system for translating customer requirements into appropriate company requirements at every stage, from research through product design and development, to manufacture, distribution, installation and marketing, sales and service. (Ungvari, 1991)

It is equally valid to think of QFD as a way of identifying the true voice of the customer (Sullivan, 1986) at an early stage and making sure that it is heard all the way through the design/production/delivery process to achieve high levels of customer satisfaction. QFD is not truly a quality technique; it is rather a planning technique used to focus teamwork where it really matters – on customer satisfaction.

The need for QFD

Due to the 'over the wall' (Cohen, 1995) nature of the traditional approach to establishing a product or service design, there is great potential for customer requirements to get lost or distorted. Organizations need to have some way of codifying this process and ensuring that the whole of the message from the final customer is gathered and translated sensibly into useful data.

Technological change presents a further problem to companies pursuing customer satisfaction. Should new technology be incorporated simply because it is state of the art or should the organization stick to what it knows? Innovation is inherently risky and to make economically viable decisions a tool is required which allows an organization to understand where innovation will be beneficial by being closely aligned to real customer needs. Sensible use of such a technique can ensure that a company is customer- rather than technology-driven.

The principles of QFD

The core principle of QFD is that the design and development process, be it product or service, should be driven by the needs of the customer. QFD is a methodology for adding structure to this process; for clearly specifying the customer's wants and needs and for systematically evaluating company capabilities in terms of meeting those needs (Cohen, 1995). By making all relationships explicit and by establishing linkages between current performance and customer satisfaction it generates a clearer view of design options.

QFD uses a matrix-based approach to derive critical product/service features to support the customer requirements and to establish the relationship between the desired end results and the necessary enabling features. By reviewing customer priorities, current performance and technical difficulty QFD facilitates the development of priority 'sales points' (Sullivan, 1986) where maximum impact on customer satisfaction can be gained for the applied company effort.

QFD embraces all customer needs and expectations, avoiding internal assumptions, and focuses on the positive aspects of quality ('how do we get the best deal for the customer?') rather than the negative ones ('how do we put this mistake right?'). QFD also creates a culture of customer focus by attending to the process for satisfying customer requirements and expectations.

Who is the customer in QFD?

This question is often more complex than it seems. Take the simple case of a packet of breakfast cereal. The producer has three basic customers: The supermarket, the purchaser and the consumer. In some cases the purchaser and the consumer may be combined, but the producer still has to make the product attractive to all three customers. At times the requirements of different customers will conflict, if this is the case the organization needs to understand the relationship between all customer groups in order to make rational decisions about how to respond to such conflicts.

When designing a new product/service, the design team will need to establish the proposed market and identify target customers. This may well be an iterative process, with designers altering product/service parameters if sufficient market interest is not originally forthcoming (Shen *et al.*, 2000). It must be further noted that there may be natural segments in the market for example, executive and family car drivers. Early decisions on the target market will drive later approaches to information gathering and option definition.

The one type of customer with whom care must be taken in using QFD is the internal customer. The requirements of these customers may not coincide with those of the external customers. For example, the desire for ease of assembly may not be reconcilable with the final customer's needs. In such cases the end product or service may be compromised by satisfying internal requirements. Since it is only by satisfying external customers that a company stays in business they cannot afford to place too much emphasis on the needs of internal customers in the QFD process. Organizations should, of course, be aware of internal problems and opportunities related to external customer needs so that they can begin to address these issues at an early stage.

Businesses must also be careful not to bias their data by only speaking to customers of a certain type. For instance, if they only ask their own customers, the chances are that they will be relatively homogeneous (and fairly positive). They need to capture data from a full cross-section of the potential market, including people who do not yet purchase in the market but who might be expected to, given an appropriate offering.

The customer view of quality

The Kano model of quality

The Kano model of quality (Figure 3.1) shows that customers' perceptions of quality are more complex than is often supposed (adapted from Kano *et al.*, 1984).

There are three key elements to Kano's model of the perception of quality:

Basic Quality relates to items where customers will assume that appropriate performance levels will be met as a matter of course. If the product meets all of these requirements, no significant positive satisfaction will be generated. However, if it fails fully to satisfy one of these criteria high levels of dissatisfaction may result. Examples of basic quality might be crashworthiness and driver/passenger safety in cars, or staff politeness in a bank.

Spoken Performance issues will take the form 'I would like the product/service to achieve this level of performance'. If the performance meets or exceeds this level the customer will be satisfied on that issue. If it does not then the customer will be dissatisfied. The model assumes a roughly linear relationship between performance against the specified criteria and customer satisfaction in that area. This may be an oversimplification (Tan and Shen, 2000); below certain threshold dissatisfaction may increase more quickly and above another level indifference may set in, and satisfaction increase more slowly. It

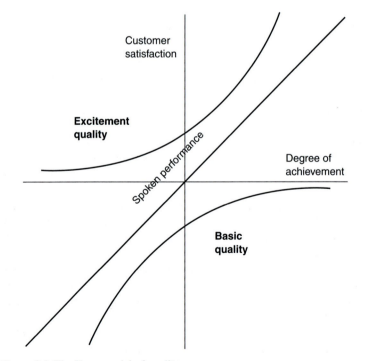

Figure 3.1 The Kano model of quality.

is, however, a workable assumption for the region of performance where customers are most concerned with the characteristic. Spoken performance items would include things like acceleration performance or fuel consumption rates in cars and waiting time at a bank.

Excitement Quality refers to giving customers something they didn't know they wanted. Clearly, customers cannot be dissatisfied because you didn't give them something they didn't know they wanted, but providing such features may generate extraordinary customer satisfaction. An example would be the leap-frogging of each generation of VCR video recorder with functions which most people wouldn't have asked for, but which they can now not do without.

The model is hierarchical in nature. If 'Basic Quality' requirements are not met then the customer will not be concerned about the 'Spoken Performance' elements. Similarly, should the product or service fail to meet the customers' spoken requirements the 'Excitement Quality' factors would not make up for this omission. For example, a car that boasts an advanced navigational aid but can seat only three people in comfort is unlikely to appeal to families of four. Even if a car meets all expressed requirements with the addition of excitement elements such as advanced navigational aids it will not sell if it proves to be unsafe, which is a basic purchase requirement for most users.

Implications of the model for QFD

From the above we can see that, although spoken performance issues are important, there are two other key areas where you may reduce ('Basic Quality') or increase ('Excitement Quality') customer satisfaction. Furthermore, these are areas where the customer will not generally volunteer the requirements, but where there is a need to get closer to customers to understand in more detail how they view the product or service. This will not typically be achieved by standard marketing techniques, which will tend to focus on the spoken performance elements.

If an organization wishes to be first choice for its customers it will need to meet all of the first category, be competitive with market leaders in the second category, ensuring a lead in at least a few, and offer some elements in the 'Excitement Quality' category. All successful 'Excitement Quality' features offered will put pressure on competing providers to match or exceed them and provide unique selling points until this happens. To this extent they offer an opportunity to lead the market and establish dominance. In terms of the QFD approach, it is possible to use the methodology proposed by Kano *et al.* (1984) to establish into which category requirements fall, and apply the logic above to underpin decisions on what action to take. This can also be useful in establishing where few requirements have been uncovered for any of the categories, indicating the need for further research.

Over time previous 'Excitement Quality' features will move into the 'Spoken Performance' category and, as the feature becomes more commonplace across suppliers it will eventually become a 'Basic Quality' item. An example of this would be the migration of electric windows in cars through the spectrum over time. This has an implication for the timeliness of delivery of products to market (Shen *et al.*, 2000). To get benefit from 'Excitement Quality' items they must be early to market in comparison to competing products, otherwise they may have dropped down the hierarchy before the customer experiences them. As a product matures and loses its technical advantages, levels of service may emerge as critical differentiators (Hassan *et al.*, 2000).

Establishing the requirements

Introduction

This is fundamental to any QFD effort. Organizations must establish what the customers need and expect.

Gathering customer data

There are a large number of possibilities for gathering this customer data. The two main approaches are as follows:

- *Questionnaire Techniques:* These can be postal, telephone interview or face-to-face interview.
- *Discussion Techniques:* These can include clinics where a large number of customers congregate and where they can experience the product or service, compare it to competitors and give feedback. Focus groups are a cross-section of the population (not necessarily customers) who are invited to discuss issues relating to the product or service. Listening to customer comments at trade exhibitions or at retail outlets can provide further information of this type.

Innovative ways of interacting with customers need to be developed in order to access the basic and excitement items. Focus groups and clinics are highly applicable in business-to-business situations but their value in open market situations may be limited by the difficulty that many customers' experience in expressing their views and requirements in what can be an intimidating forum. In such a situation carefully controlled visits to customers in their own situation might provide more insight through observation rather than discussion. One example of this is Rubbermaid's 'consumer encounter' programme (Rings *et al.*, 1998) where semi-structured customer visits are used to establish key customer views.

There are three elements to the customer data that is required for QFD. The elements (often described as the Voice of the Customer) are listed below, and some advice on how best to generate such data.

Customer needs: This will often be in their own words, which may not lend themselves to action within the company. Customers might want a car to 'look nice', 'sound good' or 'handle well'. The traditional reaction to such information would be to interpret what we think the customer means by these imprecise statements. This is wholly wrong and puts us at risk of starting off with a set of requirements that are about the company view of the customers rather than the customers' actual opinions. This danger is exacerbated by the presence in the information chain of a large number of individuals who may all put slightly varying interpretations on the statements. The customer must be asked to elaborate on their comments in order to tie down the true need. This may also be useful on occasions when a customer identifies a solution (e.g. driver airbag) when the requirement is actually, safety in a frontal crash.

These are best collected by face-to-face interviews. Mail and telephone surveys will not generate the level of understanding required due to the inability to interrogate responses adequately and to control the scope of the responses. Focus groups may be useful, or semi-structured customer visits, but it is estimated that face-to-face interviews are more cost effective and that interviewing 20–30 customers will elicit 90–95 per cent of requirements (Griffin and Hauser, 1993). Kano's approach can be used at this point to classify the requirements (Kano *et al.*, 1984).

Relative importance ratings: These establish a hierarchy of customer needs. These are best collected by mail/telephone surveys due to the volume of data required for statistical significance (>100). These will usually be collected using 5- or 9-point scales, although more elaborate scales may be used (Griffin and Hauser, 1993).

Competitive analysis: This is where customers rate the performance of the company and competitors on the customer needs (usually on a 1–5 scale). Accordingly, it should be gathered at the same time and in the same fashion as the previous point. Note that, since customers should only rate products or services of which they have direct experience, the sample size will need to be even bigger to get data on all parties.

The key criteria is to set up a data gathering system which will reflect accurately and in detail the views of the whole market place. A balance needs to be struck between making the system simple for customers and extracting the correct level and amount of data. A significant amount of the expense and effort involved in QFD will be incurred here, but if you do not get this right the whole of your product/service development process is at risk (whether or not QFD is used).

QFD case study

The application of QFD is illustrated below by the use of elements of a study performed on the design of a mountain bike. The data has been simplified to show the points more clearly.

Organizing the requirement data

In order to understand better the customer requirements and add structure to a large amount of disparate linguistic information, a process called the 'affinity diagram' technique is usually applied (Bossert, 1991). This technique generates a hierarchy of primary, secondary and tertiary requirements, and the process of grouping the requirements strongly assists the development of the QFD team's understanding of the customer requirements.

The affinity diagram technique is a bottom-up technique, which means that customers provide the tertiary requirements, which are placed in logical groupings by the QFD team. The team then defines a title for each group, which becomes the secondary level requirement for that group of tertiaries. The process is repeated for the secondary level requirements in order to generate the primaries. The team will then review the hierarchy for completeness and add any elements that may have been missed by the customer. Such additions will need to be carefully checked with the customer base to ensure that they reflect real customer requirements and not a team misconception. To this end the process is usually completed before questionnaires are sent to customers to establish relative importance ratings and competitive analysis.

QFD deals with tertiary requirements since these are most closely related to the actions an organization can take to satisfy its customers. It is these highly detailed requirements that drive the QFD process.

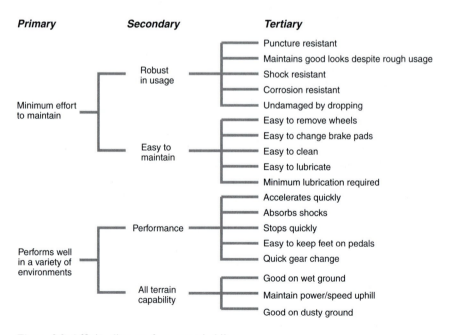

Figure 3.2 Affinity diagram for mountain bike.

Building the QFD chart

Positioning the customer information

The three elements of customer information appear on the chart as shown in Figure 3.3. Note that the requirements list stays as close as possible to the words of the customer and maintains the structure generated in the affinity diagram process.

Further analysis of the raw data may reveal opportunities for product stratification. If, for example, half the customers rate the feature 'easy to keep feet on pedals' as 9 and half as 1 it may indicate that this feature would be a good option to offer, but including it as standard may be wasteful as half the customers don't care.

The customer performance-rating graph is effectively an exercise in competitive benchmarking, but is clearly focused on the elements of the product or process that the customer believes to be important.

The customer data is the key to establishing priorities within the chart (see Analysis section). Additional information is often added to the matrix to aid analysis. One of the most common elements is warranty and customer complaints data, indicating which customer requirements have attracted complaints or claims and in what quantity. This provides additional data on dissatisfiers for customers while recognizing that a lack of dissatisfaction is not the same as satisfaction.

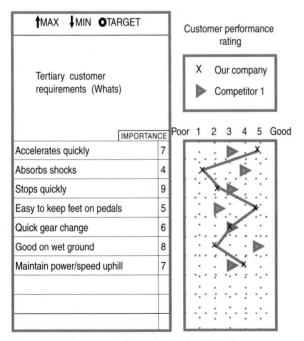

Figure 3.3 Customer information in the QFD chart.

Having gathered and organized the customer data, the QFD team generates the information in the rest of the matrix.

Linking customer requirements to product features

The translation of the voice of the customer into language meaningful to the designer of the product or service is a very important step in the QFD process and should be carried out carefully to ensure that this voice is not distorted. Care must be taken at this stage to avoid the assumption that current practice is right. This is a time to be creative in the examination of each of the requirements, remembering to confine this creativity to the technical response to the requirement and not to its interpretation.

Figure 3.4 develops the product characteristics for the mountain bike requirements shown in Figure 3.3. The diagram has been simplified in order to aid understanding by only allocating one or two product features per customer requirement. A key feature of this element of the matrix is that each product feature should be measurable and significant (Sullivan, 1986).

The design characteristics (or product features) are shown across the top of

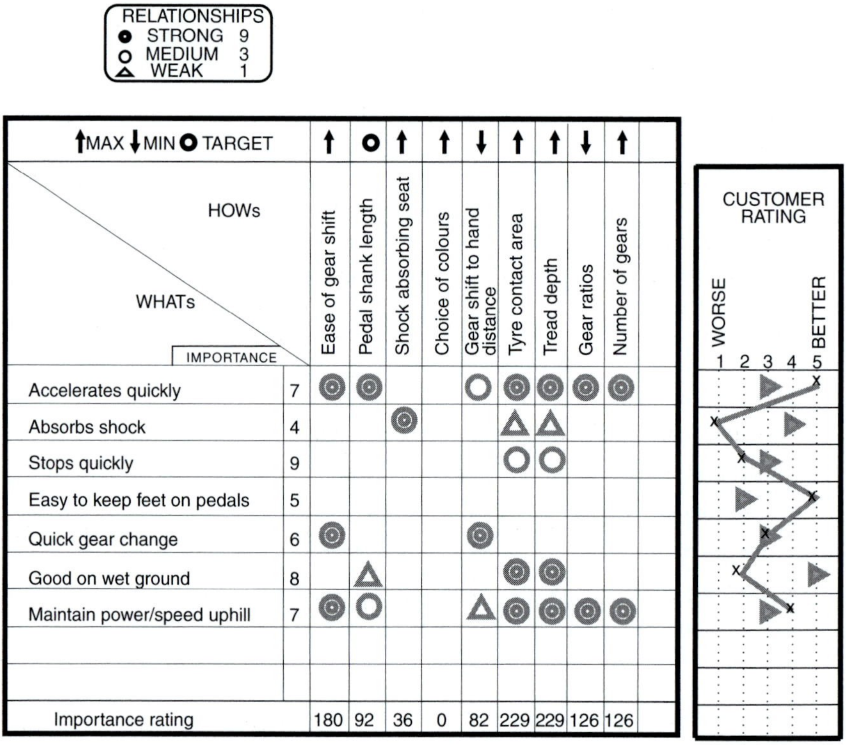

Figure 3.4 Linking customer requirement to product features.

the matrix and denoted as the 'hows'. These represent what the designers can control and have been derived by asking, for each 'what', the question 'which design features might help us to satisfy this customer requirement?' Any 'how' which affects more than one 'what' is still written down only once.

The relationship matrix represents all possible relationships between 'whats' and 'hows'. Each location represents a particular 'what'/'how' combination.

The relationship symbols indicate the strength of the perceived relationship between a 'what' and a 'how'. A blank indicates that no relationship exists, a triangle that only a possible or weak relationship exists, a circle that a medium-strength relationship exists and a double circle that a strong relationship exists. The team generates these symbols from their knowledge of the product and the market.

This part of the process is often the most time-consuming and difficult as it involves the team in exploring their understanding of the relationship between the customer requirements and possible design elements. That this often requires significant debate and even recourse to experimentation is perhaps indicative of the failings of traditional approaches to design in fostering this knowledge. The quality of the outcome of this element of the process will strongly depend upon the product, process and customer knowledge of those taking part.

The product feature importance ratings are generated from the 'what' importance ratings and the relationship strengths as shown. This gives an overall value as to the features that are most important to get right from the customer's point of view.

The relationships are given numerical weightings according to their strength: Using the traditional system, a strong relationship is weighted 9, a medium one 3, and a weak relationship is weighted 1 (Akao, 1990). Note that this scoring system may be varied (e.g. Franceschini and Rupil, 1999) although this is the most common scheme. The importance of each 'how' is the sum of its importance to each of the individual 'whats'. The relationship for each 'how' and the 'what' combination is deemed to have a multiplicatory effect. Thus, for the 'ease of gear shift' in column one the following logic and calculation apply:

Its importance to achieving customer satisfaction is:

> Importance to 'accelerates quickly' + Importance to 'quick gear change' + Importance to 'maintain power/speed uphill'

For each 'what' the importance of the associated 'how' is determined as follows:

> Importance to the customer of the 'what' $\times$ Strength of the relationship

So, for column 1 we get:

> {relationship 1 $\times$ importance rating 1} + {relationship 2 $\times$ importance rating 2} + {relationship 3 $\times$ importance rating 3}
> {9 $\times$ 7} + {9 $\times$ 6} + {9 $\times$ 7} = 180

It is important to note that this is a relative figure, and for comparison purposes only. It gives a pecking order to the key features, but does not remove the drive to optimize all parameters.

Clearly, there is a risk that inaccuracies in rating of requirements or relationships will affect the outcome. The logic of the 1–3–9 rating system has also been questioned and, for example, the analytical hierarchy technique suggested (Fung *et al.*, 1998). See critical review of QFD for further comment.

Interactions between product parameters

The triangular matrix which has been added at the top of the matrix in Figure 3.5 is known as the 'correlation matrix' since it is concerned with identifying interrelationships between the design requirements. It is analysed by reading right up the appropriate angled column from the left-most requirement of the two under consideration and left from the other until the two columns meet.

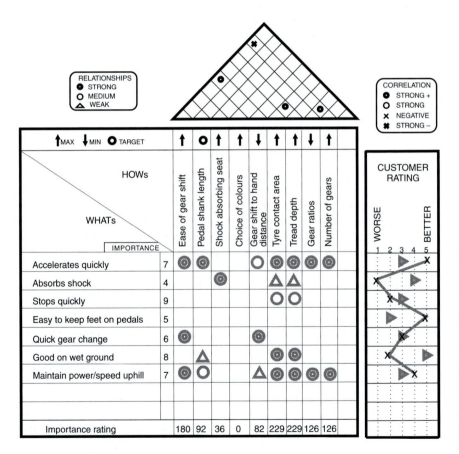

Figure 3.5 Adding the correlation matrix.

There can be one of four symbols, indicating both the nature and strength of the inter-relationship. We can see two distinct types of relationship here:

- *synergistic (positive):* where achievement of one design characteristic assists the achievement of the other;
- *trade-off (negative):* where achievement of one design characteristic interferes with the achievement of the other.

Each of these relationships may be characterized as strong or weak as indicated in the legend of the figure above. We can see, for instance, that there is a synergy between 'ease of gear shift' and 'gear shift to hand distance' (the closer to the hand the shift mechanism the less effort to change), while there is a trade-off between 'ease of gear shift' and 'number of gears' (difficulty in finding the correct gear if there are many to select from).

The benefit of this part of the QFD matrix is that it forces designers to consider rigorously all possible interactions between design features, some of which may be missed by a less systematic approach. It is thus possible to pick up trade-offs and synergies at a very early stage in the design process (this may not normally occur until the development phase in many cases). It is important to note that all trade-offs should be made in favour of the customer (i.e. in favour of the highest overall importance rating, taking into account all other interactions). A more pro-active way to look at trade-offs is to see them as an opportunity to move the state of the art forward to remove the trade-off. That is to say, approaching the question as 'how can we maximize customer satisfaction despite apparent internal inconsistencies' as opposed to 'which of these features should we give the customer most of'.

Ratings and targets for the 'hows' and technical difficulty

The final additions to consider are shown in Figure 3.6.

First, the objective target values define what level of a feature is 'right' for the market under consideration. This might be done by further market research in the case of such things as general dimensions of the bike, or designed experimentation, which might help to establish the best gear ratios.

Competitive assessment indicates how the company product compares with that of competitors against the objective target values set for the design requirements. This is a market focused (in that only those features having a direct impact on customer satisfaction are considered) technical assessment carried out in house by those involved with the service or product.

The technical difficulty ratings (in this case shown as points on a 1–5 scale, where 1 is easy and 5 is very difficult) are an important part of the decision-making process (Mizuno and Akao, 1994). Clearly, real commitment to deliver the design features which will satisfy a customer need must be given with due regard to the difficulty and cost of this activity. These difficulty figures should not be used to avoid satisfying a given need, but to generate buy-in across all concerned for the effort required.

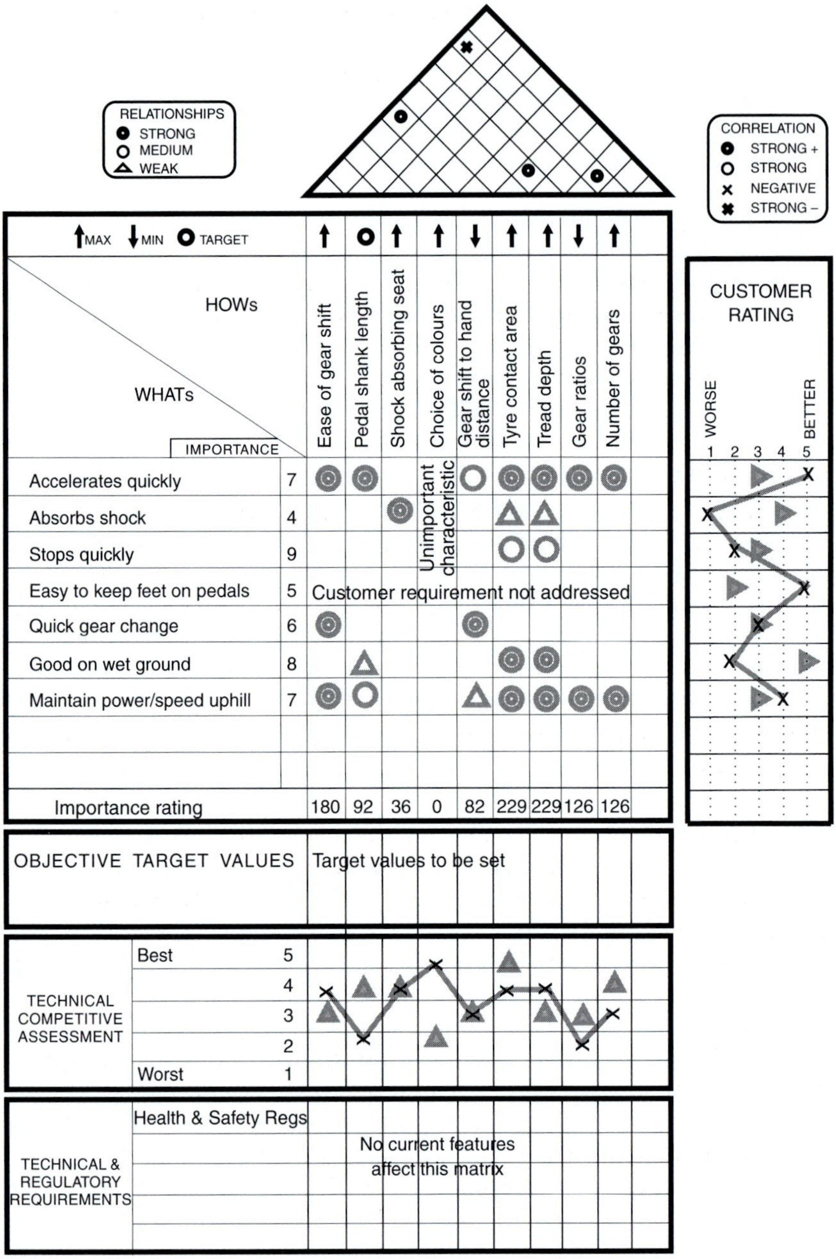

Figure 3.6 Completed QFD chart.

The customer requirements, as identified, will not cover regulatory requirements or the technical requirements that the company imposes upon itself (for
example, if we wished to make the design suitable for automated manufacture).
These requirements are kept in a separate matrix since they are generally somewhat different in nature to the customer requirements. They can be viewed as
setting the parameters within which the company must operate.

Analysing the chart

The purpose of completing a QFD chart is to draw conclusions as to where
product and process development effort can best be applied. This requires an
analysis of the whole chart in order to make sensible decisions. There are several
key elements to consider.

Logical gaps and inconsistencies

There are several logic checks within the QFD process to ensure that consistent
thinking is applied. An empty row in the main matrix indicates that there is a
customer need that is not being attended to by planned features. An empty
column indicates that some features do not appear to be focused on the customer. There are examples of this in the matrix in Figure 3.6. 'Choice of
colours' appears to affect no known customer requirement, and no design features appear to address the customer need of 'easy to keep feet on pedals'. QFD
would thus indicate the two main errors committed in the early stages of product
and process design: spending effort on things that do not matter or failing to
respond to a customer requirement within the design.

At the assessment stage inconsistencies between the two measurements can be
identified. This means that a poor rating from the customer on a particular
requirement would be expected to correlate with poor ratings for the factors
affecting that requirement in the technical assessment. Conflicts between the two
metrics indicate a mismatch between customer and company assessments of
performance.

In Figure 3.6 it can be seen that the customer rating for 'Absorbs shock' is
poor, but the technical rating for the most significant contributing feature,
'Shock absorbing seat', is good. In such a case the assumption has to be that the
customer perception is correct. The incorrect company view may relate to poor
setting of targets, or to failings in the generation of design features or in completion of the relationship or correlation matrices. The team should establish where
the problem lies and correct it.

Setting priorities for action

The key elements to making a decision about where to target development effort
are the answers to these two questions:

1   *'Does this characteristic matter to the customer?'* This is essentially answered by the customer importance rating. As it is a relative scale, the team needs to decide by looking at the pattern of these ratings what level to consider significant.
2   *'How does the customer view our present provision in relation to the competition?'* The customer performance rating answers this question. High priorities would be attached to requirements where the opposition were rated significantly better than the company, or all providers were rated poorly.

The assessments generally establish three principal levels of priority (providing that the requirement is important to the customer):

1   *Where we lag and need to catch up.* A higher performance rating is given to our competitors than to us. For example, 'Good on wet ground' in Figure 3.6.
2   *Where there is a gap in the market.* Both our competitors and ourselves receive low ratings. For example, 'Stops quickly' in Figure 3.6.
3   *Where we are ahead and need to maintain the lead.* We receive a higher rating than our competitors. For example, 'Accelerates quickly' in Figure 3.6.

For each level there are clearly several sub-levels depending on the significance of the difference (e.g. a priority 1 where the opposition gets a 5 and we get a 1 would be more significant than a 4 to 2 gap).

By implication it can be seen that areas where the customer is already well satisfied by all providers would not attract much effort, as it will be difficult/expensive to gain competitive advantage. Nor would areas where customers are relatively indifferent to the requirement being satisfied.

Having identified key customer requirements. it is possible to link these back to the most strongly related design features so that effort can be targeted in terms of what needs to be done rather than what the outcome needs to be. Considering 'good on wet ground' as a key priority would lead to focus on 'tyre contact area' and 'tread depth' as the principal features affecting this requirement. Correlations between design features will also be important here; in this case they are supportive.

Once this stage in the assessment is reached the organization can come to a series of decisions about what needs to be done in terms of design of the service or product to ensure customer satisfaction. They can rank in order of importance what needs to be got right and the difficulty in doing so. They can compare themselves to their competitors, both from the customer's viewpoint and in technical terms to see where the best business opportunities lie. The outcome of this analysis will be a number of key design requirements that will drive the more detailed design process.

The expanded QFD process

The matrix, which has been discussed in some detail so far, is the first level of the full QFD process. In practice many companies do not go much further than this and it can be seen that a significant benefit is to be gained from this exercise. However, to ensure the voice of the customer is cascaded throughout the whole company the QFD process can be extended to include other parts of the product life-cycle. There are various approaches to this deployment, the most popular being the four-phase deployment (Clausing, 1994).

The deployment activity is driven by the key 'Hows' from the previous phase becoming the 'Whats' in the subsequent phase.

Design deployment

This matrix is concerned with identifying the critical component characteristics to support the design requirements established in the previous matrix.

Manufacturing planning

The process planning matrix allows critical processes to be identified which are key to the successful creation of the product. This stage is designed to determine critical process operations and critical process parameters.

Production planning

This chart is designed to ensure the smooth transition from development into manufacture. This stage aims to minimize controllable variations in the manufacturing processes.

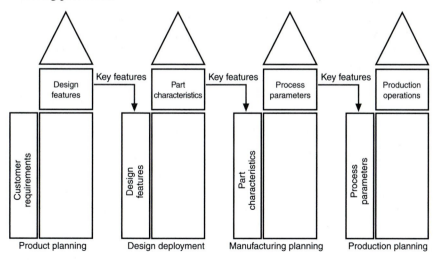

Figure 3.7 The expanded QFD process.

Source: adapted from Cohen (1995).

Managing QFD

The QFD team

The various data inputs that are required for QFD necessitate the use of a multi-disciplined team. Cohen (1995) suggests 'all important functional groups involved in design, development, building, delivering and servicing the product or service' should be represented. This team should also include key people in the design process as QFD should be part of this overall process and this will help the join to be seamless. Maintaining continuity maximizes the chances of carrying the benefits of the QFD approach through into the final product or service. The selection of team members requires the usual care in blending skills, knowledge and personalities for optimum effect.

Role of the facilitator/manager

QFD requires active management as a process, particularly early in an organization's experience of the technique. Cohen (1995) notes the importance of a facilitator/manager in achieving successful outcomes and describes this role as involving the following:

- Gaining management, functional and technical support for the approach both prior to and during implementation.
- Agreeing and clarifying the objectives of the process.
- Selecting, training and supporting the team, including explanations of each step of the process.
- Acting as an interface with senior management and functional groups, keeping them informed of progress and decisions in order to maintain commitment to the process.
- Ensuring that the team sticks to a sensible timetable and that things get done.
- Obtaining consensus during all phases of the activity and acting as a prompt to ensure decisions are based on as much data as is possible, given the uncertain nature of the information at the early phases of product/service design.

Making QFD successful

As with all techniques the success of QFD is heavily bound up with senior management commitment. They must actively promote the approach, linking it to corporate strategy and showing faith in its outcomes if others are to be persuaded. They are also responsible for ensuring that enough time is allowed for the process and that the correct resources (particularly people) are available.

QFD is principally a different way of inter-relating all of the information that goes into any design and development activity. As such it should not be introduced as a 'new technique', simply a more rigorous approach to something that the organization is committed to doing anyway. Hence the importance of continuity of team members for the whole of the design project as well as the QFD phase.

QFD requires significant upfront effort (40 hours is typical to complete the first matrix when all data has been gathered). This effort is, however, repaid many times in downstream activities. In fact, QFD often covers more ground faster than other, less structured, techniques (Cohen, 1995).

It is vital to pilot QFD as a process, once expertise has been built up most new or revised products or services can be put through the system. However, the first attempt may produce an avalanche of paperwork if not properly controlled and this can be disastrous if too many or too large projects are tackled early on.

Keep teams focused on delighting the customer rather than on doing the chart, avoid regression to old practices, such as team members filling in the charts from their own 'experience'.

Don't expect too much too soon. Be aware that initial applications may only show small tangible benefits but they will form the basis for future success by moving you closer to the customer, improving communications etc.

Ensure that the outcome of QFD is measured on items such as cost, customer satisfaction, time to market etc. in order to understand where and how the benefits have come (Zairi, 1993). Establish these metrics at the start of the project to focus the efforts of the team.

QFD applications

QFD has been used across a wide variety of product and service applications including training/education, software development, healthcare, automotive manufacturing, electronics, information technology systems and policy implementation (see Ziari, 1993; Cohen, 1995; Tan *et al.* 1998 among others).

There is evidence that although common principles apply, significant customization may be required for QFD to work in service organizations. This is due to the difficulty in differentiating between what benefits the service delivers to the customer and how the service is provided, and in measuring service elements (Franceschini and Terzago, 1998). This is not a significant problem, as QFD is a highly customizable technique. The basic rule with QFD is that what appears to the team to add value to their analysis should be used. This is the reason that very few QFD exercises look alike. QFD is a very flexible tool and, provided commonsense is applied, organizations should be prepared to make use of that flexibility.

The benefits of QFD

Detailed discussion of the benefits of QFD can be found in many textbooks and papers (e.g. Zairi, 1993; Sullivan, 1986). The QFD process supports focus on what the customer wants at a very early stage, and to apply a team working approach to carry this through all of the steps from this stage to delivery to the final customer. This can be seen to have many direct benefits including:

- *less time in development*: due to better up-front planning;
- *fewer and earlier changes*: due to better and earlier identification of problems;
- *fewer start-up problems and lower start-up costs*;
- *fewer field problems*: due to a better understanding of customer requirements and the conditions of service;
- *satisfied customers*: due to improved customer focus;
- *a better knowledge base within the company*: due to not needing to re-invent the wheel each time the design process is repeated.

Overall QFD has strong positive effects on both customer satisfaction and time competitiveness for an organization launching new or modified products or services. There are also likely to be indirect benefits such as:

- *development of cross-functional teams;*
- *increased customer focus in the organization;*
- *improved internal communications.*

The application of QFD now goes far beyond the support of product or service design and development and extends into developing how organizations plan any activity (Cohen, 1995). If used comprehensively, QFD can act as a philosophy, which helps to move the culture of the organization towards true customer focus. In particular, it encourages culture change in the following ways (Zairi, 1993):

- It calls for clear, detailed and complete information on customer needs and expectations and for these to remain the focus of the design and development process.
- It places emphasis on teamwork and multi-functional contributions and makes the goal of delivering to the final customer a company goal, rather than delegating it to one lead department (usually production or operations).
- It places emphasis on the visibility of information, which is gathered from several points of view: capability of meeting requirements from the customer's point of view, technical capabilities from a company point of view, and level of competitiveness from a market point of view.

Critical review of QFD

There can be little doubting the positive potential of QFD as a technique. In a ten-year study entitled the Global Manufacturing Futures Project, Miller *et al.* (1992) reported the top ten programmes for both attention and pay-off; QFD was on both lists. Criticism of the technique tends to relate more to the detail of how the technique works and falls into the following categories:

- the complexity of the charts;
- potential distortion of the voice of the customer due to the vagueness of the customer data collected and the subjective basis of the numerical analyses performed in the matrix.

Chart complexity issues

Bouchereau and Rowlands (2000) note that the need to input and analyse large amounts of subjective data into the matrix is difficult and time-consuming, that the matrix can become very large and complex and that QFD development records are rarely kept. Several researchers (e.g. Lyman, 1995; Ginn *et al.*, 1998) indicate that these factors can make QFD difficult to implement. In extreme cases, this may lead to loss of momentum, abandonment of the programme or questioning the validity of QFD.

Such concerns are doubtless justified, and Clausing (1994) notes the need for a cultural fit with the organization to generate the best results. However, proper preparation, careful management of the activity, and recognizing the QFD activity as a learning process as well as a product development process should minimize these concerns. In particular, there is a clear need for QFD to be piloted on small projects in order to build the confidence and expertise of the team in applying the logic and deriving conclusions.

Vagueness of data and subjectivity of analysis

This area is perhaps the single most researched area in QFD over the last few years. Vanegas and Labib (2001) note that the voice of the customer tends to be 'linguistic and non-technical in nature' and can thus be difficult for engineers to translate into technical terms for further action. Franceschini and Rupil (1998) focus on the use of an 'arbitrary' metric to codify gathered data and the likely difference in interpretation of the same scale by different evaluators. Chan *et al.* (1999) note that customer ratings for their needs are also prone to the vagueness of customers' perceptions.

Improvements to QFD have been postulated in order to reduce the impact of such vagueness and subjectivity. They range from the use of the Analytical Hierarchy Process (Fung *et al.*, 1998), artificial neural networks (Bouchereau and Rowlands, 2000), to various applications of fuzzy logic (Fung *et al.*, 1998; Wang, 1999; Vanegas and Labib, 2001). The logic of most of this work is impeccable; however, the jury is still out on the impact it will have on the practical application of QFD in industry. There is strong evidence of the positive impact QFD in its current form has had in a variety of applications (examples can be found in, among others, Zairi, 1993), and little firm evidence of practical improvements in decisions generated by incorporation of these different approaches. What is certain is that such analyses will add significantly to the complexity of a technique that, as noted above, is already seen as difficult.

This is by no means to diminish the frailties of QFD in this regard, but as essentially a prioritization technique it is generating a generally sound priority list which matters. Subtle variation in the ordering of priorities is not very significant, provided that no major issues are missed and no minor ones elevated to priority status. Where a direct comparison of traditional and fuzzy approaches has been attempted evidence of such gross shifts is limited. Chan *et al.* (1999), for example, saw no difference in ranking when they substituted Triangular Fuzzy Numbers for crisp numbers in a case study, and while Franceschini and Rupil (1998) demonstrated a reversal of priority for two engineering character-istics by changing ranking systems, they did not establish that this would significantly affect the design outcome.

Perhaps the best advice which can be given in this area is to suggest that there may be an opportunity for some sensitivity analysis when significant design expenditure is at stake. It would be possible to test the effect of customer ratings being, say, 6 rather than 7, or relationship values being medium rather than strong on the outcomes. However, in complex situations it is perhaps unlikely that all errors will work in one direction so as to inflate one characteristic at the expense of another. Indeed, it could be argued that such an event would indicate a systemic lack of understanding of relationships which would undermine what-ever system was in use.

Conclusion

QFD is a well-proven technique with the potential to provide significant insight into the product or service design and development activity. It has been applied to a wide variety of planning/development activities in a vast array of organi-zations with great success; the improved customer focus and early identification of design conflicts generating reduced costs and improved time to market with better products.

As with all techniques, it is vulnerable to poor levels of management commit-ment and particularly to loss of momentum due to its complexity and time-consuming nature. Commitment to all of the resource and cultural implications of a QFD activity must be obtained from all stakeholders before embarking on the process.

QFD is also criticized for a lack of precision. However, it provides much greater level of confidence in results than traditional means and proposals to improve precision seem to add much complexity without a proven significant impact on the quality of decisions made.

On balance, it is fair to conclude that the benefits of QFD as a process and a paradigm outweigh its perceived weaknesses in analytical precision.

References

Akao, Y. (1990) *Quality Function Deployment*. Cambridge, MA: Productivity Press.
Bossert, J.L. (1991) *Quality Function Deployment, A Practitioner's Approach*. New York: ASQC Press, Marcel Dekker.

The Boston Consulting Group, Product Development Consulting & The Management Roundtable (1993) *Review of Findings, International New Product Development Survey*.

Bouchereau, V. and Rowlands, H. (2000) Methods and techniques to help quality function deployment (QFD), *Benchmarking, An International Journal* **7**(1), 8–19.

Chan, L.K., Kao, H.P., Ng, A. and Wu, M.L. (1999) Rating the importance of customer needs in quality function deployment by fuzzy and entropy methods, *International Journal of Production Research* **37**(11), 2499–518.

Clausing, D. (1994) *Total Quality Development: A Step-by-Step Guide to World-Class Concurrent Engineering*, ASME Press.

Cohen, L. (1995) *Quality Function Deployment: How to Make QFD Work for You*. Reading, MA: Addison Wesley.

Cooper, R.G. (1993) *Winning at New Products* (2nd edn). Reading, MA: Addison Wesley.

Deming, W.E. (1990) *Out of the Crisis*. Cambridge, MA: MIT Centre for Advanced Engineering Study.

Deming, W.E. (1993) *The New Economics for Industry, Government and Education*. Cambridge, MA: MIT Centre for Advanced Engineering Study.

Franceschini, F. and Rupil, A. (1999) Rating scales and prioritisation in QFD, *International Journal of Quality & Reliability Management* **16**(1), 85–97.

Franceschini, F. and Terzago, M. (1998) An application of quality function deployment to industrial training courses, *International Journal of Quality & Reliability Management* **15**(7), 85–97.

Fung, R.Y.K., Popplewell, K. and Xie, J. (1998) An intelligent hybrid system for customer requirements analysis and product attribute targets determination, *International Journal of Production Research* **36**(1), 13–34.

Ginn, D.M., Jones, D.V., Rahnejat, H. and Zairi, M. (1998) The QFD/FMEA interface, *European Journal of Innovation Management* **12**(1), 1–27.

Griffin, A. and Hauser, J.R. (1993) The voice of the customer, *Marketing Science* **1**(1), 7–20.

Hassan, A., Baksh, M.S.N. and Shaharoun, A.M. (2000) Issues in quality engineering research, *International Journal of Quality & Reliability Management* **17**(8), 858–75.

Juran, J.M. (1989) *Juran on Leadership for Quality*. New York: Free Press.

Kano, N., Seraku, N., Takahashi, F. and Tsuji, S. (1984) Attractive quality and must be quality, *Hinshitsu (Quality, The Journal of The Japanese Society for Quality Control)* **14**(2), 39–48.

Lyman, D. (1995) Are they my QFD rules or are they new QFD rules?, or how to change technology, *Transactions from the Seventh Symposium on Quality Function Deployment*, 11–13 June, 101–10. Novi, MI.

Miller, J.G., De Meyer, A. and Nakane, J. (1992) *Benchmarking global manufacturing: understanding international suppliers, customers and competitors*. Homewood, IL: Business One Irwin.

Mizuno, S. and Akao, Y. (1994) *QFD: The Customer Driven Approach to Quality Planning and Deployment*. Tokyo: Asian Productivity Organisation.

Rings, C.M. *et al.* (1998) *Consumer Encounters of The Third Kind; Tenth Symposium on Quality Function Deployment*, 14–17 June, 89–99, Novi, MI, USA.

Shen, X.X., Tan, K.C. and Xie, M. (2000) An integrated approach to innovative product development using Kano's model and QFD, *European Journal of Innovation Management* **3**(2), 91–9.

Sullivan, L.P. (1986) Quality Function Deployment, *Quality Progress*, June, 39–50.

Tan, K.C. and Shen, X.X. (2000) Integrating Kano's model in the planning matrix of quality function deployment, *Total Quality Management* **11**(8). 1141–7.

Tan, K.C., Xie, M. and Chia, E. (1998) Quality function deployment and its use in designing information technology systems, *International Journal of Quality and Reliability Management* **15**(6), 634–45.

Ungvari, S. (1991) Total Quality Management & quality function deployment, *Third Symposium on Quality Function Deployment*, 24–25 June, Michigan, USA.

Vanegas, L.V. and Labib, A.W. (2001) A fuzzy quality function deployment (FQFD) model for deriving optimum targets, *International Journal of Production Research* **39**(1), 99–120.

Wang, J. (1999) Fuzzy outranking approach to prioritise design requirements in quality function deployment, *International Journal of Production Research* **37**(4) 899–916.

Zairi, M. (1993) *Quality Function Deployment: A Modern Competitive Tool*. TQM Practitioner Series, Technical Communication (Publishing) Ltd., Letchworth, UK.

4 Taguchi methods of experimental design for continuous improvement of process effectiveness and product quality

Jiju Antony

Introduction

Quality improvement using statistical planning and design of experiments is a major concern for many organizations today. Design of experiments (sometimes referred to as experimental design) is a powerful approach to product and process design and development, and for improving the yield and stability of an on-going production process (Montgomery, 1992). It is a direct replacement of One-Factor-At-A-Time (OFAAT) approach to experimentation, which is often unreliable, unpredictable and may yield false optimum conditions for the process (Logothetis, 1994). Experimental design, in contrast, is a systematic and structured approach to experimentation, whereby we study the effect of all the factors on a certain response (or quality characteristic) simultaneously. Here response or quality characteristic is the output which is of interest to experimenters and will have a significant impact on customer satisfaction.

Experimental design was first introduced and developed by Sir Ronald Fisher in the early 1920s at the Rothamsted Agricultural Field Station in London. In his early applications, Fisher used experimental design to determine the effect of factors such as rain, fertilizer, sunshine, condition of soil etc. on the final condition of the crop. Since that time, much development of the technique has taken place in the academic environment, but not as many applications in the manufacturing environment. Dr Taguchi, a distinguished electrical engineer and statistician, carried out extensive research on experimental design techniques in the early 1950s. He was successful in integrating the statistical methods into the powerful engineering process for process optimization problems. Dr Taguchi has developed and promoted a powerful methodology for solving product and process quality related problems in industry (Antony and Roy, 1998). Taguchi recommended the use of orthogonal arrays (OAs) for studying the effect of a number of process parameters (or design parameters) or factors on the process output performance (or product quality characteristic). Orthogonal arrays assist an experimenter to study a large number of parameters (or factors) in a limited number of experimental trials and thereby slash the experimental budget and resources.

A number of successful applications of Taguchi methods of experimental design for improving product quality and process performance have been reported by many US and European manufacturers over the last 15 years (Quinlan, 1985; Kackar and Shoemaker, 1987; Brassington, 1990; Sirvanci and Durmaz, 1993; Antony and Kaye, 1996). This chapter discusses the Taguchi methods of experimental design, the real benefits of Taguchi methods in industrial world, a methodology for Taguchi method of experimental design, application of Taguchi method of experimental design in a manufacturing company and a discussion on the advantages and disadvantages of Taguchi methods.

Experimental design using the Taguchi approach

In order to plan and design industrial experiments, Taguchi used orthogonal arrays (OAs). An orthogonal array (OA) is a matrix of numbers arranged in rows and columns. Each row represents the levels (or states) of the selected factors in a given experiment, and each column represents a specific factor whose effects on the process performance (or product quality characteristic) can be studied. Orthogonal arrays have a balanced property which entails that every factor setting occurs the same number of times for every setting of all other factors considered in the experiment. Taguchi has developed the application of a series of designs utilizing orthogonal arrays handling a large number of factors and levels, quantifying likely interactions and optimizing factor levels during the experiment (Dale, 1994). Taguchi and Konishi provide the complete list of standard orthogonal arrays that can be used for conducting real world experiments in industry (Taguchi and Konishi, 1987). Taguchi's orthogonal array designs are widely used in screening experiments to identify the most important factors from a large number of factors. An OA is usually represented by the following notation:

$$L_a(b^c)$$

Where: a = number of experimental runs or trials;
b = number of levels of each factor;
c = number of columns in the array.

The 'L' notation implies that the information is based on the Latin square arrangement of factors.

For example, $L_4(2^2)$ can be used for studying two 2-level factors in four experimental runs or trials. Here the term level refers to a specified setting of a factor. Table 4.1 illustrates a four-trial OA for studying two 2-level factors (1 represents level 1 and 2 represents level 2 of that factor). Taguchi considers the ability to detect the presence of interactions to be the primary reason for using

Table 4.1 A four-trial OA for studying two 2-level factors

Trial number	Factor 1	Factor 2
1	1	1
2	1	2
3	2	1
4	2	2

orthogonal arrays. To minimize the experimental budget and due to time constraints, the experimenter often attempts to employ the smallest OA, which will meet the objective of the experiment.

Although the OAs are based on the earlier works of Finney (1945) and Plackett and Burman (1946), Taguchi has developed a series of linear graphs which diagrammatically demonstrates how and where each factor and its interactions has been assigned to the column of an OA. However the use of linear graphs do not provide the complete confounding relationships among the factors or interactions to be studied for the experiment (Tsui, 1988). Here the term confounding refers to the combining influences of two or more factor (or interaction) effects in one measured effect. In other words, one cannot estimate factor effects and their interaction effects independently. The confounding nature of factors among different columns in an OA can be obtained from Taguchi's interaction table or confounding tables (Phadke, 1989).

Applications and benefits of Taguchi methods in industry

Taguchi methods of experimental design were introduced into the US in the early 1980s. Taguchi's introduction of the method to several major American companies, including AT & T, Xerox and Ford, resulted in significant improvement of product and process quality (Antony, 1997). Taguchi methods were introduced into the UK industry in the late 1980s and early 1990s. Taguchi methods have proved to be successful in many manufacturing areas including plastics, automotive, metal fabrication, process and semi-conductors and today even the service industry is using this powerful technique for tackling service delivery time-related problems (Rowlands *et al.*, 2000). Table 4.2 gives the applications and benefits of Taguchi methods in the manufacturing industry. The manufacturing sectors are classified into plastics, chemical, automotive, metal fabrication, electronics and semi-conductors and food. Kumar *et al.* (1996) provide an excellent application of Taguchi's experimental design technique to improve service performance of a small software export company in the US.

The use of Taguchi methods in a non-manufacturing environment is still not much reported. It is important to note that Taguchi methods can be applied to the service industry as long as the output performance can be identified and measured accurately. Moreover, service process performance depends a great deal on the behaviour of human beings involved in delivering the service. The

Table 4.2 Typical applications of Taguchi method in manufacturing sector

Process/product	Nature of problem	Experiment size	Benefits
Injection moulding process	High scrap rate due to excessive process variability	Eight trials	Annual savings were estimated to be over £40,000
Injection moulding process	Excessive warpage with the moulded part	Eight trials	Reduced percentage rework from 50% to less than 5%
Cylindrical lapping	Poor surface roughness	Sixteen trials	Improved the surface roughness by 20%
Diesel injector	High rework rate	Sixteen trials	Annual savings were estimated to be over £10,000
Extrusion process	Unacceptable variation in the thickness of extruded rubber hoses	Eight trials	Increased process capability from 0.7 to above 1.5
Welding process	Low weld strength	Sixteen trials	Annual savings were estimated to be over £16,000
Casting process	High scrap rate due to a casting defect called 'shrinkage porosity'	Eight trials	Scrap rate dropped from 15% to less than 4%, estimated annual saving was nearly £20k
Chemical process	Low process yield	Eight trials	Process yield was improved by over 10%
Biscuit	Excessive variability in biscuit length	Sixteen trials	Biscuit length variability was reduced by over 25%
Wire-bonding process	Low wire pull strength	Sixteen trials	Annual savings were over £30,000

following are the potential applications of Taguchi methods of experimental design in the service industry (Blosch and Antony, 1999):

- comparing competitive strategies on the development of new services;
- minimizing the time to respond to customer complaints;
- minimizing errors on service orders;
- reducing the service delivery time to customers (e.g. banks, hospitals, restaurants etc.);
- reducing processing errors in transactions at banks;
- reducing waiting time at the check-in counter of an airport;
- reducing the length of stay in an emergency room in hospitals;
- minimizing the number of billing errors from a utility company.

The Taguchi's quality philosophy

The term quality can be defined in different ways and it has different meanings to different people. However in order to achieve a competitive status through quality, it is desirable to have a definition for quality that reflects customers' expectations or needs. Taguchi's approach to quality differs from other world leading quality gurus such as Juran, Deming, Crosby, Feigenbaum and Garvin in that he focuses on the engineering aspects of quality rather than on management philosophy. He advocates the use of statistical design of experiments for reducing variation in the functional performance of products and processes around a specified target value. The following seven points briefly embrace the discerning features of Taguchi's quality philosophy in assuring product and process quality. A detailed description of each point can be obtained from the paper entitled 'Taguchi's Quality Philosophy: Analysis and Commentary' (Kackar, 1986).

- *Quality of a product/service is the loss imparted by the product/service to society from the time the product is shipped (if it is related to a product) or from the time the service is rendered to the customer*

The meaning of the word 'quality' changes with the context in which it is being used. According to Taguchi, quality is measured as a deviation in the functional performance of a product/service from its target performance. The larger the deviation in the functional performance, the greater the loss. Some examples of loss incurred by a product/service to the society include:

- failure to meet customer requirements for a certain service;
- failure to meet the desired performance and harmful side effects caused by the product;
- cost of customer dissatisfaction which may lead to loss of company reputation, and so on.

- *Continuous improvement of product/process/service quality and cost reduction programmes are essential for organizations to sustain their competitive advantage*

According to Bessant *et al.* (1994), continuous improvement has been defined as a company-wide process of focused and incremental innovation. An analysis of the level of development of continuous improvement across all departmental operations provides a good indicator of company's future competitive potential. In today's modern and competitive global market place, a business that does not earn a reasonable profit cannot stay in business for long. In order to increase market share, products must be produced at high quality and low costs (includes R&D costs, manufacturing costs and maintenance costs). Taguchi accentuates the use of parameter design (Taguchi, 1987) to accomplish the above objective. The objective of parameter design is to make product performance robust at minimal costs.

- *A continuous quality improvement programme has to aim continuously at reducing functional performance variation of products about a specified target performance*

In many organizations, quality is viewed as merely conforming to specification. This view of quality in organizations must be a first step, not a final goal. The objective of a continuous quality improvement programme is to continuously reduce the variation of the product functional performance characteristic about their target levels. Inconsistency of product performance due to excessive variation is a sign of poor quality. Organizations must strive to reduce functional variation in product performance characteristic around the target value, which is the key task of parameter design.

- *The quality loss is approximately proportional to the square of the deviation in the functional performance characteristic of a product from its target value*

The term 'quality loss' is the deviation in the functional performance of products from their target value. This 'loss' includes the costs associated with customer dissatisfaction (due to loss of reputation of the company), costs associated with failure to meet customer requirements for a certain service, and so on. Taguchi argues that the loss in financial terms is proportional to the square of the deviation in the functional performance characteristic from its target of a product from its target value. The loss function takes the following basic quadratic form:

$$L(y) = k(y - m)^2 \qquad\qquad (4.1)$$

where: L(y) is the loss in monetary terms;
m is the target value for a certain performance characteristic;
y is the individual performance characteristic;
k is a constant called cost constant or quality loss coefficient, which depends upon the financial importance of the product characteristic.

- *The final quality and cost (R&D, manufacturing and other operations) of a manufactured product are determined to a large extent by the engineering designs of the product and its manufacturing process*

It is important to recall the point that 'quality cannot be achieved by the traditional process of inspection and screening'. Quality should rather be designed and built into products at the design phase so as to make the product performance robust in the manufacturing phase. Countermeasures against variation in the product's functional performance caused by undesirable external influences can be built into the products only at the product design stage. Companies who strive to make their product and process design and also manufacturing processes insensitive to all sorts of variation (e.g. environmental, product-to-product etc.) will thus sustain their competitive position in the global market place.

- *Variation in product (or process) performance can be reduced by exploiting the non-linear effects of the product (or process) parameters on the functional performance of the product*

A robust product or a robust process is one whose output performance is least sensitive to all noise factors. The output performance of a product depends on the values of control and noise factors through non-linear function. The objective of robust design is to exploit the non-linearity to find a combination of process parameter values (or product design parameter values) which yields minimum variation in the performance characteristic around its nominal value. By exploiting non-linearity, one can minimize the quality loss without increasing the product cost (Phadke, 1989).

- *Statistically planned and designed experiments can be used to identify the product (or/and process) parameter settings that reduce variation in the performance characteristic of products*

Statistically planned and designed experiments are used for determining the optimal process or/and product parameter settings that reduce variation in the functional performance of products around its desired target value. In order to accomplish this objective, one may need to identify the key parameters which have significant impact on the mean process performance and performance variability through carefully planned experimental design approach.

A systematic methodology for the Taguchi approach to experimental design

This section describes a systematic methodology for Taguchi methods of experimental design to tackle product and process quality related problems in industries. The methodology consists of four important phases; planning, conducting, analysing and implementing the solution (see Figure 4.1).

The major steps to complete an effective designed experiment are listed in the following text. The planning phase includes seven steps as follows:

Planning phase

Step 1: *Problem recognition, formulation and organization of the team*

Problem recognition and formulation is crucial for the success of any industrial designed experiment. It is important to ensure that the problem at hand requires an experimental approach to determine a suitable solution. A clear and succinct statement of the problem contributes substantially to a better understanding of

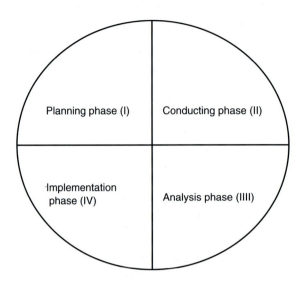

Figure 4.1 The four phases of the methodology.

the problem. Some of the generic process problems in manufacturing where experimental approach can be utilized are:

- development of new processes or products or improvement of existing processes or products;
- improve the performance characteristics of the product/process relative to customer needs and expectations;
- low process yields as the process is not operating at the optimum condition;
- excessive process variability which leads to poor process capability, and so on and so forth.

Once the problem and the objective of the experiment are decided upon, a team which will perform the study can be formed. Coleman and Montgomery (1993) stress that objective(s) should be specific, measurable and must yield practical value to the company. The team approach to experimental design encourages unbiased objectives of the experiment. The team may include a DOE specialist, process engineer, production engineer, quality engineer, operator and a management representative.

Step 2: *Selection of quality characteristic (QC) and measurement system*

The selection of an appropriate quality characteristic from the customers' point of view is critical to the success of an industrial experiment. The selection of quality characteristics to measure as experimental outputs immensely influences the number of experiments that will have to be carried out to be statistically meaningful (Ross, 1996). The output(s) of an industrial experiment can be either variable or attribute in nature. Variable characteristics (e.g. dimensions, efficiency, viscosity, strength etc.) generally provide more information than attribute characteristics (good/bad, pass/fail, etc.). Moreover variable characteristics require fewer experiments (or samples) than characteristics which are attribute in nature to achieve the same level of statistical significance. It is important to ensure that the selected quality characteristic for the experiment should be related as closely as possible to the basic engineering mechanism of the product. In Taguchi methods of experimental design, we generally consider the following five types of quality characteristics:

1   **Smaller-the-Better (STB) quality characteristics:** this type of quality characteristic is selected for the experiment when the experimenter measures characteristics such as tool wear, surface finish, porosity, shrinkage, impurity content in a chemical, number of defects etc.
2   **Larger-the-Better (LTB) quality characteristics:** this type of quality characteristic is selected for the experiment when the experimenter measures characteristics such as efficiency, hardness, strength etc.
3   **Nominal-is-the-Best (NTB) quality characteristics:** this type of quality characteristic is considered for the experiment when the experimenter measures characteristics such as length, thickness, diameter, width, force, viscosity etc.
4   **Classified attribute quality characteristics:** this type of quality characteristic is selected for the experiment when the experimenter classifies the data into good/bad, grade A/B/C/D, and so on.
5   **Dynamic characteristics:** these characteristics are considered for the experiment, when the strength of a particular parameter has a direct effect on the output quality characteristic. Such a parameter with a direct impact on the output quality characteristic is called a signal factor. For example, in a fabric dyeing process, the quantity of dye will have a direct impact on the dyeing performance and therefore can be considered as a signal factor. Similarly, in an injection moulding process, the dimension of the die will have a direct influence on the dimension of the injected part. Therefore, the dimension of the die is a signal factor.

It is also important to define the measurement system (what to measure and units, where to measure, how to measure) prior to experimentation to understand the contribution of variation accounted for by the measurement system. There is always uncertainty in every measurement that is taken and this can be attributed to a number of key inputs, such as gauges, parts, operators, methods and environment. All these inputs are sources of variation within the measurement process. One may have to ensure that the measurement system variation would not bias the results of experiment. In other words, the measurement system should be capable, stable and robust (i.e. insensitive to changes of operator or environmental conditions). One comprehensive and practical method to achieve this goal is through the use of Wheeler's Evaluating the Measurement Process (EMP) technique (Wheeler and Lyday, 1989).

Step 3: *Selection of design/process parameters (or factors) that may influence the QC*

It is important to assure that the selected design/process parameters (or factors) really provide the necessary and relevant information about the problem. Prior knowledge and experience of the product/process are useful in the identification of design/process parameters. Brainstorming, flowcharts and cause and effect analysis are useful tools for determining which parameters (or factors) must be included in initial experiments. This step is the most important of the experimental design procedure. If important factors are unknowingly left out of the experiment, then the information gained from the experiment will not be in a positive sense.

How many design/process parameters should be studied in the first round of experimentation? This commonly asked question is related to the experimental size and experimental budget and resources. It is a good practice to conduct a screening experiment to identify the most important parameters which influence the QC of interest. In screening experiment, the number of levels is kept as low as possible, usually at two. It is not a good practice to conduct a large experiment involving many design/process parameters. For example, one may be able to study up to seven factors using just eight experimental runs. It is advisable not to invest more than 25 per cent of the experimental budget in the first phase of any industrial designed experiment such as screening (Antony, 1999).

Step 4: *Classification of design/process parameters into control, noise and signal factors*

Having selected the design/process parameters (or factors), the next step is to classify them into control, noise and signal factors. Here control factors are those factors which can be controlled by a design engineer in the design of a product/process or by a manufacturing process/production engineer in a production environment. Noise factors are those factors which cannot be controlled or difficult to control or in many cases even expensive to control during actual production conditions or customer environment. Signal factors are those which affect the target performance of the characteristic but generally have no influence on variability in the performance characteristic of the product/process. If we consider an injection moulding process, control factors may be injection speed, cure time, injection pressure etc.; noise factors may be ambient temperature, machine operators etc. and signal factor may be the dimension of the die which determines the size of the final mould.

Step 5: *Determination of the number of levels for design/process parameters*

The selection of the number of levels of a factor depends on the nature of the design/process parameter, i.e. whether or not the chosen parameter is qualitative or quantitative. For quantitative parameters (e.g. pressure, speed etc.), generally two levels are required especially in the early stages of experimentation. However for qualitative parameters such as type of material, type of supplier etc., more than two levels may be required in initial experiments.

Product or process technical expertise is essential for the selection of appropriate values for the design/process parameter levels. The levels need to be in an operational range of the product or process. Taguchi recommends the use of three levels if non-linearity is expected in the main effect of control factor on the quality characteristic. Taguchi's principle for selecting the test levels of noise factors is as follows (Kackar, 1985):

Suppose the mean and standard deviation of the distribution of noise factor (N_I) are m_I and s_I respectively. If N_I is assumed to have a linear effect on the quality characteristic, then it should have two test levels: $(m_i - s_i)$ and $(m_i + s_i)$. On the other hand, if N_I is assumed to have a curvilinear effect on the quality characteristic, then it should have three test levels: $(m_i - s_i . \sqrt{(3/2)})$, m_i, $(m_i + s_i . \sqrt{(3/2)})$. These choices of test levels are in fact based on the assumption that noise factors have approximately symmetrical distributions. If noise factors cannot be studied, it is then recommended to repeat the experimental run (or trial) in a random manner to capture variation due to unknown sources.

Step 6: *Determination of the interactions to be studied*

Interaction between two design/process parameters exists when the effect of one parameter on the quality characteristic is different at different levels of the other parameter. If the interactions between control factors need to be studied, then it is advisable to list the potential interactions of interest. The questions one should always ask, include 'Should an interaction be replaced by an additional factor?' and 'Do we need to study the interactions at all in the first phase of the experiment?' The team must be prepared to answer these questions prior to choosing an appropriate experimental layout for the experiment. It is not common in industrial designed experiments to study the interactions among the noise factors or signal factors. Exploring the interactions among the noise and signal factors are just a waste of resources. Nevertheless, it is wise to explore the interaction between control and noise factors for achieving robustness. In other words, it is advisable to determine the optimum levels of the control factors which alleviate the effect of noise factors on the performance characteristic of the product/process.

Step 7: *Choice of appropriate orthogonal array(s) and assignment of design/process parameters and their interactions*

Orthogonal arrays (OAs) allows experimenters to study the effect of a large number of control and noise factors on the quality characteristic in a minimum number of trials. If noise factors are considered for the experiment, then two OAs will be required. Taguchi proposes the use of OAs for planning the design/process optimization experiments. The choice of OA is very critical as it depends on the number of factors to be studied for optimization, number of interactions to be examined, number of levels required for each factor, objective of the experiment and, of course, availability of experimental budget and resources. To assure that the chosen OA design will provide sufficient degrees of freedom for the contemplated experiment, the following inequality must be fulfilled:

> Number of degrees of freedom for the OA ≥ Number of degrees of freedom required for studying the main and interaction effects

Having chosen the appropriate OA design (s) for the experiment, the next step is to assign factors and locate interactions. For some experiments one may have to use the standard OA or in some cases modifications need to be done on the selected OA. Interaction tables and confounding structures must be constructed while assigning the factors and the interactions of interest to the OA. This will assist experimenters to envisage how factors are confounded with interaction effects.

Conducting phase

Step 8: *Conducting the experiment and recording the results*

It is important to note that an optimization experiment can be carried out in one of the two ways: physical experiment or computer simulation. It is vital to monitor the process carefully to ensure that everything is being done according to plan. Thorough preparation is critical to the success of any industrial experiment. Errors in the experimental procedure at this stage will destroy experimental validity. It is worth while considering the following points prior to performing the experiment.

- Selection of suitable location – it is important to select an appropriate location which is unaffected by external sources of noise. The experimental environment should ideally be as close to an exact replicate of the user's environment.
- Availability of experimental resources – make sure that the necessary equipment, operators, materials etc. required for the experiment are available before the start of the experiment.
- Cost-benefit analysis – verify that the experiment to be performed is neces-

sary and justify that the benefits to be gained from the experiment will exceed the costs associated with the experiment (such as material cost, labour cost, data analysis etc.).

- Preparation of data sheets – it is advisable to use the uncoded data sheets for running the experiment and coded data sheet for analysing the data. The data sheet should list the levels of each factor, date and time of the test and who has conducted the experiment. The data sheet should also have the space to enter the recorded response or output values.
- Randomize the experimental trials or runs (if necessary) – randomization is critical to ensure that bias is evaded during data gathering. Whether or not to randomize the experimental trials depends on two main considerations: the cost of randomization and whether a time-dependent factor (known or unknown) will disturb the results of the experiment. It is good to randomize the trials as it averages out evenly the effect of lurking parameters which are expensive or difficult to control.
- Replicate the experiment – replication is a process of running the experimental trials in a random order. It requires resetting of each trial condition and therefore costs involved in replication should be taken into account. Schmidt and Launsby provide a useful table for the number of replicates (i.e. sample size) required for an experiment using OA with the aim of identifying a significant factor effect (Schmidt and Launsby, 1992).

Analysis phase

Step 9: *Analysing the experimental data and interpreting the results*

In this step, statistical methods must be used to analyse the data so that objective conclusions can be drawn out. Moreover, statistical methods provide objectivity to the decision-making process. If the experiment has been planned properly, designed correctly and conducted in accordance with the data sheet, then statistical analysis will provide sound and valid conclusions. In design/process optimization experiments, the following are the possible objectives to be achieved from the experiment by the team:

- determination of design/process parameters which affect mean performance of the product/process;
- determination of design/process parameters which influence the variability of product/process performance;
- determination of design parameter levels which yield the optimum performance from a technical and functional point of view;
- determination of whether or not further improvement in the performance of product/process is possible.

In Taguchi methods of experimental design, we use a performance statistic called the signal-to-noise ratio (SNR) which yields the predictive performance of a product/process in the presence of noise factors or lurking variables. The factor levels which yield highest SNR will be selected. Higher SNR value implies better performance of the product/process. Analysis methods include the analysis of variance (ANOVA) for identifying the key design/process parameters and the key interactions, analysis of SNR for achieving process/design robustness and the prediction of performance at the optimum condition. A confidence interval around the predicted mean performance can then be constructed. The equations and calculations involved in the SNR can be obtained from Taguchi's system of experimental design (Taguchi, 1987). The selection of an appropriate SNR depends on the type of quality characteristic which has been measured during the experiment. For multiple quality characteristics, it is recommended to use multiple signal-to-noise ratio derived from Taguchi's quality loss function (Antony, 2000).

The methodology also provides modern graphical tools such as Pareto plot, normal probability plot, and so on. These graphical tools will yield a better understanding of the results to engineers with limited statistical competency. Data interpretation is useful to assist people with limited statistical expertise in understanding the results and to take necessary actions on the design/process. Having interpreted the data, it is advisable to ensure that the experimental conclusions are supported by the data, and that they are meaningful in the stakeholder's world.

Implementation phase

Step 10: *Confirmation run/experiment (or follow-up experiment)*

In order to validate the conclusions from the experiment, performing a confirmatory experiment (sometimes called a follow-up experiment) is suggested. During the confirmation experiment, the insignificant design/process parameters should be set at their economic level. If the results from the confirmation experiment fall outside the confidence interval determined in Step 9, possible causes must be identified. Some of the possible causes may be:

- wrong choice of OA for the experiment;
- incorrect choice of quality characteristic;
- missing of some important parameters which have not been included in the experiment;
- inadequate control of noise factors which causes unpleasant variation in the performance of the product/process;
- some fundamental mistakes have been made during the experiment and/or measurement;
- some important interactions were left out of the experiment.

If the results from confirmation experiment fall inside the confidence interval determined in Step 9, then improvement action on the product/process is recommended. The new design/process parameter settings should be implemented with the involvement of top management. Once the solution has been implemented, it is recommended to construct suitable control charts on the quality characteristic or key design/process parameters.

Case study[1]

The purpose of the study was to investigate the possibility of using lightweight plastics in a modern braking system. In order to achieve this task, an experiment was performed based on Taguchi's orthogonal arrays (OAs) with the aim of optimizing the production process of retaining a metal ring in a plastic body by a hot forming method. Experimental design based on Taguchi methods was chosen due to the limited budget and also for acquiring a quick response to the experimental investigation. The production process consists of a heated die, which is then forced down by air pressure on to a valve body forming a plastic lip into which a retaining ring was inserted.

Although the process was fairly straightforward, it was felt that the maximum pull-out strength was not being achieved by the engineering team of the company involved in this process. In order to simulate the production process, a test rig was designed and a suitable metal insert made to the dimensions of the metal ring into which a tensometer could be screwed in order to measure the pull-out strength. The company had initially performed an experiment based on varying one-factor-at-a-time. However the results obtained from this experimentation was neither repeatable nor predictable. This method did not seem to point towards achieving the best pull strength and the supply of valve bodies available to the project was rapidly being consumed. At this stage, it was decided to design an experiment based on Taguchi methodology as it provides a systematic approach to study the effects of various production parameters in a limited number of experimental trials and hence limited budget and resources (Taguchi, 1987).

The objective of the experiment was to identify those control factor settings which provided maximum pull-out strength with minimum variation. A brainstorming session consisting of senior design engineers, plastic engineers and operator identified a list of production process parameters (also called control factors) which were thought to influence the pull-out strength. Table 4.3 illustrates the list of control factors. The control factor die temperature was studied at four levels and all other factors were kept at two levels for the experiment. The levels for each factor were selected by the design and plastic engineers based on their knowledge and experience of the production process.

The strain rate pull-out was used as a noise factor and controlled at two levels for the experiment to simulate a varying load on the product when in use. Due to the difficulties and expense of manufacturing valve bodies to different dimensions and with variations in material, it was decided not to include this in the experiment. For the present case study, it was decided to measure pull-out strength in Kilo Newtons (KN).

Table 4.3 List of control factors for the Taguchi experiment

Control factor	Level 1	Level 2	Level 3	Level 4
Die temperature (A)	180°C	200°C	220°C	240°C
Hold time (B)	5 sec.	15 sec.	–	–
Batch no. (C)	1	2	–	–
Maximum force (D)	6 KN	7 KN	–	–
Force application rate (E)	5 KN/sec.	1 KN/sec.	–	–

As a reference for the results of the experiment, based on the experience of the engineers, the following levels were considered to give the best performance: A2 B1 C1 D1 E1.

For the experiment, we had to study one factor at four levels, four factors at two levels and also the interaction between hold time (B) and force application rate (E) were of interest to the team. Therefore the degrees of freedom required for studying all the effects is equal to 8. The closest number of experimental trials (from the standard OAs) which will meet this objective is an L_{16} OA. However the standard L_{16} OA contains 15 two level factor columns. In other words, this array is used to accommodate only two level factor columns. Hence it was essential to modify the standard L_{16} OA in order to study the four level factor. As a four level factor consumes three degrees of freedom, it was decided to combine columns 2, 4 and 6 of the standard array. Table 4.4 illustrates the modified L_{16} OA with experimental results. It is important to note that each experimental design point was repeated three times to obtain adequate degrees of freedom for the error term.

Table 4.4 Experimental layout used for the study

Run	B	A	C	D	E	B×E	y^1	y^2	y^3
1	1	1	1	1	1	1	2.18	2.10	2.14
2	1	1	2	2	2	2	2.68	2.65	2.67
3	1	2	1	1	1	1	2.46	2.57	2.52
4	1	2	2	2	2	2	2.92	2.59	2.76
5	1	3	1	1	2	2	2.83	2.74	2.79
6	1	3	2	2	1	1	3.61	3.22	3.42
7	1	4	1	1	2	2	3.31	3.40	3.36
8	1	4	2	2	1	1	4.02	3.98	4.00
9	2	1	1	2	1	2	3.08	3.14	3.11
10	2	1	2	1	2	1	3.07	2.97	3.02
11	2	2	1	2	1	2	3.35	3.15	3.25
12	2	2	2	1	2	1	3.46	3.21	3.34
13	2	3	1	2	2	1	3.42	3.81	3.62
14	2	3	2	1	1	2	3.56	3.70	3.63
15	2	4	1	2	2	1	4.33	4.90	4.62
16	2	4	2	1	1	2	4.77	4.70	4.74

For the present case study, the first step was to analyse the signal-to-noise ratio (SNR), which measures the functional robustness of product or process performance in the presence of undesirable external disturbances (Kapur and Chen, 1988). In this case, as we need to maximize the pull-out-strength with minimum variation, SNR for larger-the-better quality characteristic was selected. The higher the SNR, the better the product performance will be. The SNR for larger-the-better quality characteristic is given by the following equation:

$$SNR = -10\log\left\{ \frac{\sum\limits_{i=1}^{n} \frac{1}{y_i^2}}{n} \right\} \qquad (4.2)$$

where y_i = each individual quality characteristic value, n = number of replications (or repeated observed values) per trial or run.

Having obtained the SNR values, the next step was to calculate the average SNR at each level of each factor. For interaction effect, it is important to analyse the SNR corresponding to each factor level combination. Table 4.5 provides the average SNR values for all the factors and the interaction between hold time (B) and force application rate (E).

Analysis of variance (ANOVA) was performed to determine the most important control factors and the interaction between hold time and force application rate. Control factors or the interaction among them with low sum of squares can

Table 4.5 Average SNR values

Factor/interaction effect	Average SNR
Factors	
B_1	9.25
B_2	11.15
A_1	8.64
A_2	9.37
A_3	10.47
A_4	12.33
C_1	9.81
C_2	10.59
D_1	9.85
D_2	10.56
E_1	10.26
E_2	10.14
Interaction effect	
B_1E_1	9.33
B_1E_2	9.18
B_2E_1	11.20
B_2E_2	11.11

be pooled to obtain adequate degrees of freedom for error and hence error variance can be computed (Roy, 1990). Here control factors C, D, E and interaction between B and E have been considered for pooling and the results of the ANOVA on SNR are shown in Table 4.6.

Table 4.6 shows that factors A and B have significant influence on the SNR. Factors C, D, E and interaction between B and E have no impact on the SNR.

Determination of optimal condition

The optimal condition is the optimal control factor settings which yield the optimum performance. In this case, it is the control factor settings which provide the highest pull-out strength with minimum variation. The optimal condition is obtained by identifying the levels of significant control factors which yield the highest SNR. As both factors A and B have significant impact on the SNR, it was important to determine the optimal levels of these factors. The optimal settings based on SNR are: A_4B_2. The levels of other control factors were selected based on the analysis of mean response. It was found that $C_2D_2E_1$ yields highest pull-out strength. The final optimal condition was hence determined as follows:

$$A_4B_2C_2D_2E_1$$

The predicted mean pull-out strength $(\hat{\mu})$ at the optimal condition (based on the most important factors) is given by:

$$\hat{\mu} = 4.18 + 3.66 - 3.31$$
$$= 4.53 \, KN$$

A set of confirmation trials were carried out and the average pull-out strength was calculated. It was observed that the average pull-out strength was close to the prediction and fell within the calculated confidence limits. Here confidence limits represent the variation of the predicted value of the mean response (or quality characteristic) at the optimum condition at a certain confidence level. In

Table 4.6 Results of pooled ANOVA on SNR

Source of variation	Degree of freedom	Sum of squares	Mean square	F-ratio	Percent contribution
B	1	14.48	14.48	30.25**	27.65
A	3	30.89	10.30	21.51**	58.17
Pooled error	11	5.26	0.48	–	14.18
Total	15	50.63	3.38	–	100

From F-tables: $F_{0.01,1,11} = 9.65$, $F_{0.05,1,11} = 4.84$, $F_{0.01,3,11} = 6.22$ and $F_{0.05,3,11} = 3.59$
**implies that both factor effects A and B are statistically significant at the 5 per cent and 1 per cent significance levels.

Taguchi methods, we use both 95 per cent and 99 per cent confidence levels. If the observed value during the confirmation trials falls outside the predicted value, it implies the presence of interactions. For the above case study, the pull-out strength from experimentation shows a significant improvement (more than 35 per cent) compared to the average pull-out strength before experimentation. Moreover a significant reduction in variability of pull-out strength values was also achieved from the experiment.

A critique of Taguchi approach to experimental design

This section is focused on a critique of the Taguchi approach to experimental design. Though Taguchi approach to industrial experimentation has proved to be successful in many organizations, it suffers from some technical problems. It is important to note that Taguchi's philosophy is inherently sound and his attempt to integrate statistical methods into the powerful engineering process is absolutely praiseworthy. However, his approach to experimental design and of course data analysis methods could be enhanced by integrating other alternative but powerful methods developed by researchers in the area. The following are the various technical issues which undermine Taguchi's approach to experimental design.

• *Little emphasis on interaction effects*

Taguchi has maintained a dogmatic attitude towards the treatment of interactions. He recognizes the presence of interactions and recommends methods for reducing their effect on the quality characteristic of interest. He claims that it is possible to eliminate the interaction between factors by selecting the appropriate quality characteristic and design/process parameters. He recommends a small follow-up experiment to verify whether or not the objective of the experiment has been accomplished. If interactions are present, the predicted results will be different from the results of follow-up experiment. It is important to note that follow-up experiments can only confirm the optimal settings of the parameters considered and it cannot 'rediscover' interaction effects that were ignored in the first place.

• *Size of the experiment is large due to the use of inner-outer array experimental layout*

Taguchi recommends a crossed array (inner-outer array) structure for determining the robust design/parameter settings. If the number of experimental trials in the inner-array is 16 and the number of trials in the outer-array is four (assume two noise factors to be included in the outer-array), then the total size of the experiment will be 64. Is it really necessary to conduct 64 experiments to determine the effect of noise factors and hence determine the control factor settings which are least sensitive to external disturbances (i.e. noise)? A better strategy is to use a combined array structure that incorporates both control and noise factors (Miller *et al.*, 1993–94). This experimental layout will always lead to a significant reduction in the number of experimental trials and provides sufficient information to enhance process understanding.

- *Use of linear graphs often lead to misleading conclusions*

Taguchi recommends the use of linear graphs to assign factors to the columns of the orthogonal array. The use of linear graphs can lead to inefficient designs (Antony, 1996). Taguchi's linear graphs do not provide the complete confounding relationships among the factors or interactions. Taguchi advocates the use of interaction tables to understand fully the confounding relationships among the columns in the OA. However this does not seem user friendly and is incomplete. A more efficient approach to determine the complete confounding relationships is to use a defining relation and then generate the confounding (sometimes called aliasing) structure as explained in Box *et al.* (1978).

- *Use of inappropriate SNR as a measure of process/design performance*

Taguchi recommends the use of SNR for analysing experiments in which both the mean and the standard deviations are under study. The logic behind the SNR is to uncouple location effects (control factors which affect only the mean quality characteristic) and dispersion effects (control factors which affect variability in quality characteristic). It is hard to separate those factors affecting mean quality characteristic (or mean response) and those affecting standard deviation. SNR could produce a mean bias if the response standard deviation and the response mean are not linearly connected. A much safer and efficient approach is to analyse the mean and standard deviation of the response separately. In this way, one can develop separate response surface models for mean response and response variability.

- *Disregarded modern graphical and analytical methods for rapid understanding*

Taguchi neglects some of the powerful modern analytical and graphical tools for performing the data analysis from industrial designed experiments. For example, the use of appropriate data transformation, probability plotting, residual analysis, response plots etc. are completely ignored. All these data analysis techniques could be easily integrated into his approach to experimental design and analysis.

- *Discouraged the adaptive, sequential approach to experimentation*

Taguchi's approach to industrial experimentation are 'one-shot' experiments (i.e. pick the winner) which can lead to unsatisfactory conclusions. If some initial assumptions go wrong at any stage of the experiment, a significant waste and loss of management support may result. A better strategy is to conduct a sequence of smaller experiments at the beginning stages to characterize the processes rather than trying to learn everything from one large experiment.

Conclusion

Industrial designed experiments are powerful for both design/process optimization problems. This chapter briefly elucidates the importance of industrial designed experiment based on Taguchi. The benefits of Taguchi methods of experimental design in both manufacturing and service organizations were demonstrated. A systematic methodology for design/process optimization is also presented with the aim of assisting people with limited knowledge in experimental design to apply it in a structured manner. This follows a case study with the objective of optimizing a production process of retaining a metal ring in a plastic body by a hot forming method. A significant improvement on the pull-out strength with minimum variability was achieved from a modified L_{16} OA with three replications at each trial condition. The final part of the chapter reveals a critique of experimental design approach advocated by Taguchi.

Note

1   This case study has been reproduced with the permission of MCB University Press. *Source:* Process Optimization using Taguchi Methods of Experimental Design, Antony, J. *et al.*, Work study, 2000.

References

Antony, J. (1996) Likes and dislikes of Taguchi methods, *Productivity* **37**(3), 477–81.
Antony, J. (1997) A strategic methodology for the use of advanced statistical quality improvement techniques, PhD thesis, University of Portsmouth, UK.
Antony, J. (1999) Ten useful and practical tips for making your industrial experiments successful, *The TQM Magazine* **11**(4), 252–6.
Antony, J. (2001), Simultaneous optimisation of multiple quality characteristics in manufacturing processes using Taguchi's quality loss function, *International Journal of Advanced Manufacturing Technology*, vol. 17, No. 2, pp. 134–8; Spring-Verlag publishers.
Antony, J. and Kaye, M. (1996) Optimisation of core tube life using experimental design methodology, *Quality World Technical Supplement*, IQA, 42–50.
Antony, J. and Roy, R.K. (1998) *Quality Assurance Journal* **6**(2), 87–95.
Bessant, J., Caffyn, S., Gilbert, J. and Webb, S. (1994) Rediscovering continuous improvement, *Technovation* **14**(1), 17–29.
Blosch, M. and Antony, J. (1999) Experimental design and computer-based simulation: a case study with the Royal Navy, *Managing Service Quality* **9**(5), 311–19.
Box *et al.* (1978) *Statistics for Experimenters.* New York: John Wiley.
Brassington, K. (1990) Optimisation of a robotic welding process, *Third European Symposium on Taguchi Methods*, December.

Coleman, D.E. and Montgomery, D.C. (1993) A systematic approach to planning for a designed industrial experiment, *Technometrics* **35**, 1–27.

Dale, B. (1994) *Managing Quality* (edited), London: Prentice Hall.

Finney, D.J. (1945) Fractional replication of factorial arrangements, *Annals of Eugenics* **12**, 291–301.

Kackar, R.N. (1985) Off-line quality control, parameter design and Taguchi methods, *Journal of Quality Technology* **17**, 176–88.

Kackar, R.N. (1986) Taguchi's quality philosophy: analysis and commentary, *Quality Progress*, December issue, 21–9.

Kackar, R.N. and Shoemaker, A.C. (1987) Robust design – a cost effective method for improving manufacturing processes, *AT & T Technical Journal*, 39–50.

Kapur, K.C. and Chen, G. (1988) Signal-to-noise ratio development for quality engineering, *Quality and Reliability Engineering International* **4**, 133–41.

Kumar, A., Motwani, J. and Otero, L. (1996) An application of Taguchi's robust experimental design technique to improve service performance, *International Journal of Quality and Reliability Management* **13**(4), 85–98.

Logothetis, N. (1994) *Managing for Total Quality*. Englewood Cliffs, NJ: Prentice-Hall.

Miller, A. *et al.* (1993–94) Are large Taguchi-style experiments necessary? A reanalysis of gear and pinion data, *Quality Engineering* **6**(1), 21–37.

Montgomery, D.C. (1992) The use of statistical process control and design of experiments in product and process improvement, *IIE Transactions* **24**(5), 4–17.

Phadke, M.S. (1989) *Quality Engineering Using Robust Design*. Prentice-Hall International.

Plackett, R.L. and Burmann, J.P. (1946) The design of optimum multifactorial experiments, *Biometrika* **33**, 305–25.

Quinlan, J. (1985) Process improvement by application of Taguchi methods, *Transactions of the Third Symposium on Taguchi Methods*, MI, 11–16.

Ross, P.J. (1996) *Taguchi Techniques for Quality Engineering*. New York: McGraw-Hill.

Rowlands, H., Antony, J. and Knowles, G. (2000) *An Application of Experimental Design for Process Optimisation* **12**(2), 78–83.

Roy, R. (1990) *A Primer on the Taguchi Method.* New York: VNR Publishers.

Schmidt, S.R. and Launsby, R.G. (1992) *Understanding Industrial Designed Experiments.* Colorado Springs, CO: Air Academy Press.

Sirvanci, M.B. and Durmaz, M. (1993) Variation reduction by the use of designed experiments, *Quality Engineering* **5**(4), 611–18.

Taguchi, G. (1987) *System of Experimental Design: Engineering Methods to Optimise Quality and Minimise Costs*, Vols. 1 and 2, UNIPUB/Kraus.

Taguchi, G. and Konishi, S. (1987) *Orthogonal Arrays and Linear Graphs*, ASI Press.

Tsui, K.-L. (1988) Strategies for planning experiments using orthogonal arrays and confounding tables, *Quality and Reliability Engineering International* **4**, 113–22.

Wheeler, D.J. and Lyday, R.W. (1989) *Evaluating the Measurement Process*. Tennessee: SPC Press, Inc.

5 Statistical process monitoring in the twenty-first century

Michael Wood

Introduction

The term 'Statistical Process Control' (SPC) refers to a loosely defined collection of techniques for monitoring a process so as to prevent deterioration and facilitate improvement. These techniques are used for monitoring a process (Box and Kramer, 1992), so the phrase 'process monitoring' seems more appropriate than 'process control' and I have used the former in the title. However, this is just a matter of terminology: SPC techniques always were about monitoring rather than control, and as the use of the word control causes problems – as we will see below – it is sensible to replace it with a more accurate term. I will use the term SPC/M in this chapter.

The most prominent of these techniques, and the traditional focus of SPC/M, is the Shewhart control chart, named after its originator, Walter Shewhart. There are different types of Shewhart charts: the most widely used are charts for the mean (*X-bar*) and range (*R*), proportion defective (*p*), and number of defects (*c*). In each case, a graph of the appropriate statistic (mean, range, etc.) of successive samples is plotted, and 'control lines' superimposed to indicate points which are 'out of control'. These indicate 'special' or 'assignable' causes of variation which should be investigated and, if appropriate, action taken to adjust the process.

There are also a number of more sophisticated control charting methods (although, according to Gunter, 1998, these are 'rarely used'). These include multivariate methods for monitoring several related variables simultaneously (Montgomery, 1996), methods for monitoring a single measurement (as opposed to one based on a sample) such as moving average charts and exponentially weighted moving average (EWMA) charts (see, for example, Montgomery, 1996), and cumulative sum (cusum) methods which are more sensitive than Shewhart charts for detecting small but consistent changes in the level of the measurement (Hawkins and Olwell, 1998).

In addition to control charts, the conventional SPC/M package incorporates ways of establishing the capability of a process (Rodriguez, 1992) – the most commonly used index here being c_{pk} – and a number of more elementary methods for solving problems and improving quality. For example, Montgomery (1996: 130) lists the 'magnificent seven': histogram or stem-and-leaf-display, check sheet, Pareto chart, cause and effect diagram, defect concentration diagram, scatter diagram, as well as the control chart.

These methods, their implementation, and the concepts and philosophy underlying them, are covered in the many texts on SPC/M and related areas, e.g. Oakland (1999), Woodall and Adams (1998), Montgomery (1996), Bissell (1994), Mitra (1993). Woodall and Montgomery (1999) provide a helpful recent review of current issues and research in the area.

The purpose of this chapter is not to provide a summary of SPC/M and how to implement it. There are many excellent texts – such as those mentioned above – to which readers can refer for the technical and organizational details of the procedures, and an analysis of their potential benefits. Instead, this chapter aims to provide a critique of SPC/M, and some suggestions about how it needs to be adapted to the twenty-first century. I am assuming that the reader has some familiarity with the main SPC/M techniques – although not necessarily with the details of formulae or the more advanced methods.

The value of SPC/M has been widely recognized over the last half century. According to Stoumbous *et al.* (2000)

> control charts are among the most important and widely used tools in statistics. Their applications have now moved far beyond manufacturing into engineering, environmental science, biology, genetics, epidemiology, medicine, finance, and even law enforcement and athletics.

However, there is little recent, empirical evidence of widespread benefits from SPC/M in business, and, indeed, a few suggestions that all is not well. For example Gunter (1998: 117) suggests that 'it is time to move beyond these now archaic and simplistic tools [control charts]' and complains that

> We have become a shockingly ingrown community of mathematical specialists with little interest in the practical applications that give real science and engineering their vitality.

Woodall and Montgomery (1999) suggest that the problem is that 'in much of academia, the rewards are for publications, not usefulness' (p. 18). In the world of real applications, on the other hand:

> Many, if not most of the users of control charts have had little training in statistics. Thus, there is a reluctance to introduce more complex topics, such as the study of autocorrelation, into training materials (p. 17).

The result of this situation is, as might be expected, disappointing. Dale and Shaw (1991: 40), on the basis of research in the late eighties, concluded that

> The findings of this piece of research must bring into question the effectiveness of the current methods of educating company managements on the use

of SPC/M. The time, resources, and cost committed to SPC/M by organizations has been considerable and if a cost benefit analysis were to be performed it would be unfavourable.

Hoerl and Palm (1992) also comment on the 'limited success' of many efforts to use Shewhart charts in industry, which, they say, is typically due to using the wrong formula, a poorly chosen sampling plan, or that the 'improvement work demanded by the charts is so radical in the context of the organization's culture that the organization is unable to properly respond' (p. 269).

This chapter explores issues such as these. It starts with a discussion of the purpose and potential benefits of SPC/M. However, as we have seen, this is not the whole story; there are difficulties in practice. The section after gives a brief case study, based on a small manufacturing company, which illustrates many of the difficulties of trying to implement traditional SPC/M techniques, as well as some of the benefits. This leads on to a systematic discussion of these difficulties and how they might be resolved.

The philosophy, purpose and potential benefits of SPC/M

The purpose of a control chart is to monitor a process so that patterns and trends over time are seen, and problems can be picked up in time to prevent defective output being produced. The control lines are designed to pick out those fluctuations which are too large to be normal 'chance' fluctuations; the purpose of this is to avoid wasting time and money and disturbing the process unnecessarily by reacting to 'normal' or 'common cause' variations.

Figure 5.1, for example, shows the mean times taken for patients to reach the admissions ward from casualty in a hospital. This is based loosely on the situation described by Jefferson (see Chapter 8). Each point on the graph is the mean of the times taken by a random sample of 20 patients on the day in question. For a variety of obvious reasons, the times taken by individual patients will vary, with the result that the daily means will also vary; the control lines on the graph are calculated statistically to encompass 99.8 per cent of these random fluctuations. Points within the control lines should be ignored – because the chart suggests that only 'common causes' of variations are in play here.[1] On the other hand, points outside, such as Day 7, indicate that there is a 'special' cause which should be investigated – in this case to see if anything can be learned from it to improve the process. (This chart is for monitoring the *mean* time; care obviously needs to be taken when comparing these means with the maximum allowable time for an *individual* patient.)

The other techniques in the SPC/M toolbag (e.g. the 'magnificent seven' referred to above) support control charts in monitoring processes, and in finding ways to improve them. By detecting and dealing with special causes of variation at particular points in time, control charts stabilize a process, but other techniques may be useful to improve the process as a whole. SPC/M can be used for service and administrative processes as well as manufacturing processes,

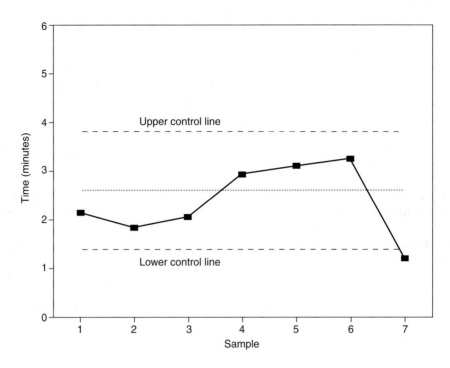

Figure 5.1 Mean chart of hospital journey time.

although care needs to be taken when adapting techniques developed in a manufacturing context to another context (Wood, 1994). This means that SPC/M is
relevant across the whole spectrum of business processes, and is likely to be an
important component of any Quality Management strategy.

There are a number of assumptions underlying SPC/M which are worth clarifying. The key problem is seen as *variation*: in any process there will always be
differences from one hour (or day or month) to the next. In manufacturing contexts such variation is usually unwelcome, and so one aim of SPC/M is to reduce
this variation. This is not necessarily the case in a service context (Wood, 1994)
– a hospital is not, for example, in a position to reduce the variation between its
patients even if it wanted to – but variation is still a problem in that it may hide
underlying changes in the system.

This leads on to the second key assumption: the main task is to manage the
underlying *process*, and to avoid reacting to chance events – which is likely to
be counterproductive. If SPC/M is used for critical processes, this will help to
ensure that the whole system will produce adequate and consistent quality
levels. It is for this reason that the use of SPC/M is an important part of various
quality standards, and TQM initiatives.

SPC/M is specifically concerned with monitoring processes *through time*.
Typically, historical data is used to measure the performance of a process, and

then a control chart established to monitor changes over time. This is a continuous improvement model, based on the assumption that the best way of improving is to make a detailed study of past performance. There are, needless to say, other possibilities, e.g. BPR (business process re-engineering) is concerned with discontinuous change, and the benchmarking principle involves learning from other processes. Statistics can also, of course, be used for other quality-related purposes besides SPC/M. Examples include the design of experiments (Antony, see Chapter 4), and the use of SERVQUAL for analysing service processes (Capon and Mills, see Chapter 7).

SPC/M is undoubtedly widely used. To take one example, the Ford Motor Company makes extensive use of SPC/M methods, and requires its vendors to do likewise. There are many other companies, large and small, in a similar position.

The benefits which should follow from SPC/M are similar to those from any other useful quality strategy: improved quality levels, reduced costs, enhanced reputation and improved market share. However, there is a disappointing lack of recent statistical evidence of the extent to which these benefits have been realized. One recent textbook on SPC/M (Oakland, 1999), for example, cites no references to empirical research in the section on *Successful users of SPC/M and the benefits derived*. This is perhaps understandable given the difficulties of research in this area, but it is unfortunate.

An illustrative case study

This section is based on one of the cases outlined in Wood and Preece (1992). It illustrates some of the difficulties, as well as the benefits of SPC/M.

Company A makes small plastic components by an injection moulding process. Each component has a hole in it; the size and shape of this hole is crucial to performance. The quality problems which may occur are that the hole may be the wrong size – this is checked by measuring the rate at which air flows through the hole (the 'flow rate'); the hole may have irregularities – checked by a visual inspection; or, most seriously, the hole may not exist at all – this can be picked up by the flow rate or the visual checks.

A number of changes have recently been made to the Quality Management system. Before these changes, the company operated an inspection system which worked as follows: after each hour's production a sample of, typically, twenty components was chosen at random and inspected visually and by means of a flow rate test, and the entire hour's production was scrapped if any component in the sample did not meet the specification. The inspections were not carried out by the operators, but by a separate inspection department.

There were a number of difficulties with this system. It was very expensive in labour – the number of inspectors was approximately the same as the number of operators; it led to conflicts between the operators and the inspectors; it tolerated a considerable amount of scrap; and the small sample sizes meant that problems with the manufacturing process were not always picked up.

Two changes have now been made. First the quality department has been reorganized: the inspectors have been replaced by a smaller number of auditors whose role is to assist and train the operators so that these operators can carry out the inspections themselves. Fortuitously, this change occurred at a time when orders were increasing so more operators were needed and no redundancies were necessary. The operators then have the responsibility for the operation of the machines and the control of quality. This change was welcomed by all concerned.

The second change was the design and installation of equipment to measure flow rates automatically. This equipment could take a large sample of components (typically several hundred instead of twenty), measure the flow rates of each, and then analyse and display the data on a VDU. The software, written specifically for this purpose by a software house, was designed to produce control charts (mean and sigma), capability indices, and to display a histogram of the sample of data and thus indicate whether all components were within the specification.

Before the introduction of the automatic testing equipment there was a certain amount of apprehension that the operators/inspectors would be unable or unwilling to use the new automatic system. These fears proved quite unfounded: after a short induction period the new equipment was being used with few difficulties and considerable enthusiasm – as it replaced a particularly monotonous manual task. However, the control charts and capability indices are not used; rather the histograms are used to check for any components outside the specification, and, just as before, each hour's production is only accepted if all components in the sample are within specification. The sample size used is now much larger (hundreds rather than tens) which clearly means that the sensitivity of the monitoring process has increased: problems are now more likely to be noticed. However, this was not an *intended* change, but just an accidental byproduct of the changed technology.

The quality manager had considered implementing a 'proper' statistical control chart system. (He had experience of a statistical approach to quality in a previous post.) He gave the following reasons for not doing so:

1   his pressure of work and therefore lack of time;
2   the operators and setters of the machines would be wary of a system which appears to be tightening the controls;
3   there was little point, anyway, in tightening the control further;
4   the flow rate, which, in his view, was the obvious parameter to chart, was not really the critical one (the system for monitoring flow rates automatically was set up before his arrival);
5   it would be difficult to apply standard techniques because different batches for different customers have different specifications, and because a number of other special features of the processes made them difficult to fit into standard techniques;
6   he was particularly concerned when a defect arose in one of the cavities of a

moulding machine which meant that components produced from that cavity had no hole at all. If this fault was not spotted, and components with no holes were passed as acceptable, this would have very costly repercussions. The problem here is not the problem of monitoring a drift, but of preventing disaster.

All this (particularly the last two points) meant that the situation was seen as a 'non-standard' one and so difficult to deal with using the standard textbook techniques for quality control. In fact, the standard techniques can be adapted to cope with the problem of changing specifications, and it is possible to use probability theory to calculate how large a random sample must be to be almost sure of detecting a fault leading to the absence of holes:[2] but the ability to work out things of this type seems most unlikely to result from a short training course in SPC/M techniques.

The impetus for the changes that were made appeared to be the experience of the quality manager who had seen various techniques working in a previous job in the motor industry, and his perception that the existing situation was unsatisfactory. The company experienced only a limited amount of pressure to use specified approaches, such as control charts. Most customers made only very general enquiries about the quality system – which were not sufficiently explicit to drive the company down one direction rather than another.

The company has managed to achieve considerable benefits from the new system. The reorganization of the quality department eliminated the conflicts between operators and inspectors by eliminating the inspectors, and, by giving the operator some of the responsibility for the whole process, increased the likelihood of inspection data being used constructively to monitor and improve the process. The monitoring process is undoubtedly cheaper and more efficient now, which has obvious implications for costs and quality.

However, the control charts are not used, and the checking process is still clearly oriented towards inspection and rejection, rather than improving the manufacturing process. This is despite the fact that the process clearly did have room for improvement: one sample of data showed scrap rates ranging from 3 to 12 per cent, with problems picked up by the flow rate test being the largest category.

An example of the type of control chart produced (but not used by the operators) by the automatic testing equipment appears in Figure 5.2. This chart is a simplified version of the one actually produced – which includes a standard deviation chart and capability indices as well. Figure 5.2 is a control chart monitoring the mean of a sample of 200 components, and clearly shows that the process is well 'in control', i.e. all points are well inside the control lines. However, the control lines are incorrectly calculated:[3] the correct picture (according to the standard textbook procedure) is as in Figure 5.3, which shows that the penultimate sample is *out of control*, i.e. just outside the control lines, and that corrective action should be taken. Figure 5.3 provides evidence that the process mean has *changed* very slightly, despite the fact that *it is still well within the specification*; this would provide the operator with the means to make the necessary adjustments *before* the process approaches the limits of the specification, thus preventing the production of future scrap. Figure 5.2, on the other hand, does not achieve this; the control lines here are much too far apart.[4] The erroneous calculation of the control lines was not noticed by the developers of the software, or by anyone at Company A.

Figure 5.3 is not, however, ideal either. This shows a monitoring system which can detect very small changes and is more sensitive than necessary; this is because the sample size (200) is determined by the capabilities of the monitoring equipment rather than the requirement of process monitoring. We will discuss the implications of this in the next section.

As we have seen, the quality manager in this company was reluctant to use many aspects of SPC/M. The next section looks at some of the reasons behind this reluctance.

SPC/M in practice: problems and suggested solutions

There are a number of inter-related problems, which, for convenience, I will divide into four clusters of issues – each of which can be tackled in ways that are, in principle, straightforward.

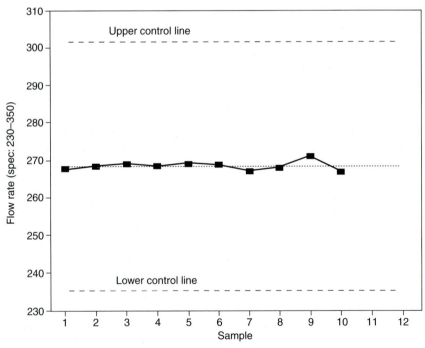

The estimate of the standard deviation of the individual measurements is 11.1, and the size of each sample is 200.

Figure 5.2 Mean chart similar to actual charts used.

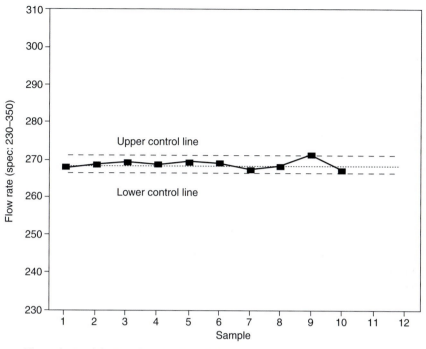

The estimate of the standard deviation of the individual measurements is 11.1, and the size of each sample is 200.

Figure 5.3 'Correct' version of the mean chart.

Polarized views on the scope of the statistical approach

Statistics is a subject which tends to polarize people. There are those who think that all problems should be tackled statistically, and there are those who think that no problem should be tackled statistically. Needless to say, both of these attitudes are counter-productive; the best approach is likely to lie between these two extremes. This polarization of attitudes may be a problem if it leads to lost opportunities.

Figure 5.1 above shows a mean chart based on a process in a hospital. Jefferson points out that relying on a numerical measure inevitably means that the detail of the particular situation is ignored; this detail is obviously important to any improvement strategy. On the other hand the statistical approach shows general patterns which may alert us to general trends and problems, and may suggest which particular incidents are worth looking at – this is, of course, the whole point of an control chart.

The quality manager in the case study company was reluctant to embrace SPC/M wholeheartedly because he felt – rightly – that SPC/M was useful for detecting a drift in the hole size, but it was unhelpful for the more urgent problem of dealing with components with no hole at all. This latter problem needs a suitable method of sampling,[2] and then an investigation of *every* problem found – rather than a statistical analysis of the numbers of such problems. A sensible strategy would have been to have used this tactic, *and* SPC/M for the hole size.

Wood and Christy (1999) distinguish between statistical inferences, and illustrative inferences that can be drawn from specific cases. Both styles of investigation are useful and likely to complement each other: statistical analysis and the detailed investigation of possibilities, such as particular modes of failure.

The changing nature of business processes and technology

Control charts were originally designed for manufacturing processes in the 1920s and 1930s. The potential applications of SPC/M now encompass service processes, and manufacturing processes far more diverse than those for which SPC/M was originally developed. In addition, the methods of monitoring are now often automated, as are some aspects of the statistical analysis. This has a number of implications.

The greater diversity of processes means that the standard methods are now less likely to be appropriate: an approach may well have to be crafted for each particular set of circumstances. As an example, Company A's quality manager was correct in thinking that standard methods were not the answer to some of his problems: a customized solution was required.[2] This may be provided by a statistical specialist, although the danger here would be that the users of customized techniques may not have an adequate understanding to use them to their full effect.

The fact that the data for the monitoring process at Company A could be obtained automatically meant that samples were now much larger. This is a general trend (Gunter, 1998; Woodall and Montgomery, 1999): the costs of data may be reduced to almost zero in some cases, so SPC/M may have access to far more data and far bigger samples. With large samples control lines are simply not necessary because sampling error[5] is negligible. The width of the control lines in Figure 5.3 gives an indication of sampling error: this is obviously negligible in comparison to the specification interval. The sample is large enough for *any* noticeable fluctuation to be meaningful. Control lines were introduced to help distinguish random fluctuations from real change, but with large samples this is not an important problem. This means that control charts would be simple line graphs of a key measure plotted against time – provided that this measure is based on a large sample so that sampling error can be ignored.

Sometimes, there may be too much data. The problem now is one of monitoring so that important trends are noticed without being overwhelmed by the quantity of data. Gunter (1998) suggests that new techniques for data reduction and visualization should become part of the new SPC/M toolkit for dealing with 'data smog'.

Another possibility raised by new technology is that of making automatic *adjustments* to the process, as well as *monitoring* it. This goes some way beyond traditional SPC/M which relies on human intervention to react to the signals produced by the monitoring system. The relationship between the two approaches is discussed by Box and Kramer (1992). There are technical problems in incorporating methods for making automatic process adjustments into SPC/M systems (discussed by Box and Kramer, 1992 – the details are too complex to summarize here), but in some contexts extending SPC/M in this direction may be very useful.

Difficulties of understanding statistical concepts and consequent misinterpretation, misuse or non-use

Some of the authors cited in the introduction draw attention to the difficulties of learning and understanding statistics, and the problems this causes. This would be confirmed by the comments of many students who have studied statistics: statistics is a discipline which is hard to master. In the case study above, the fact that nobody at the company noticed that the control charts were incorrectly calculated (and the difference between Figures 5.2 and 5.3 is not trivial) illustrates this problem. In another of the case studies in Wood and Preece (1992), reference was made to the 'horrendous' difficulties of understanding even seemingly elementary statistical concepts such as the standard deviation. Needless to say the 'skewness and kurtosis checks of normality' (produced by the software used) created even more difficulty. And this was despite an extensive training programme incorporating sophisticated technology such as interactive video.

An obvious response to this problem is to try to make the statistics easier. This can be achieved by getting employees to learn and practise 'the simple mechanics of the X-Bar-R chart without being exposed to derivations, exceptions ... [or] "standard deviation" or "rational subgroups"' (Evans, 1987: 37). Those who have difficulty with calculation can be tutored or can ask someone else to do their calculations.

The difficulty with this approach is that it is likely to lead to people carrying out computations by rote without any understanding of the underlying rationale. In essence, people are trained to do what a computer could do better. It does not address the problem of the quality manager at Company A who had insufficient appreciation of the rationale behind the formulae to see the error in the software.

This approach does not tackle misconceptions on the conceptual side. The most serious of these is the typical misconception surrounding the word 'control'. The phrase 'in control' is often viewed as meaning that the process manager has *real* control, i.e. the necessary control to ensure that the process delivers what its customers want. This, after all, is what the term 'control' implies in ordinary English. In fact, however, the word control, and the control lines, refer to a statistical fiction: namely the behaviour of the process when it is influenced only by 'common causes of variation'.

The notion of statistical control as the state of a process under the influence of common or random causes of variation only is a subtle one. Levi and Mainstone (1987: 26) cite evidence that 'people tend to perceive patterns and meaning in random events, and to impute more predictability to events than is warranted', which suggests that control charts are likely to be difficult to understand because they conflict with deep-seated intuitions (although the fact that these intuitions need to be corrected does indicate the importance of the charts' message). What exactly are the common or random causes of variation which are incorporated in the notion of statistical control? In fact, the answer depends on the control chart model that is used (Wood *et al.*, 1999), which means that the formulae and the interpretation are inextricably interwoven, and are far more subtle than SPC/M trainers tend to assume.

One way of tackling difficulties of this kind is to revise or rename the concepts. For example, the 'in control' state of a process could be called 'ordinary conditions', the corresponding zone between the control lines called the 'expected zone', and the control lines themselves could be called 'surprise limits' (Wood *et al.*, 1998). Then, of course, Statistical Process *Control* needs renaming: Statistical Process Monitoring being an obvious alternative. Similarly, process capability indices[6] could be replaced by something along the lines of 'predicted defectives per million' (Wood *et al.*, 1998), and the (deliberately?) mystifying slogan 'six sigma' replaced by the equivalent, but more transparent, 'one defective in one thousand million'.[7]

It is also possible to use methods which are more transparent to non-statisticians than the conventional ones. Some suggestions are made in Wood (1995), Wood *et al.* (1998) and Wood *et al.* (1999). Some of these suggestions are rough approximations to standard methods, but others, chiefly those based on resampling (Diaconis and Efron, 1983; Gunter, 1991; Gunter, 1992a; Gunter, 1992b; Simon, 1992; Wood *et al.*, 1999) are often as rigorous and accurate as conventional methods, and sometimes more so. Resampling methods tend to be used by professional statisticians because they perform *better* than standard methods, or will provide answers to questions which standard methods cannot. It is against this background that Jones and Woodall (1998) conclude, on the basis of a simulation study of several resampling methods for control charting, that they 'do not perform substantially better than the standard method' (p. 374), but, by implication, they might perform slightly better.

To illustrate this, resampling could be used to establish the control, or 'surprise', limits for Figure 5.3. The procedure is to use the data on which Figure 5.3 is based to generate a large number of random samples of the appropriate size (called resamples for obvious reasons), work out the mean of each such sample, and then use the resulting distribution to assess the variability of sample means under 'ordinary conditions', and to read off the appropriate 'surprise' limits. This is easily done with a computer; the process is entirely transparent and free of all statistical concepts except the mean, percentiles and tally charts. In particular, no mention is made of standard deviations or the normal distribution. Essentially the same approach can be used to set up limits for a range chart, *p* chart, *c* chart (although this is not quite so straightforward), or for many other possibilities (see Wood *et al.*, 1999, for more details). This approach has the advantage of flexibility: it can, for example, easily be adapted to the case study quality manager's problem of deciding how large a sample is required to be reasonably sure of picking up the problem of the absence of holes in the components.[8]

Of course, if the samples are large and it is cheap to gather data, and control lines are deemed unnecessary for the reasons discussed above, then none of these techniques is called for. On the other hand, useful statistical analysis may benefit from going beyond the standard techniques to topics such as – to take the examples cited above – autocorrelation (Woodall and Montgomery, 1999), or data reduction and visualization techniques (Gunter, 1998). Stoumbous *et al.* (2000) point out two gaps: one between applications and developments published in applied research journals, and the other between these and theoretical statistics journals. Most practitioners are receiving little benefit from recent developments: if they are to do so the educational problem becomes even more urgent.

Conflicting purposes and interests

Another explanation for the relative lack of success of many SPC/M applications is the possibility that SPC/M may not sit comfortably with the predominant culture of an organization (Bushe, 1988; Hoerl and Palm, 1992; Preece and Wood, 1995): the time-scale for SPC/M to produce benefits may be too long, or there may be a reluctance to use a technique which shows up problems, for example. These points may result in SPC/M being ignored or abandoned, or it may lead to SPC/M techniques being (mis)interpreted in ways which suit the interests of particular stakeholders. Such reinterpretation is more likely to occur if there is little real appreciation of the nature of the underlying concepts – as we suggested above was often the case.

The espoused philosophy of SPC/M emphasizes its role in understanding a process, diagnosing potential problems in time to prevent defective output, and in recognizing opportunities for improvement. In practice, however, it may have two other functions, which conflict with this role: its role in quality assurance, and its role for demonstrating that a process is 'in control'. Given the potential benefits of SPC/M, its use is sometimes seen as ensuring satisfactory quality levels. This is the (perfectly sensible) rationale behind its incorporation into various quality standards and the insistence of some organizations that suppliers use SPC/M. However, the difficulty in practice is that this may result in the application of the letter of the law (of SPC/M) but not its spirit. Company A had no such pressure, and so did not bother to set up a formal SPC/M system. However, Company B, a supplier of the Ford Motor Company (see Wood and Preece, 1992) carried out various statistical calculations but made little use of them. Their motivation was to satisfy Ford that they were implementing SPC/M, not to gain any of the direct benefits of the application. As they also had problems understanding and interpreting the statistical techniques, this was perhaps inevitable. This corruption of the spirit of SPC/M is clearly less likely if the techniques and the ideas underlying them are properly understood by all parties concerned.

The second, related, potential 'function' of SPC/M is as a way of demonstrating that a process is 'in control'. The suggestion that the operators at Company A would be wary of the control imposed by control charts is clearly based on this assumption. If the key goal of the SPC/M application is in demonstrating that the present and past process is in control, rather than to monitor the process to diagnose problems and improve the future process, it is hardly surprising if the SPC/M methods are manipulated to achieve this end, possibly at the expense of their effectiveness at improving the future process. For example, Figure 5.2 was undoubtedly a more comfortable picture to the operators and managers at Company A, than was Figure 5.3, because 'out-of-control' signals were clearly much less likely. This seems a plausible explanation for the refusal to accept that Figure 5.3 was the correct version. In general, smaller sample sizes produce charts with wide control lines like Figure 5.2. If Company A had decided to use control charts, they could have ensured charts with the 'control' lines a comfortable distance apart by using small samples. This, however, clearly makes little sense from the diagnosis point of view, since the equipment measuring the flow rates will cope with large samples, and obviously larger samples provide more information. One means of resolving this conflict would be to perform two *separate* analyses: one for future-oriented diagnosis and monitoring, and a second, separate analysis for present- and past-oriented performance measurement (Wood, 1994).

Similar issues arise in relation to Figure 5.1. Jefferson (this volume, Chapter 8) points out the danger of numerical measures being manipulated to suit particular interests. This danger might be reduced by having separate measures that are used for diagnosis purposes via SPC/M charts, but which are not used for audit purposes.

Conclusion

Statistical monitoring of processes is as necessary now as it has ever been. However, techniques which made good sense seventy years ago may now be problematic from various points of view. Traditional methods may need adapting to the modern context. We can distinguish four main clusters of problematic issues for the implementation of SPC/M in the twenty-first century.

1   The first is that of clarifying the role of the statistical approach. Statistics almost always has a role to play, but there is also almost always a role for non-statistical methods. The quality manager of the case study company could have used SPC/M to monitor gradual drifts in the hole size, but he also needed to have a system which was capable of immediate detection of the problem of components being made without any hole.

2   Difficulties in interpreting and using the concepts and methods are more important than is often supposed and need attention. This is partly a matter of education, but there is also scope for adjusting terminology to clarify the nature of the technique (e.g. avoiding the word 'control' in control charts),

and introducing more transparent methods. The goal should be that of ensuring that all parties appreciate how the statistical methods should be used and their results interpreted. There are many contexts in which benefit would be gained from the use of more advanced techniques than those traditionally used, which can only exacerbate this problem.

3   SPC/M is sometimes viewed as a means of demonstrating quality to third parties. This may lead to manipulation of methods and data to give a favourable impression. Similarly SPC/M might be seen as a means of tightening control by management. The diagnostic and improvement functions of SPC/M are far more likely to be achieved if monitoring schemes for improving future performance of a process are kept separate from those used for measuring past performance.

4   Finally, the changing business and technological environment means that SPC/M needs to be applied in an ever greater diversity of circumstances. The traditional toolkit of techniques is no longer likely to be adequate. Flexible, transparent methods are particularly valuable as they can be adapted to each particular context. Alternatively, new approaches must be crafted for each particular situation. The problem of determining a suitable sample size for the case study quality manager to detect the production of components without holes illustrates the possibilities well. Note[2] is the standard mathematician's approach, whereas note[8] is a general purpose simulation approach adapted to this context. On the other hand, some changes may make the statistical problems easier. When automation means that data samples are large, the traditional problem of computing control limits – the source of so many statistical problems, misconceptions and distortions – disappears because sampling errors are negligible and control lines are not worth plotting.

Notes

1   Sometimes inner 'warning' lines are included at the 2.5 and 97.5 percentiles, and the process investigated if two successive points fall outside the same warning line.

2   The problem of changing specifications in different batches can be catered for by taking the deviation from the specification as the variable; and the required sample size is given by:

$$\log(p)/\log(1-1/c)$$

where 'p' is the probability of *failing* to find the fault and 'c' is the number of cavities on the moulding machine.

3   The formulae used for the control lines in Figure 5.2 are:

$$(\text{overall mean} - 3*s) \text{ and } (\text{overall mean} + 3*s), \text{ instead of}$$

$$\left(\text{overall mean} - 3\frac{s}{\sqrt{n}}\right) \text{ and } \left(\text{overall mean} + 3\frac{s}{\sqrt{n}}\right)$$

where 'n' is the sample size and 's' is the sample standard deviation.

4   It is true that the control lines are inside the specification limits, but they are close. If the mean were to drift down to the lower control limit, the variation between individual components might mean that some components would be outside the specification.

5   Sampling error refers to the error, when drawing conclusions from a sample, which is attributable to the normal variation between one sample and another. Obviously, sampling errors will usually be smaller with large samples: this is the whole point in taking a large sample.

6   These indices are distinctly odd. For example a value for c_{pk} of 1 indicates a defective rate of around 0.27 per cent. The reason for this odd equivalence is bound up in the mathematics of the normal distribution, which is surely an irrelevance.

7   Six sigma means that the tolerance limit is six standard deviations (sigmas) away from the mean. This corresponds to this probability level if the process is centred, as the reader should be able to confirm using the normal distribution function in a spreadsheet. If the process is not centred the level of defectives will obviously be larger.

8   If there are c cavities, of which one is defective, the proportion of the output which is defective is $1/c$. This fact can be used to simulate a batch of output, from which a sample of, say, 50 components can be drawn. If this process is repeated, say 1000 times, the probability that samples of 50 will find the fault can easily be estimated. If this is unacceptably low, the simulation could be run again for a larger sample size. This crude, trial and error approach, is not as efficient as the formula given above, but its rationale is entirely transparent, and it could easily be adapted to different circumstances.

References

Bissell, D. (1994) *Statistical Methods for SPC/M and TQM*. London: Chapman & Hall.

Bushe, G.R. (1988) Cultural contradictions of statistical process control in American manufacturing organizations, *Journal of Management* **14**(1), 19–31.

Box, G. and Kramer, T. (1992) Statistical process monitoring and feedback adjustment – a discussion, *Technometrics* **34**(3), 251–67.

Dale, B.G. and Shaw, P. (1991) Statistical process control: an examination of some common queries, *International Journal of Production Economics* **22**, 33–41.

Diaconis, P. and Efron, B. (1983) Computer intensive methods in statistics, *Scientific American* **248**, May, 96–108.

Evans, W.D. (1987) Statistics-free SPC/M, *Manufacturing Systems*, March, 34–7.

Gunter, B. (1991) Bootstrapping: how to make something from almost nothing and get statistically valid answers – Part 1: brave new world, *Quality Progress*, Dec., 97–103.

Gunter, B. (1992a) Bootstrapping: how to make something from almost nothing and get statistically valid answers – Part 2: the confidence game, *Quality Progress*, Feb., 83–6.

Gunter, B. (1992b) Bootstrapping: how to make something from almost nothing and get statistically valid answers – Part 3: examples and enhancements, *Quality Progress*, Apr., 119–22.

Gunter, B. (1998) Farewell fusillade: an unvarnished opinion on the state of the quality profession, *Quality Progress*, Apr., 111–19.

Hawkins, D.M. and Olwell, D.H. (1998) *Cumulative Sum Charts and Charting for Quality Improvement*, New York: Springer-Verlag.

Hoerl, R.W. and Palm, A.C. (1992) Discussion: integrating SPC and APC, *Technometrics* **34**(3), 268–72.

Jones, L.A. and Woodall, W.H. (1998) The performance of bootstrap control charts, *Journal of Quality Technology* **30**(4), Oct., 362–75.

Levi, A.S. and Mainstone, L.E. (1987) Obstacles to understanding and using statistical process control as a productivity improvement approach, *Journal of Organizational Behavior Management* **9**(1), 23–32.

Mitra, A. (1993) *Fundamentals of Quality Control and Improvement*, New York: Macmillan.

Montgomery, D.C. (1996) *Introduction to Statistical Quality Control* (3rd edn). New York: John Wiley & Sons.

Oakland, J.S. (1999) *Statistical Process Control* (4th edn). Oxford: Butterworth-Heinemann.

Preece, D. and Wood, M. (1995) Quality measurements: who is using the sums and for what purpose? *Human Resource Management Journal* **5**(3), 41–55.

Rodriguez, R.N. (1992) Recent developments in process capability analysis, *Journal of Quality Technology* **24**(4), Oct., 176–87.

Simon, J.L. (1992) *Resampling: the New Statistics*. Arlington, VA: Resampling Stats, Inc.

Stoumbous, Z.G., Reynolds Jr, M.R., Ryan, T.P. and Woodall, W.H. (2000) The state of statistical process control as we proceed into the 21st century, *Journal of the American Statistical Association* **95**(451), Sept., 992–8.

Wood, M. (1994) Statistical methods for monitoring service processes, *International Journal of Service Industry Management* **5**(4), 53–68.

Wood, M. (1995) Three suggestions for improving control charting procedures, *International Journal of Quality and Reliability Management* **12**(5), 61–74.

Wood, M., Capon, N. and Kaye, M. (1998) User-friendly statistical concepts for process monitoring, *Journal of the Operational Research Society* **49**(9), 976–85.

Wood, M. and Christy, R. (1999) Sampling for possibilities, *Quality & Quantity* **33**, 185–202.

Wood, M., Kaye, M. and Capon, N. (1999) The use of resampling for estimating control chart limits, *Journal of the Operational Research Society* **50**, 651–9.

Wood, M. and Preece, D. (1992) Using quality measures: practice, problems and possibilities, *International Journal of Quality and Reliability Management* **9**(7), 42–53.

Woodall, W.H. and Adams, B.M. (1998) Statistical process control. In H.M. Wadsworth Jr. (ed.), *Handbook of Statistical Methods for Engineers and Scientists*, 2nd edn, pp. 7.3–7.28. New York: McGraw-Hill.

Woodall, W.H. and Montgomery, D.C. (1999) Research issues and ideas in statistical process control, *Journal of Quality Technology* **31**, 376–86.

Part III

Case studies in Quality Management

6 TQM in higher education institutions

A review and case application

Jaideep Motwani and Glenn Mazur

Introduction

Higher education institutions (HEIs)[1] have felt the pressure to change and reform during the last few years. Changing student demographics, declining student performances, diminishing government funding, rising dropout rates, and dramatically increased competition have been the driving forces for change (Brown and Koenig, 1993; Francis and Hampton, 1999). As a result, many institutions of higher education have started to study and apply Total Quality Management (TQM), in one or more forms.

TQM can be defined as a general management philosophy and set of tools which allow an institution to pursue a definition of quality and a means for attaining quality; with quality being a continuous improvement ascertained by customers' contentment with the services they have received (Blow, 1995). The customers of HEIs are the different group of actors that affect the education process, namely; existing and potential students; employees; employers, government; and industry. Owing to their different characteristics, they exert certain demands that affect the behaviour of the education system (McGettrick and Mansor, 1999).

According to Narsimhan (1987), the first application of TQM in US HEIs was at Fox Valley Technical College (FVTC). TQM helped FVTC to become more efficient in areas such as placement of graduates, employer satisfaction with contracted training programmes, acceptance of college credits at receiving institutions, and improvement in learning environments. Later, many institutions began to join the TQM bandwagon, including Virginia Commonwealth University, Oregon State University, Pennsylvania State University, University of Pennsylvania, Kansas State University (Cowles and Gilbreath, 1993; Coate, 1993; Lozier and Teeter, 1996), among others. Rubach (1994) showed that 415 HEIs in the United States are involved in implementing either quality improvement practices in their administrations or quality-related courses in their curricula, or both. HEIs that have successfully adopted the principles offer success stories of improved communication, higher employee morale, increased productivity, improved process efficiency, and reduction in defects and costs (Matthews, 1993).

The purpose of this chapter is to discuss the implementation of TQM in HEIs and its contribution to the institutions' performance and business excellence. The chapter is divided as follows. First, the reasons for implementing TQM in HEIs are discussed. Secondly, the definition of 'customer' of HEIs is provided. A review and classification of pertinent literature on TQM in HEI, into four different research streams, forms the third section of the chapter. Next, a discussion and a case application of Quality Function Deployment (QFD), a powerful TQM tool, at the University of Michigan are explained. The QFD application has increased the student to teacher ratio in the course, grown from one section to three, and continuously sends student teams into various departments in the university and local businesses to improve their quality programmes. This chapter shows the step-by-step application of QFD that focuses both on external evaluators of the university (companies that hire graduates) and internal evaluators of the university (the students themselves). In the final section, issues relating to TQM in HEI that need to be addressed in the future are suggested.

Why implement TQM in HEIs?

Quality is what the customer says it is, particularly in the case of HEIs because the 'product' generated by higher education is not a visible, tangible product that can be held, analysed, and inspected for defects. If customers are perfectly happy with the services provided to them by institutions, then quality is acceptable. This is the reason that the definition of an institution's customer is such an important and necessary task. You must know your customer to be able to determine the success or failure of your commitment to quality (Motwani, 1995).

There are many advantages and disadvantages to pursuing the TQM program in any business, whether it is a product-oriented business or a business providing services, as in the case of HEIs. For many universities, a selling point for a quality program is the leaner budgets and higher efficiency and productivity inherent in certain quality programs (Cyert, 1993).

As budgets continue to tighten and as individual grants and gifts dwindle, HEIs will have to be more vigilant and tenacious in their pursuit of providing quality education at a lower cost. In 1991, for the first time in 30 years, state funding for higher education dropped. Three-quarters of the university and college presidents in the United States believe mounting operating costs and shrinking revenues are the largest problems with which they have to contend in the 1990s. Growing costs, decreasing enrolment totals, and economic-induced slashes in funding from the legislatures have produced a 'decade of scarcity' in which colleges and universities have to trim their budgets and raise tuition to meet their financial needs (Coate, 1993).

These predicaments have forced many HEIs to begin to consider ways to make the change to a 'leaner and meaner' organization as early as possible. This is one of the many reasons that HEIs have begun to turn to TQM programs as a source of relief. If one follows a quality program completely and intently, the business will inevitably run on a lower budget and make more efficient use of manpower due to the nature of the 'beast' that is total quality (Edwards, 1991).

Defining the 'customer' in HEIs

The question of 'customer' for higher education poses a very sticky problem. No college or university seems willing or able to settle on a specific definition of customer. There appears to be something inherently ominous about defining a HEIs customer as the student. This poses all kinds of dilemmas for administrators. Faculties balk at the idea of having a student as the customer, as in 'the customer is always right'. This tends to engage faculty to the boiling point because they believe that giving the student what they want will not necessarily lead to higher quality education. This belief is based on the assumption that a happy student is one merely passes classes and graduates, so students are only concerned with short-term satisfaction (making the grade), as opposed to actually learning and growing (long-term gains). Faculty and administrators tend to hold the belief that they know what the student *needs*, whereas the student may not necessarily be privy to the information at the early stages of their educational development (Harris and Baggett, 1992).

Examples of their fear of using the student alone as the customer are reflected in the definitions used by the leaders of the TQM movement in HEI. Samford University defines their customer as the student customer but states that 'many contemporary academics feel the term "customer" is too crass a commercial term, denoting a cash exchange' (Harris and Baggett). Harvard University defines their customer thus: 'The customer is defined as anyone to whom we provide information or service' (Hubbard, 1994: 21). Oregon State University, perhaps the most highly touted TQM follower in higher education, considers their customer in this light: 'Our students are our purpose of existence' (Coate, 1993: 7). They go on to divide their customer base into external and internal groups to encompass every possible customer. Northwest Missouri State University bases their customers focus on the following percept: 'in the classroom, the student along with the instructor, are "suppliers" who produce a "product" (knowledge) that future "customers" (employees or graduate schools) will evaluate' (Hubbard, 1994: 95). Syracuse University does call their student their customer; however, 'some balked at the term "customer". Their fear was that by serving students, we might risk relinquishing control of the academic experience' (Shaw, 1993: 26) Fox Valley Technical College believes their customer to be 'students who use our services and employers who are ultimate customers of our graduates' (Spanbauer, 1987: 179).

Based upon these definitions of customer, as well as the many others found in the literature (Mahoney *et al.*, 1993; McNeill, 1995; Stein, 1994), one could see the myriad problems with defining the student as customer. None of the universities or colleges cited, however, can exclude the student from the final definition of customer. No matter what term one chooses to use, the student is the foremost component of the clientele served by HEI.

In summary, it appears that all of the above-mentioned colleges and universities believe their customer consists of either the employer or student or both. There are two universities that chose to broaden their definition to include everyone everywhere. After shifting through the numerous definitions, the basic definition of the customer of HEI proposed by this chapter is as follows:

The **customer** of HEI is the student as the consumer of knowledge and services, the future employer or graduate school as a consumer of the student product, and society as a whole as taxpayers and beneficiaries of the educational operations of the institution.

Classification of literature on TQM in HEI

The research done in the area of TQM implementation in the HEI can be conveniently grouped as follows.

Definition and overview articles

Several research studies provide comprehensive definitions of the term Quality Management in HEIs (Marchese, 1991; Helms and Key, 1994). The overview articles, on the other hand, include topics such as important elements that separate TQM in the HEIs from TQM in other industries (Cloutier and Richards, 1994), roadblocks to implementing TQM (Thurmond, 1993; Chappell, 1994) and discussion of various measuring instruments to determine the quality of products or services (Hogan, 1992; Parsuraman *et al.*, 1985), among others.

TQM is viewed variously as a philosophy, which emphasizes that quality is the responsibility of everyone in an organization; as a process for managing change; as a strategy to improve organizational competitiveness and effectiveness; a value system that emphasizes striving for quality in product or services; and an approach to doing business that covers the whole organization (Marchese, 1991; Tang and Zairi, 1988a,b).

TQM is customer-driven and it is a strategy based on the desire to satisfy the customer's expectation. With the blessings of and commitment from the top-level management, it encourages and motivates employees to participate in continuous improvement of the product, service and operations. Overteit (1993) defined 'three aspects of quality ... that need to be part of a comprehensive quality measurement system: customer-or client-quality, professional- or technical-quality, and management quality'. Parsuraman *et al.* (1985) defined 'service quality as the discrepancy between consumers' perceptions of services offered by a particular firm and their expectations about the firm offering such services'.

TQM is also viewed as a management 'unification' process (Stuelpnagel, 1988/89) that emphasizes teamwork and employee empowerment. Employees at all levels are organized and motivated with knowledge and responsibility for managing and improving the processes. Thus, TQM is far more than simply statistical quality control and quality assurance. It is concerned with 'changing the fundamental beliefs, values and culture of a company, harnessing the enthusiasm and participation of everyone', with the ultimate goal of doing the job right first time.

In providing a definition of quality or TQM in HEIs, there is a need to recognize that (1) customers understand the meaning of quality at different levels, (2) giving weight on quality depends on the quality judgement, and (3) the definition of quality is not absolute, judgement of quality is more of the concept of 'fitness for purpose'. Harvey and Green (1993) make it clear that 'quality' depends on the perspectives of different sets of people, on different things that have been given the same label and, in addition, 'quality' is sometimes viewed in relation to some idea of a 'normal' standard. TQM in HEIs embraces three broad categories: goals, the processes deployed for achieving these goals, and how far these goals have been achieved. Of necessity, there are interactions between these categories.

The roadblocks to implementing TQM in HEIs are as follows. First, there is a substantial outlay of resources (including cash and employee time) and personnel required when implementing any new program. The outlay involved when an institution decides to plunge the whole organization into the total quality plan at one time, requiring a complete and systematic change to the culture, can be overwhelming or unjustifiable to sceptics and local bodies. This is the reason that many HEIs choose to take the slow-implementation route. This entails starting a few departments at a time on the total quality plan and adding to them until the whole institution is involved in the total quality plan over a period of time.

Faculty, also, may feel that TQM means an increase in committee work, which is true in that more time must be invested, for which there is no professional benefit for the faculty member individually. Another obstacle to TQM implementation could be the inability to define outcomes and standards in an educational setting, thus making TQM unmeasurable and groundless. Above all, most people who get involved with TQM expect to see results immediately, and this is usually not the case. It takes time to plan, organize, and implement TQM.

Lastly, various measuring instruments have been also developed in order to determine service quality in HEIs. Hogan (Hogan, 1992) uses the Malcolm Baldridge criteria to evaluate service quality of administrators of HEIs; however, the items used do not cover the needs of various stakeholders of HEIs. Lastly, Owlia (1996) introduced a model for measuring the quality of engineering programs at universities in the UK. Although the instrument can be applied to the whole institution, it does not indicate the importance of each factor.

Prescriptive articles

The second stream covers the gamut of normative studies done mainly by practitioners. These deal with the importance of TQM, both to the overall organization, as well as functional areas of the organization. It also provides normative suggestions for institutionalizing TQM strategies in HEIs. Normative suggestions for TQM include: the need for a proactive, rather than a reactive approach to TQM, steps for building a TQM system (Schragel, 1993); factors that must be considered in implementing a TQM program in HEI (Fisher, 1993; Rubach and Stratton, 1994), examples of how HEIs have successfully institutionalized TQM strategies (Barrier, 1993; Fam and Camp, 1995), and the benefits of implementing TQM (HBR, 1991). This stream covers a medley of studies whose main thrust is to emphasize the importance of TQM. Written largely by practitioners, these studies are all prescriptive in approach and without any kind of methodological rigour. However, one cannot dismiss their contributions to the field because the authors, for the most part, speak from field experience.

Theory building

The third research stream is concerned with developing conceptual models for assessing and implementing Quality Management strategies. Several researchers suggest specific models and/or steps for implementing the principles of TQM (Helms and Key, 1994; Dale, 1996) or for selecting an effective set of measures for institutions practicing TQM (Hogan, 1992). Some of these models have also been successfully applied to HEIs. Even though the models/steps suggested by the above authors are detailed, the main criticism against this stream is that there has been little effort to use existing theory to develop a comprehensive model of TQM in HEIs.

Some of the specific TQM models that have been implemented by various HEIs are as follows. The TQM implementation model established by the Office of Quality Improvement at the University of Wisconsin-Madison comprised the following steps: (1) identify their natural leadership team, who then begins to learn about the concepts and methods and decides whether or not to implement. If they decide to move ahead, they develop the following, involving all staff at various steps. (2) Identify their mission or purpose of the unit, in support of the campus mission. (3) Identify their customers – for whom do we want to do? – and their needs. (4) Develop a vision – where do we want to head? (5) Identify critical processes. (6) Pilot one or two projects aimed at critical needs. (7) Provide training in the concepts and methods to all staff in a continuously learning process. (8) Develop a plan for continuous improvement and learning about customer needs (University of Wisconsin, 1994).

Babson College has designed a Quality Improvement Process that consists of nine key steps. These steps are: (1) identify output; (2) identify customers; (3) identify customer requirements; (4) translate requirements into supplier specifications; (5) identify steps in work process; (6) establish measurements; (7) assess process capability; (8) evaluate results; (9) schedule periodic reviews (Babson College, 1994).

Mathews (1993) has developed his own version of a TQM model for HEI. His model comprises the following seven steps: (1) identify the institution's primary stakeholders; (2) develop a specific competitive quality based mission; (3) establish internal measures for quality and excellence in specific and identified areas; (4) determine who has to commit to the chosen standards; (5) establish motivation for those unwilling to commit to quality and excellence; (6) form quality progress teams; (7) report, recognize and reward success.

Harvard University has been able to pare their quality process to the following six steps: (1) management behaviour/actions – includes components such as performance management, planning, financial management, staff meetings and so forth; (2) education and training – is composed of LUTE (learn, use, teach, evaluate), competitive benchmarking, and keeping employees 'evergreen'; (3) communication – covers listening for understanding, flow of information, consensus building and consistency; (4) tools and measures – consists of planning processes, reporting/reviews, and so forth; (5) transition teams – deal with time and resource commitment, long-term plan commitment and other such items; (6) recognition and reward – focuses on things such as meetings, gifts, salary review, and thank you notes.

Kanji's Business Excellence model (Kanji, 1998) comprises four principles: delight the customer; management by fact; people-based management; and continuous improvement. Each principle is further divided into two core concepts, namely: customer satisfaction and internal customers are real; all work is process and measurement; teamwork and people make quality; and continuous improvement cycle and prevention. Although Kanji has not used the term 'critical success factors', the author emphasized that the higher education system has to be guided through the TQM principles and core concepts by top management leadership in order to achieve business excellence.

Freed and Klugman's approach (1999) is essentially an organization development approach to TQM. Taking systems view of higher education, the authors identify the external and internal drivers for the quality initiative and then trace the elements of successful efforts through the critical organizational components: goal-setting, team-building, leadership, culture, human resources development and communication.

Lastly, Oregon State University has developed their own TQM model that consists of nine steps. Their model is a combination of the Hoshin Planning Model and the Baldridge Award Criteria (Coate, 1990).

Theory testing

The fourth stream, which can be the culmination of all research done in TQM, deals with the assessment and successful implementation of current practices of TQM by HEIs (Coate, 1990; Nagy *et al.*, 1993; Seymour, 1993). Most of the research under this stream, done through field studies, questionnaire surveys or case studies, illustrates how TQM can create a competitive advantage.

For example, Oregon State University's (OSUs) states: 'By so far, we consider TQM a real success at OSU. We now have 15 teams operating and the results have been spectacular. Time has been saved, costs have been reduced, people have been empowered at all levels, and morale has skyrocketed' (Coate, 1993: 21). OSU is regarded as one of the fledging leaders of the TQM in HEI movement. OSU has gone so far as to develop 'success criteria' (Coate, 1993: 17) as part of its ongoing efforts. Another leader in the TQM in HEI movement, Northwest Missouri State University, has had their 'success' at implementing TQM defined as: 'Enrolment is now at capacity; the budget is balanced; faculty salaries are higher than average; and about 10 per cent of the budget has been shifted from administration to instruction' (Anonymous, 1994).

OSU and Northwest Missouri are two universities who believe they have successfully implemented TQM programs at their respective universities (noting, of course, that TQM is a continual process of never-ending improvement and growth). In the early nineties, Syracuse University began to implement TQM in its processes and report success based on the following: 'the teams . . . have sustained a high level of enthusiasm . . . the number of calls to the bursar's office has dropped dramatically, and so has the incidence of standing in line to register . . . the financial aid area . . . busy signals . . . dropped period' and have developed 'a new focus on customer's needs and request' (Shaw, 1993).

According to Hubbard (1994), Harvard University successfully joined the TQM bandwagon during that period. The program, which began with its Office for Information Technology, resulted in a $70,000 per year savings on software licenses from the elimination of unused or unnecessary software packages, a $120,000 credit from New England Telephone from reconciling reporting processes, a 40 per cent reduction in paper used for billing, new billing formats, a reduction in Harvard University's copy centre data entry timing from two days to 1.5 hours, and the creation of a telephone service, among other things. Other success stories of TQM implementation programs at universities include: Boston, Columbia, Leigh, Northern Arizona, Tennessee, among others (Mahoney *et al.*, 1993; McNeill, 1995; Stein, 1994; Marchese, 1991).

In addition, several universities, colleges and junior colleges in the US have used quality circles to increase their effectiveness in areas of classroom teaching, residential life, student learning support, work life management of college employees, college administration, library facilities, and student services (Kogut, 1984; Kaplan, 1991; Sell and Mortola, 1985). Most of the reported experiences with the quality circle implementation in higher education have been positive. However, there is some evidence that the success of quality circle programs may be jeopardized by problems, such as inadequate training, problematic group membership, exclusion of supervisors etc.

Relatively little has been written about the application of TQM in UK HEIs. Initially, the reason for strong interest in TQM in UK universities was due to key legislative changes, coupled with UK Department of Education's intention to establish an explicit link between quality assessment and funding (Kanji, 1996). Later, TQM was adopted by universities to deal with impending problems, such as decline in student funding; commensurate encouragement to increase alternative sources of funding, drop in student performance; and dissatisfied employers of quality of graduates (Doherty, 1993). In the UK, the higher education sector is also facing unprecedented and increasing levels of market accountability fuelled by the legislative processes of subsequent administration (Tang and Zairi, 1988a, b). Some varied and positive experiences reported on UK universities are cases at Aston University, South Bank University, the University of Ulster, the University of Bradford and the University of Wolverhampton (Doherty, 1993; Tang and Zairi, 1988a, b). According to Harrison (1994), quality in universities in the UK was three-tiered. First, there existed an internal quality assurance system. Secondly, the system was evaluated by an external audit. Thirdly, a judgmental apparatus linked to the funding agency capped them. In 1998 the Quality Audit Agency proposed a new framework, based on institution's internal validation as well as reviews by academics, for assessing education quality. Forty-two subject benchmark groups were identified that would be used as national subject benchmark standards. These developments are moving UK HEIs closer to adopting TQM by way of their increased customer focus, the need for Quality Management and enhancement, and the utilization of benchmarks.

Kanji and Malek (1999a, b) provide an excellent overview of quality in UK higher education. In this study, the authors surveyed 51 UK HEIs, and concluded that: (1) there were only four institutions that implemented TQM in UK HEIs; (2) 72.5 per cent defined quality as 'fitness for purpose'; (3) the nine TQM critical success factors that influence performance and business excellence of UK HEIs were: continuous improvement, leadership, external customer satisfaction, people management, teamwork, process improvement, internal customer satisfaction, measurement of resources, and prevention; and (4) most institutions use financial measures as indicators of organizational performance (60.8 per cent). The nine critical factors found in this study are consistent with the TQM principles and core concepts described in the *theory building* and *theory testing* literature described earlier.

In other parts of the world, TQM has not been practised rigorously, except for some isolated cases of TQM implementation in Malaysia, and New Zealand. Kanji and Malek (1999a, b) reported the findings and conclusions of recent exploratory research conducted on the application of TQM in HEIs in the US and Malaysia. Altogether, 60 Malaysian HEIs and 72 US HEIs participated in the study. The authors concluded that TQM institutions outperformed non-TQM institutions in organization performance. Also, in both countries, especially in the US, good quality performance was associated with good organizational performance.

Application of TQM in HEI: a case study

In this section, by means of a case study, a successful application of quality functional deployment (QFD), a powerful TQM tool, in a TQM course is provided. Since, the second author of this chapter played a very critical role in the success of this application, we felt that it would be beneficial for our readers if we discussed the process of implementation of this important TQM tool. Prior to the case study discussion, the different application of QFD in the educational literature is provided.

QFD applications in HEIs

QFD has been applied to university and other educational institutions in North America, Europe and the Pacific Rim since the late 1980s. One of the earliest uses of QFD in education was by Ermer at the Mechanical Engineering Department of the University of Wisconsin, Madison in 1991 where the department chairman used it to assess and respond to the needs of his faculty. Application reports began appearing at the North American QFD Symposia in 1992 with a case study for a high school guidance program (Stamm, 1992) in which she reported outstanding improvements in student involvement in college planning activities. Krishnan and Houshmand (1993) demonstrated their use of QFD to balance between research and teaching at the University of Cincinnati Department of Industrial Engineering. In this case, various customers such as businesses and students were identified, and their needs were translated through QFD into 'product features' such as 'communication skills, practical knowledge' etc. which were translated into 'process features' such as 'presentations, project reports, lab experiments' etc. QFD was used by Lakeshore Technical College in Wisconsin to increase the variety of course offerings and other structural issues such as parking etc. for its students (Grimes *et al.*, 1994). Curriculum was addressed again in 1995 by Hillman and Pionka of Wayne State University (Hillman and Pionka, 1995), which portrayed the strong relationship between the needs of industry and the employability of engineering graduates. A full engineering curriculum update by Rosenkrantz led to an almost course-for-course match to SME Curricula 2000 recommendations at California State Polytechnic University (Rosenkrantz, 1996). A new application of QFD to strategic planning and funding was done at the University of Vermont by Hummel (1996).

QFD activities to improve European institutions have also been taking place. Clayton (1995) reported on the use of QFD to build a degree program in the Department of Vision Sciences at Aston University in the United Kingdom. Nilsson *et al.* (1995) reported on the use of QFD to develop a Mechanical Engineering Program more responsive to the needs of changing industries in Sweden. QFD was applied by Seow and Moody (1996) to design an MSc degree in Quality Management at University of Portsmouth in the UK. Conjoint analysis has been recently employed in the market research end of QFD and a study was conducted by Gustafsson *et al.* (1996) at the University of Linköping, Sweden to develop a TQM course curriculum.

In Japan, Akao, Nagai and Maki (1996) have systematized a process for identifying and analysing both the internal and external evaluators of higher education and using QFD to identify and improve critical and conflicting needs. Tiede (1995) polled the perception of Australian high school educators about QFD after students, parents, and staff used it to strengthen the understanding of school policies.

Application of QFD in TQM 401: a senior and graduate course in TQM

In 1993, the College of Engineering at the University of Michigan introduced a course in TQM in the Department of Industrial and Operations Engineering. Capitalizing on many of the quality control techniques gaining popularity in the automobile industry, such as Taguchi Methods, $C_p k$ measurements, SPC etc., a professor assembled a course to cover these techniques. After its initial offering, the professor invited Glenn Mazur (the second author of this chapter) to take over the class. Because of the author's exposure to many advanced quality techniques, such as QFD, he decided to apply these to structuring the course according to customer needs.

The benefits of using QFD were that he could focus the constrained resources, in my case time, on those areas that mattered most to the customers of my course. The word 'customer' must be interpreted broadly. Traditionally, instructors do not look at their students as customers, but more like 'raw materials' to be moulded into a 'product' that industry and society will accept. A more capitalistic interpretation is that students spend money and have choice. What the author expected QFD to achieve was a course that would give students' marketable knowledge and skills, and would be packaged such that the best students would choose it over other course options. The author knew the starting point was to identify the customer.

Dr Akao of Asahi University and one of the founders of the QFD methodology 30 years ago, has described two groups of customers of a university, which he calls internal and external evaluators (Akao *et al.*, 1996). See Figure 6.1.

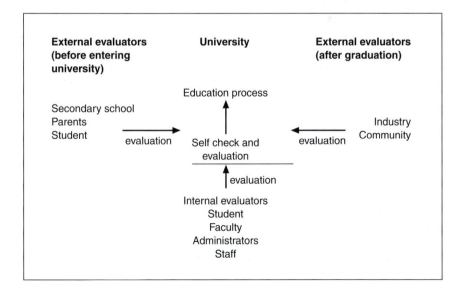

Figure 6.1 Akao's concept of university evaluators.

Since the concern of the author was for a single course rather than a full curriculum or degree program, the customers were limited to industry as the external evaluator and the student as the internal evaluator.

TQM401, being a 400 level course, was intended for graduating seniors in Industrial Engineering who would be expected to participate in ever growing TQM activities in companies that were hiring them. Thus, it made sense to focus on those industries, which frequently hired University of Michigan graduates and their future bosses as the customers. Since Michigan is the automobile capital of the world, the author consequently spoke with a number of engineering managers in the automobile, automotive parts, and also the electronics industries. The purpose was to find out what capabilities they wanted new hires to have in addition to their engineering speciality. Their responses were then grouped using the KJ™ method into an Affinity Diagram, which help structure the requirements from the customers' point of view. KJ™ method, developed in the 1960s by Kawakita Jiro, a Japanese anthropologist, is a technique for gathering and organizing a large number of ideas, opinions, and facts relating to a broad problem or subject area. It enables problem solvers to shift through large volumes of information efficiently and to identify natural patterns or groupings in the information. See Figure 6.2. When coupled with a hierarchy diagram, unspoken requirements can also be identified.

Engineering managers were also asked to prioritize their needs using the

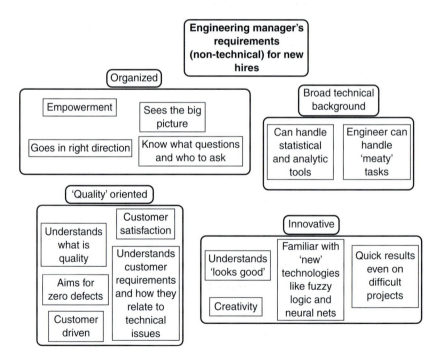

Figure 6.2 Affinity diagram of engineering managers' needs.

Analytic Hierarchy Process (AHP). The AHP uses pair wise comparisons that allow for an accurate measure of importance, including a ratio scale distance between values, unlike the more traditional rating scale used in QFD. The results are shown in Figure 6.3 using the first level of detail only.

The next phase was to translate these managers' requirements into skills and capabilities that the students must have upon completion of the course. This was done using a fishbone diagram with the need in the head as the 'effect' and the skills and capabilities in the bones as the 'causes'. This is consistent with the earliest models of QFD developed by Akao and Bridgestone Tire (Mizuno and Akao, 1994). These were then formed into a quality table with the managers' needs priorities developed from the AHP above being translated into priorities for the skills and capabilities (see Figure 6.4).

These skills and capabilities were then mapped (details omitted) into subject matter, activities, and reports in proportion to the curriculum percentages in the quality table. The author was surprised to see the close correspondence to the ten week IS course for overseas students (Fukuyama, 1994).

After fine-tuning the course contents, it was time to focus on student needs. Since students are not in as good a position to judge the content of the course, as they are the format and style, this became the focus of the next QFD study. As part

Appropriate TQM education for engineering undergraduates

Node: 0

Compare the relative IMPORTANCE with respect to: GOAL

	TECHNICA	ORGANIZE	INNOVATE
QUALITY	2.0	6.0	7.0
TECHNICA		5.0	3.0
ORGANIZE			3.0

Row element is_times more than column element unless enclosed in ()

Abbreviation	Definition
Goal	Appropriate TQM education for engineering undergraduates.
QUALITY	Quality minded in understanding customers and solving.
TECHNICA	Broad technical background to handle difficult tasks.
ORGANIZE	Organized approach to work.
INNOVATE	Familiar with innovative methods and technologies.

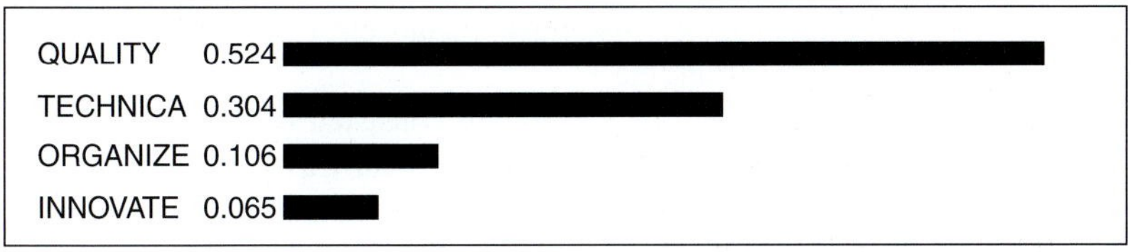

QUALITY   0.524 ████████████████████████████
TECHNICA 0.304 █████████████████
ORGANIZE 0.106 ████████
INNOVATE 0.065 █████

Inconsistency ratio = 0.09

Figure 6.3 AHP to prioritize engineering managers' requirements.

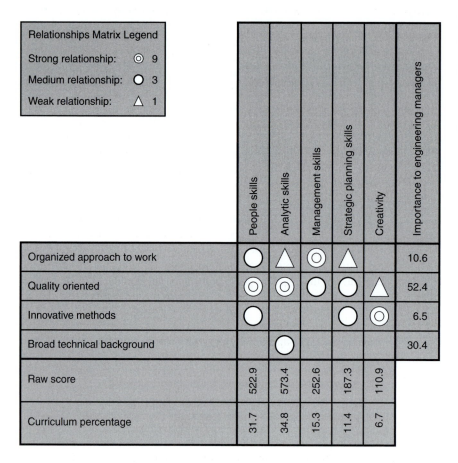

Figure 6.4 Quality table for managers' needs vs students' skills.

of the course, students form TQM teams to work directly with real organizations; the purpose is that by explaining TQM to others, they learn it better themselves.

One of the projects is the TQM course itself. The course has customers (engineering managers who hire the graduates), a manager (the instructor), different functional departments (registration, library, classroom and facilities), a service (teaching), a product (books, materials, visuals etc.), and processes (lectures, projects, grades, presentations etc.).

Unlike traditional QFD studies, the QFD team consisted of the internal customers (the students) themselves. Internal customer data was gathered from the team surveying the current students and a review of student evaluations from previous semesters. Needless to say, not all were flattering, but if improvement is to take place, than certainly a teacher of TQM should be able to demonstrate with his or her own program!

In fact, the winter 1995 semester was able to solve the over-enrolment problem, the highest priority issue that year. The problem of over-enrolment occurred after the first semester the author took over the class due to rising popularity of the subject. Due to the projects and audit style of the course, only 30 students could be accommodated in each section. After the first semester, fall 1993, the number of sections was increased to two, which immediately filled up. By winter of 1995, the demand was approaching 100 students demanding to take the course but the university was not able to add a third section so quickly. From the QFD study, the team changed the University's standard override procedure and put up a World Wide Web site so that prospective students could review the course and confirm their interest prior to enrolling. In the fall of 1995, however, demand exceeded 120 students, and so a third section has now been added. The fall 1995 team began their teamwork in much the same way, except that now there were other priorities to improve. From this study emerged a new graduate feedback process to help continuously upgrade the course content based on changing requirements in industry. Every semester, since 1995, three sections of this course are being offered. The course continues to be popular and the students continue to work on exciting projects.

Future research directions

There are several issues relating to TQM in HEI that need to be addressed in the future. These concerns can be categorized, according to the four research streams, described earlier.

Definition and overview articles

Recommendations for research under this stream deal with a definition and overview of Total Quality Management and how it relates to HEI. First, more research needs to be done to determine whether implementation of TQM is viewed as the responsibility of the board of control, president, administrators (deans), or selected group of faculty members and staff. The primary users of TQM should be the ones who direct implementation throughout the organization. Secondly, research on the regulations, attitudes, policies, and practices, which may be an impediment to continuous improvement, should be identified and eliminated.

A third concern relating to this research stream is whether there is government and congressional push and support for implementing TQM in HEI. The issues of educational reform plans, relative to TQM, and its successful implementation is in order. To gain government and congressional support, HEIs must continually stress the importance, necessity, and results of TQM.

Prescriptive articles

Research under this stream pertains to normative studies conducted by experts in the field. Several issues relating to this area deserve consideration in the future.

First, studies needed to be undertaken to examine if a dramatic time lag between the directive, training and implementation will impede the effectiveness of TQM. Future research should seek to determine the effect of time lag between the onset of the program and the final results, and turnover of senior personnel.

Another critical issue practitioners should address is the variance among TQM implementation and standards of quality within and among different HEIs. Attempts to standardize performance and quality have been less than fully successful in the past. As a result, quality standards, standard operating procedures, inspections and audits are not uniform among the various HEIs. Determination of benchmarking procedures and their usage would be helpful.

Theory building

There is a great potential for future study regarding very few integrated models linking TQM and HEI have been developed. A primary issue of concern is the need for the 'system' to work perfectly on demand. Yet, sometimes there are operational breakdowns. Models should be developed to determine where operating system breakdowns occur, why they occur, and how they can be prevented.

Secondly, there is a need for development of suitable TQM model for HEIs that incorporates various critical success factors. The existing models in the literature are difficult to apply, partly because they do not emphasize the principles and assumptions that make up TQM. In addition, they do not incorporate the critical success factors that affect TQM outcomes. The other shortcomings of these models are: (1) although it is claimed that they are successful, they have not been validated by suitable data, and (2) most models have been developed by institutions to serve their particular needs and may not be suitable for use by other institutions.

Theory testing

There is ample opportunity and necessity for future studies in this stream. First, TQM advocates typically issue strong promises that TQM will unite campuses; increase employee satisfaction, among others. Unfortunately, the empirical evidence in favour of TQM in universities is anecdotal and surprisingly sparse. Most studies do not contain any rigorous empirical evidence on the effects of TQM, only opinions and process indicators. Also, hard empirical evidence or cost-benefit studies, especially those that relate to learning and academic achievement at the university level, need to be investigated in the future.

Secondly, more comprehensive and comparative case studies of successful implementation would be helpful to those who are still struggling with this stage. Thirdly, elaborate studies, which detail the steps in building a successful TQM system in HEI and which outline specific performance measures in evaluating educational systems, are necessary. Data for such studies should be obtained from on-site observation, questioning and performance of data analysis that can lead to hypotheses to be measured by questionnaires sent to administrators who have been successful in implementing TQM.

Conclusion

Recent success of customer-driven TQM efforts in the business sector has promoted its broader application to HEIs. In this study, we discuss the implementation of TQM in HEIs and its contribution to the institutions' performance by classifying the pertinent literature into four different research streams. Based on our extensive literature review, we can conclude that there is a smaller number of TQM efforts in the UK and the rest of world in relationship to the US. In the US, HEIs have been influenced by the critical state of education in the 1980s in terms of student grades, funding and complaints from employees and parents. Results show that the institutions that have implemented TQM, regardless of the location or country, have benefited from improved student performance, better services, reduced costs and customer satisfaction. The nine TQM critical success factors that influence HEIs are continuous improvement, leadership, external customer satisfaction, people management, teamwork, process improvement, internal customer satisfaction, measurement of resources and prevention.

In addition to the literature classification, we also provide a discussion and a case application of Quality Function Deployment (QFD), a powerful TQM tool, at the University of Michigan. A step-by-step application that focuses both on external and internal evaluators of the university is provided. The QFD application has increased the student to teacher ratio in the course, grown from one section to three, and continuously sends student teams into various departments in the university and local businesses to improve their quality programs.

Note

1   Includes both universities and other higher education institutes.

References

Akao, Y., Nagai, K. and Maki, N. (1996) QFD concept for improving higher education. In *Proceedings of ASQC's 50th Annual Quality Congress*, 12–20.
Anonymous (1994) Quality, with tears, *Financial World* **163**(6), 52.
Babson College (1994) *Continuous Quality Improvement at Babson College*, Babson College, Office of Quality, Oct.
Barrier, M. (1993) Business schools, TQM, and you, *Nation's Business* **81**, 60–1.
Blow, C. (1995) An introduction to Total Quality Management, *Assessment Journal* **2**(1), 25–7.
Brower, M. (1991) The paradigm shifts required to apply TQM and teams in higher education. *Readings in Total Quality Management*, 485–97.
Brown, D.J. and Koenig, H.F. (1993) Applying Total Quality Management to business education, *Journal of Education for Business* **68**(6), 35–6.
Chappell, R.T. (1994) Can TQM in public education survive with co-production? *Quality Progress*, July, 41–4.

Clayton, M. (1995) QFD – building quality into English universities. In *Transactions from the Seventh Symposium on Quality Function Deployment, Novi, Michigan*. Ann Arbor, MI: QFD Institute, 171–8.

Cloutier, M. and Richards, J. (1994) Examining customer satisfaction in a big school, *Quality Progress*, Sept., 117–19.

Coate, L.E. (1990) TQM at Oregon State University, *Journal of Quality and Participation*, Dec., 90–101.

Coate, L.E. (1993) The introduction of Total Quality Management at Oregon State University, *Higher Education* **25**, 303–20.

Cowles, D. and Gilbreath, G. (1993) TQM at Virginia Commonwealth University: an urban university struggles with the realities of TQM, *Higher Education* **25**, 303–20.

Cyert, R.M. (1993) Universities, competitiveness and TQM: a plan of action for the year 2000, *Public Administration Quarterly* **17**(1), 10–18.

Dale, B. (1996) Benchmarking on Total Quality Management: a positioning model, *Benchmarking for Quality Management & Technology* **3**(1), 28–37.

Doherty, G. (1993) Towards TQM in higher education: a case study of the University of Wolverhampton, *Higher Education* **25**, 321–39.

Edwards, D. (1991) Total Quality Management in higher education, *Management Services* **35**(12), 8–20.

Ermer, S.D. (1995) Using QFD becomes an educational experience for students and faculty. *Quality Progress*, May, 131–6.

Fam, E. and Camp, R. (1995) Finding and implementing best practices in higher education, *Quality Progress* **28**(2), 69–73.

Fisher, J. (1993) TQM: a warning for higher education. *Educational Record*, Spring, 15–19.

Francis, J. and Hampton, M. (1999) Resourceful responses: the adaptive research university and the drive to market, *Journal of Higher Education*, Nov./Dec., 625–41.

Freed, J. and Klugman, M. (1999) *Quality Principles and Practices in Higher Education*. Phoenix, AZ: Oryx/Ace Press, Nov./Dec.

Fukuyama, H. (1994) Japan Standards Association training course for developing countries. *JSQC News*, Aug., 108.

Grimes, M., Malmberg, J. and LaBine, G. (1994) Integrating the customers' voice to improve educational services through Quality Function Deployment. In *Transactions from the Sixth Symposium on Quality Function Deployment, Novi, Michigan*. Ann Arbor, MI: QFD Institute, 359–72.

Gustafsson, A., Ekdahl, F. and Bergman, B. (1996) Conjoint analysis – a useful tool in the design process. In *Transactions from the Eighth Symposium on Quality Function Deployment/International Symposium on QFD '96, Novi, Michigan*. Ann Arbor, MI: QFD Institute, 261–85.

Harris, J.W. and Baggett, J.M. (eds) (1992) *Quality Quest in the Academic Process*. Birmingham, AL: Samford University and Goal/QP, Methuen, MA.

Harrison, M.J. (1994) Quality issues in higher education: a post-modern phenomenon? In G.D. Doherty (ed.), *Developing Quality Systems in Education*. London: Routledge.

Harvard Business Review (1991) An open letter: TQM on the campus, *Harvard Business Review*, Nov.–Dec., 94–5.

Harvey, L. and Green, D. (1993) Defining quality, *Assessment and Evaluation in Higher Education* **18**(1), 9–34.

Helms, S. and Key, C. (1994) Are students more than customers in the classroom? *Quality Progress*, Sept., 97–9.

Hillman, J. and Pionka, F. (1995) Using QFD for curriculum design. In *Transactions from the Seventh Symposium on Quality Function Deployment, Novi, Michigan*. Ann Arbor, MI: QFD Institute, 179–82.

Hogan, T. (1992) The Application of the MBNQA Criteria to the Evaluation of Quality in College Administration Services. PhD dissertation, Ohio University, Athens.

Hubbard, D.L. (1994) Higher education: continuous quality improvement – making the transition to education, *Journal of Academic Leadership* **19**(6), 401.

Hummel, K. (1996) Abstracting the QFD: applying the power of QFD to strategic planning. In *Transactions from the Eighth Symposium on Quality Function Deployment/International Symposium on QFD '96, Novi, Michigan*. Ann Arbor, MI: QFD Institute, 93.

Kanji, G. (1996) Implementation and pitfalls of Total Quality Management, *Total Quality Management* **7**, 331–43.

Kanji, G. (1998) Measurement of business excellence. *Total Quality Management* **9**, 633–43.

Kanji, G. and Malek, A. (1999a) *TQM in Higher Education*. Best of Quality: IAQ Book Series, Vol. 10. Wisconsin: ASQ Quality Press.

Kanji, G. and Malek, A. (1999b) Total Quality Management in UK higher education institutions, *Total Quality Management*, Jan., 129–53.

Kanji, G., Malek, A. and Wallace, W. (1999) A comparative study of quality practices in higher education institutions in United States and Malaysia, *Total Quality Management*.

Kaplan, R. (1991) The topic of quality in business school education and research, *Selections*, Autumn, 13–21.

Kogut, L.S. (1984) Quality circles: a Japanese management technique for the classroom, *Improving College and University Teaching*, 123–7.

Krishnan, M. and Houshmand, A. (1993) QFD in academia: addressing customer requirements in the design of engineering curricula. In *Transactions from the Fifth Symposium on Quality Function Deployment, Novi, Michigan*. Ann Arbor, MI: QFD Institute, 505–30.

Lozier, G. and Teeter, D. (1996) Quality improvement pursuits in American higher education. *Total Quality Management* **7**, 189–201.

McGettrick, A. and Mansor, N. (1999) Standards and levels – a case study, *Assessment and Evaluation in Higher Education*, June, 131–40.

McNeill, R. (1995) TQM and Northern Arizona University, Cornell Hotel and Restaurant, *Administration Quarterly* **34**(6), 92.

Mahoney, M., Boyd, M., Greensburg, R., Misch, B. and Sylvester, D. (1993) Getting started in TQM – a Tennessee experience, *Journal of Career Planning and Employment* **53**(3), 36–43.

Marchese, T. (1991) TQM reaches the Academy, *American Association for Higher Education Bulletin* 433–46.

Matthews, W.E. (1993) The missing element in higher education, *Journal for Quality & Participation*, Jan./Feb., 102–8.

Mizuno, S. and Akao, Y. (1994) *QFD: The Customer-Driven Approach to Quality Planning and Deployment* (transl. G. Mazur). Tokyo: Asian Productivity Organization.

Motwani, J. (1995) Implementing TQM in education: current efforts and future directions, *Journal of Education for Business* **71**(2), 60–3.

Nagy, J., Cotter, M., Erdman, P., Koch, B., Ramer, S., Roberts, N. and Wiley, J. (1993) Madison: how TQM helped change an admission process, *Change*, May/June, 35–40.

Narsimhan, J. (1987) Organizational climate at the University of Braunton in 1996, *Total Quality Management* **8**, 233–7.

Nilsson, P., Lofgren, B. and Erixon, G. (1995) QFD in the development of engineering studies. In *Transactions from the Seventh Symposium on Quality Function Deployment, Novi, Michigan*. Ann Arbor, MI: QFD Institute, 519–29.

Overteit, J. (1993) *Measuring Service Quality: Practical Guidelines*. Lathwork: Technical Communications.

Owlia, M.S. (1996) A Customer-Oriented Approach to the Measurement and Improvement of Quality in Engineering Education. PhD dissertation, Birmingham University.

Parsuraman, A., Zeithaml, V. and Berry, L. (1985) A conceptual model for service quality and its implications for future research, *Journal of Marketing* **49**, 41–50.

Rosenkrantz, P.R. (1996) Using TQM techniques for curriculum development: developing the manufacturing engineering curriculum at Cal Poly Pomona. *Proceedings of ASQC's 50th Annual Quality Congress*, 29–37.

Rubach, L. (1994) Fourth Annual Quality in Education listing, *Quality Progress*, Sept., 27.

Rubach, L. and Stratton, B. (1994) Teaming up to improve US. *Quality Progress*, Feb., 65–8.

Schragel, F. (1993) Total quality in education. *Quality Progress*, Oct., 67–9.

Sell, D. and Mortola, M.E. (1985) Quality circles and library management, *Community & Junior College Libraries*, Spring, 79–92.

Seow, C. and Moody, T. (1996) QFD as a tool for curriculum design. In *Proceedings of ASQC's 50th Annual Quality Congress*, 21–8.

Seymour, D. (1993) Quality on campus: three institutions, three beginnings. *Changes* **25**, 14–27.

Shaw, K. (1993) Sunflower seeds at Syracuse. *Educational Record* **74**(2), 20–7.

Spanbauer, S. (1987) *Quality First in Education, Why Not?* Appleton, WI: Fox Valley Technical College Foundation.

Stamm, G. (1992) Flowing customer demanded quality from service planning to service design. In *Transactions from the Fourth Symposium on Quality Function Deployment, Novi, Michigan*. Ann Arbor, MI: QFD Institute, 394–412.

Stein, R. (1994) *TQM Program at Colorado Tech*. Colorado Tech, Arts, Management and Logistics Dept.

Stuelpnagel, T.R. (1988/89) Total Quality Management – and academia, *Business Forum*, Fall 1988/Winter 1989, 4–9.

Tang, K.H. and Zairi, M. (1988a) Benchmarking quality implementation in a service context: a comparative analysis of financial services and institutions of higher education, Part IIi, *Total Quality Management*, Oct., 539–52.

Tang, K.H. and Zairi, M. (1988b) Benchmarking quality implementation in a service context: a comparative analysis of financial services and institutions of higher education, Part IIii. *Total Quality Management*, Dec., 669–79.

Thurmond, C. (1993) Quality strained through Japan. *School Management*.

Tiede, L. (1995) The participants' summative perceptions of the Quality Function Deployment (QFD) process as used to review a school policy. In B. Hunt (ed.), *Proceedings of the 1st Pacific Rim Symposium on Quality Deployment*. MacQuarie Graduate School of Management Pty Ltd. MacQuarie University, Australia, 235–45.

University of Wisconsin (1994) *Continuous Improvement on a Tradition to Excellence*. University of Wisconsin – Madison, Office of Quality Improvement.

7 Do customers know what is best for them?

The use of SERVQUAL in UK policing

Nick Capon and Vivien Mills

Introduction

The search for Quality Management methods which are appropriate in the service sector revolves around the key differences of a service from manufacturing:

- perishable: stocking to smooth demand not possible;
- simultaneous: no time to correct any mistakes between creating the service and the customer receiving it;
- heterogeneous: each service must be tailored to the particular customer;
- intangible: measurement of effectiveness is subjective.

The result is that manufacturing quality methods such as final inspection have no value since it is then too late to alter outcomes to customers. The variety and unpredictability of customer requirements mean that prescriptive procedures are less appropriate than in manufacturing. And the subjective nature of service makes reliable measurement difficult.

SERVQUAL meets the challenge by proposing that:

Service Quality = Expectation − Perception

In other words, in the service industry, quality is not absolute nor relative to contractual obligations, it is relative to the performance believed to be available from competitors. Improvement can be gained by managing the expectations of customers without any change in performance. Also actual performance is not the key, it is the subjective perception of that performance that it is vital to understand and enhance.

A key problem with this widely used method is doubt of its validity and reliability given the subjective nature of such measurements (Van Dyke *et al.*, 1997; Buttle, 1996). Do customers know what is best for them? And does SERVQUAL accurately and consistently measure their priorities?

This chapter describes a case study application of SERVQUAL in the UK

Sussex Police Force. It discusses the reliability and effectiveness of the method in a policing context, particularly in the ability of SERVQUAL to support UK government pressure to ensure the police service provides 'Best Value'.

The SERVQUAL method

SERVQUAL was originally proposed as a model to measure service quality by Parsuraman, Zeithaml and Berry in the mid 1980s (Parsuraman *et al.*, 1985, 1988), based on US research in the varied service industries of a repair company, a long-distance telephone company, a securities broker, several retail banks and credit companies. In 1991 the authors replicated their 1988 study, using two additional industries: fast food and dry cleaning.

The authors of SERVQUAL claim that five dimensions of Quality are generic to all services: Tangibles, Reliability, Responsiveness, Assurance and Empathy. A standard questionnaire of 22 questions (4 or 5 for each dimension) is therefore provided as a basic tool requiring adaptation of wording for use in any application (Appendix 7.1). A Likert scale of 1–7 is given against each dimension. A representative sample of customers are asked to give two scores against each question, one for expectation (E) and one for perception (P) in order to analyse the service quality gap $Q = E - P$ (known in SERVQUAL as 'Gap 5').

Customers can also be asked to identify the importance (I) of each dimension. Weighting the $(E - P)$ scores by I does not usually alter the relative ranking of results but it does increase the relative gap sizes making the presentation of outcomes clearer to see.

SERVQUAL also proposes that by using the same questionnaire with internal staff the major root cause of the $(E - P)$ gap can be established. For each question staff are asked to give four scores: customer expects (A), management policies encourage (B), actual performance (C), and our communication to customers (D).

> Total gap $(E - P) = (E - A) + (A - B) + (B - C) + (C - D)$ (by arithmetic, the internal measures A to C cancel each other out, and the method assumes $D = P$)

Gap 1 $(E - A)$ is assumed to be caused by lack of customer awareness, Gap 2 $(A - B)$ by procedures out of date, Gap 3 $(B - C)$ by staff and resource weaknesses, and Gap 4 $(C - D)$ by poor communication to customers. Mean sizes of each of the gaps 1 to 4 are calculated and their relative sizes compared to determine the largest gap. Detailed likely causes of each gap, based on the original research of SERVQUAL authors, are given to support the identification of an effective solution.

Preventive action is therefore achieved by a periodic 'health check' rather than on going control charts (Wood, this volume). A full description of the SERVQUAL method can be found in Zeithaml *et al.*, 1990.

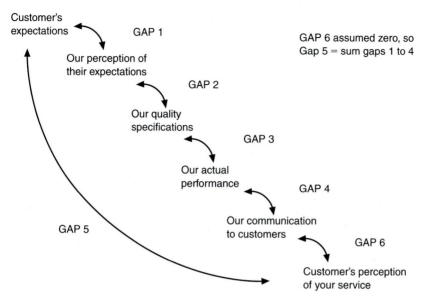

Figure 7.1 The SERVQUAL model.

Evaluating SERVQUAL

- *Scope:* Do the 22 questions and the five dimensions they represent adequately cover the full domain of service? SERVQUAL primarily addresses service quality, rather than product quality or the cost/value of quality. Total quality is likely to depend on all three dimensions (Richard and Allaway, 1993; Parsuraman *et al.*, 1994).

  An alternative to adapting the SERVQUAL questionnaire to suit a particular application is the 'clean sheet' approach of Conjoint Analysis (Green and Srinivasan, 1978, 1990; Wetzels *et al.*, 1995). This method starts with no preconceptions and derives separate dimensions of service quality in each application. The method uses focus groups or interviews with management, contact personnel and customers to collect data and uses cluster analysis to identify the relevant key dimensions of quality. The method identifies customer preferences only, rather than evaluating service quality. Other drawbacks include considerable cost, knowhow, experience and time to perform the analysis.

- *The grouping of the questions into five dimensions:* Do five dimensions accurately summarize the questions? The discriminant validity of the questionnaire is questioned by Carman (1990). Difficulty is reported over lack of independence of the five dimensions in the mind of those completing the SERVQUAL questions, e.g. is the question of opening hours more of a 'tangibles' dimension than 'empathy'?

- *Measurement:* The third concern in the literature relates to the measurement method used by SERVQUAL. SERVQUAL measures service quality as $\Sigma I.(E - P)$, where I is importance, E is expectation and P Perception. Cronin and Taylor (1992, 1994) suggest this measures short-term customer satisfaction rather than long-term service quality. Instead they propose SERVPERF which excludes the expectation comparison. The measure is also challenged by Carman (1990) due to empirical evidence that measures of performance alone have slightly better predictive power of consumer purchasing intention than a difference score. These authors suggest a single measure of 'how does current performance compare to expectation?' However the difference in results using $(E - P)$ or P alone is small (Brown *et al.*, 1993). And interest in the additional diagnostic information available prompted the authors to use SERVQUAL in this application.

- *Expectation:* A practical difficulty in measuring expectations reliably is raised by Carman (1990). When seeking customers views of 'expectation' it can be unclear whether the definition is 'desires' or 'wants', 'hoped for' or 'adequate', 'what a service provider should offer' (Parsuraman *et al.*, 1988), 'experience norms' (Woodruff, 1983) or 'excellence' (Zeithaml *et al.*, 1990). In the police context we used 'excellence' and assumed the public's knowledge of policing would reduce ambiguity.

  Teas (1993) suggests one further problem. He proposes that quality attributes are not vectors as SERVQUAL suggests, with no upper limit for improvement. Instead he suggests there is an 'ideal' quality upper limit above which quality performance should not be exceeded, e.g. excess detail on an accounting report. In this application this problem did not occur often enough to merit special attention.

- *Importance:* Zeithaml *et al.* (1991) report that using importance weights does not often change the outcome of SERVQUAL, it just amplifies the measured size of the performance gaps. However the cost of gathering importance information is not high and most writers in the literature supports its use (Carman, 1990; Hemasi, 1994).

- *Consistency over time:* Lastly there is research evidence in the literature that although SERVQUAL has ability to highlight current priorities for improvement, its value as an ongoing performance indicator is suspect. A longitudinal study by Triplett (1994), applying SERVQUAL in IT, found consistency over time in the dimensions of tangibles, reliability and responsiveness but not in the more subjective dimensions of empathy and assurance. This is regretfully likely to be true of any subjective measure.

Quality Management in policing

The police force can be seen as a major service provider in the UK, with 43 police forces in England and Wales employing 127,000 police officers. The core processes provided are emergency response to calls, reduction of crime, public order and reassurance, traffic control and community assistance (Sussex Police

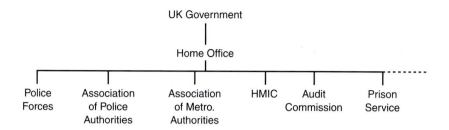

Figure 7.2 UK police organizational structure.

Annual Report 1997/8). Each force is independently managed, but all are subject to common rules, regulations and guidance set by Parliament and issued through the Home Office.

Each police force has a headquarters and local police stations. The Association of Police Authorities and Association of Metropolitan Authorities are local, independent civilian governing bodies. HMIC is Her Majesty's Inspectorate of Constabularies, typically comprising experienced senior police officers. The Audit Commission comprises civil servants who audit all government services.

Quality Management is not a separate function in policing, but is integral to the business targets set each year by the Home Office for each force. For example, in 1999 there were six key national objectives: reduce re-offending by the young, reduce local crime, target drug related crime, increase detection of violent crime, increased detection of burglaries, and rapid response to emergency calls.

The TQM concept of quality of service being defined externally by service users has three major barriers when applied in policing:

- there is doubt whether the knowledge of service users provides a sound basis for setting future standards;
- the freedom to raise private capital and income to finance all quality improvements desired by the public is restricted;
- there are perceived to be conflicting priorities across the diverse customers of the police service, e.g. general public requires visible police presence, government requires efficient value for money.

These barriers are very similar to those found in the Health Service (see Jefferson, Chapter 8).

The police definition of quality is therefore a cautious one: 'to achieve the best possible balance between professionally defined need plus customer led expectation against available resources' (Association of Chief Police Officers, 1998).

Table 7.1 Use of Quality Management tools in the 43 forces of England and Wales

Tools/standards	Forces
Business Excellence model (BEM)	43
Process mapping	26
Investors in People (IIP) accreditation	12
Balanced scorecard	9
Charter mark	7

Nevertheless, some police forces are experienced users of the latest methods of Quality Management. Survey results (Leigh *et al.*, 1999) are given in Table 7.1.

The extent of use is not measured, and some forces are in the early planning stages only. Process mapping has led to the use of Business Process Reengineering and Benchmarking and ISO 9000 accreditation is being considered in some forces.

A major incentive to measure quality improvement comes from the UK government requirement to demonstrate 'Best Value'. Best Value requires police, fire and local authorities to undertake a five-yearly programme of review for each service provided. The key elements (4 'C's) of each review are designed to ensure that each aspect of service:

- is still needed ('challenge');
- has been widely consulted on ('consult');
- has been compared to other provider's services ('comparison');
- is subject to competitive consideration ('competition').

Best Value, therefore, does not solely focus upon lowest cost, as with the previous government's Compulsory Competitive Tendering (CCT), but requires:

- efficiency (outputs compared to inputs);
- effectiveness (properly allocated resources with outcomes meeting objectives);
- quality (high standards that meet user requirements).

CCT was repealed in January 2000 and Best Value became a UK statutory requirement from 1 April 2000.

The European Foundation for Quality Management (EFQM) Business Excellence model is currently the most established technique for supporting Best Value requirements, within England and Wales, using self-assessment. However the survey of Leigh *et al.* (1999) found some disadvantages:

- costly and complex, due to the number of questions and complex question wording;

- too reliant on perceptions, due to Likert scales being used rather than evidence of results;
- highlights weaknesses not solutions, since it is a 'health check' measurement tool without supporting root cause diagnostics;
- has no built in 'challenge', since no competition nor exposure to different methods is involved.

The second most popular quality tool (see Table 7.1) is process mapping. When this uses the standard processes defined in the Police Process Classification Framework (agreed by the Association of Chief Police Officers in 1998) this method creates a common language between forces, facilitating discussion and comparison. Measures of cost and effectiveness for each of these processes then provide evidence of efficiency, creating 'challenge' and objectively establishing 'best practice' in each process, subject to consideration of the local context. However the Leigh survey again found some problems in practice:

- costly, since process mapping requires training and time;
- doesn't involve people – desk-based exercise, since the majority of time involves creation of process maps rather than creative problem-solving using them;
- focused on internal rather than external need, since there is no customer involvement (Leigh *et al.*, 1999).

Similarly, the SERVQUAL approach, which was used by the police force researched for this chapter, also has weaknesses. These include:

- reliability questionable since subjective opinions may vary;
- standard questionnaire needs adapting for each application, requiring skill to design questions to fully cover all contextual issues;
- validity of its measurement method is questioned by some academics, since short-term customer satisfaction rather than long-term service quality may be being measured (Cronin and Taylor, 1992).

However SERVQUAL has the advantages of:

- not expensive, for example four person weeks for this application to collect and analyse data for one police authority;
- involves staff and customers directly both in seeking their opinions of current opportunities for improvement and in recommending possible solutions;
- has a built in 'challenge' aspect even for monopoly providers, by comparing performance with customer expectations;
- identifies potential solutions, based on research evidence from other service companies and supported by the opinion of current staff;
- supports a culture change to a greater focus on external need, due to the majority of data used being feedback of current customer opinion.

These advantages of SERVQUAL match the weaknesses of both BEM and process mapping in supporting Best Value, hence the value of using SERVQUAL as a complementary technique.

SERVQUAL in the Sussex Police Force

Sussex Police employ 4000 staff, one-third civilian and two-thirds officers. Approximately 500 are located in the Lewes headquarters in East Sussex, and the remainder in divisions around the county. A series of Quality Management initiatives were at the early stages of development: Investors in People (IiP) initiative in personnel department, ISO 9002 in custody and Business Excellence in strategic management. The structure and style of policing embraced many of the aspects associated with TQM: strong leadership, team working, problem-solving and continuous improvement. Customer satisfaction surveys were used to canvas the views of the victims of crime and road accidents and also to gain feedback on policing priorities in preparation for the creation of Policing Plans. Examples of actions resulting from the use of these surveys included efforts to identify and consult with minority groups in Sussex and the creation of 'Citizens Panels' to build partnerships with local communities.

A SERVQUAL study was carried out in 1999 in order to examine the additional insights it revealed of public perception of the police. The standard SERVQUAL questionnaire (Appendix 7.1) was first adapted to wording suitable to a police context, resulting in the questionnaire shown at Appendix 7.2. The description of each dimension was also amended to that shown in Appendix 7.3. In contrast to the Healthcare context (Jefferson, Chapter 8), additional dimensions beyond the generic five of SERVQUAL were not found to be necessary to assess police service quality.

The main stakeholders with an interest in the level of service achieved by the police were identified by police staff as shown in Figure 7.3.

The potential variation in opinion within each of these stakeholder groups was taken to be largest from the 'General Public' and lower among 'Victims', 'Custody' and 'Police authority'. Relative sample sizes were chosen accordingly.

Figure 7.3 Who assesses the quality of our performance?

Table 7.2 Sample sizes used for external data collection

Group	Number issued	Number returned	Number used	Response
General public	50	44	39	78 per cent
Victims	20	19	18	90 per cent
Custody	20	18	17	85 per cent

The total number was estimated to be adequate to capture some examples of all types of opinion, with further samples planned to be collected for any question where high variation of replies prevented meaningful conclusions to be reached. In the event this did not prove to be necessary since the police were satisfied with the reliability of the top priorities revealed in the results.

The high response rates were due to prior contact by the authors by telephone or in person to obtain agreement to participate in each case before being given a questionnaire.

The 84 sample each completed three documents: two copies of the Expect/actual performance questionnaire (Appendix 7.2), one for expectations of an excellent police force (E) and one for perceptions of current Sussex Police performance (P), together with one copy of the Importance questionnaire (I) (Appendix 7.3). The data used below to illustrate the modelling and analysis of the results is fictitious as the actual data is confidential to Sussex Police.

Data results

Results were analysed separately for each stakeholder group, as shown in Figure 7.4.

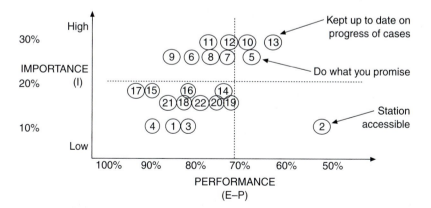

Figure 7.4 What do the Police Authority think of our performance? (22 questions asked, importance and performance of each, average results plotted; n = 10.)

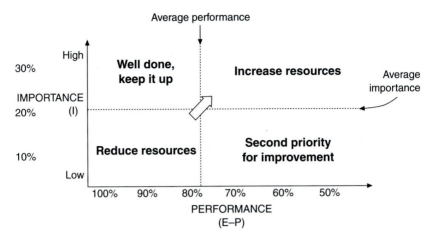

Figure 7.5 Challenge analysis.

The annotations describe the individual question content. Since the maximum and minimum possible scores are 6 and 0, percentage performance was calculated as $[6 - (E - P)] * 100/6$.

The advantage of displaying the results in this way as a two-dimensional presentation, rather than multiplying $I * (E - P)$ to give a linear priority sequence, is that it allowed the 'challenge' aspect of analysis as shown in Figure 7.5.

This analysis suggests that where responses fall in the top right quadrant (high importance, low performance) they indicate areas which are top priority for improvement. This perhaps can be at least partially achieved by reducing the excessive resources currently allocated to service aspects in the bottom left quadrant.

For Sussex Police a similar pattern emerged for each of the 'General public', 'Victims' and 'Custody', with the responses from two particular questions consistently appearing in the top 5 of the 'Increase resources' quadrant and two other questions always in the bottom left extreme of 'Reduce resources'.

Using the arithmetic mean to cluster the replies on the individual questions into the five standard dimensions (see Appendix 7.1), and combining the responses from all four customer groups, gave the results shown in Figure 7.6.

The size of the oval indicates the range of responses and the overlap between dimensions illustrates the limits of the reliability of the results.

Using factor analysis (Norusis, 1997, Soutar *et al.*, 1995) to check whether a different clustering of the questions would represent the data more accurately, revealed that responses to the questions clustered slightly differently from those dimensions predicted by SERVQUAL (see Table 7.3).

The new descriptions 'professional image' and 'sensitivity' were descriptions chosen by the authors to convey the shared meaning of the questions which cluster together.

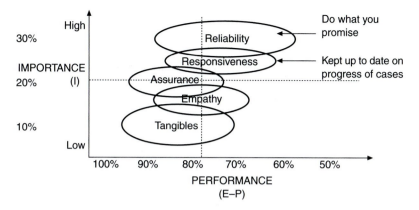

Figure 7.6 What do all customers think of our performance? (Clustering questions in groups; n = 84.)

Table 7.3 Revised dimension clusters using factor analysis

SERVQUAL standard dimensions		Factor analysis of police data	
Questions	*Description*	*Questions*	*Description*
1, 2, 3, 4	Tangibles	3, 4	Professional image
5, 6, 7, 8, 9	Reliability	5, 6, 7, 8, 9, 13	Reliability
10, 11, 12, 13	Responsiveness	10, 11, 22	Responsiveness
14, 15, 16, 17	Assurance	14, 15, 16, 17, 18, 20, 21	Assurance/ sensitivity
18, 19, 20, 21, 22	Empathy	1, 2, 12, 19	Access

In each different business similar changes from the standard SERVQUAL dimensions may occur due to modifications to the standard questions and a different business context. Using these modified dimensions gives the average responses shown in Table 7.3 and illustrated in Figure 7.7.

It appears in this case therefore that increased accuracy of dimension definition made little difference to the management implications, since the same priorities for change emerged.

The validity of the measure of (E − P) to assess service quality was supported in this case study, for example by the answers to the question on the attractiveness of police literature. The mean perception score was 4.277, but the mean expectation was also one of the lowest at 4.611. In this context, measuring P alone would result in a priority for improving literature, whereas the

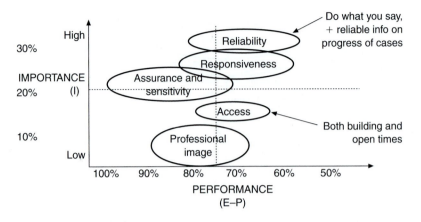

Figure 7.7 Revised results using factor analysis. (Clustering questions in groups; n = 84.)

SERVQUAL measure sensibly results in it taking low priority since both (E − P) and I are small values.

The root causes of current performance gaps emerged through an application of the Expect/Perform questionnaire to the internal police staff. A stratified random sample was used as shown in Table 7.4. 'Front line' staff comprised front line support staff, constables and sergeants.

Management staff and Chief officers were asked to complete four copies of the same questionnaire (Appendix 7.2), one each for:

1   to what extent we understand the public expect this from an excellent police force;
2   to what extent standards exist regarding this aspect, either formal or informal;
3   to what extent required standards are being met;
4   to what extent communicated promises on this aspect are being met.

Table 7.4 Sample sizes used for internal data collection

Group	Number	No. returned	No. used	Response %
Chief officers	5	5	5	100
Senior managers	15	12	12	80
Middle managers	25	20	19	76
Front-line	100	69	67	67
Total	145	106	103	71

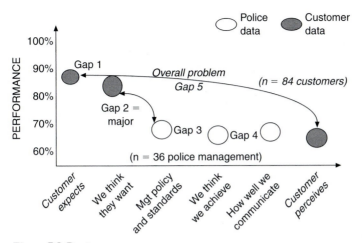

Figure 7.8 Root causes.

Front-line staff were given the same four questionnaires, but also the SERVQUAL list of likely root causes (Appendix 7.4) and were asked to identify to what extent they thought each were appropriate in Sussex Police.

The illustrative example in Figures 7.6 and 7.7 of customer data revealed an average customer expectation of 87 per cent and perceived current performance of 65 per cent, giving an opportunity for improvement of 22 per cent. In SERVQUAL this is known as 'Gap 5', shown in Figure 7.8. Results from the internal data collection were analysed as described in Figure 7.1 above to calculate Gaps 1, 2, 3 and 4. These were plotted on the same diagram (see Figure 7.8).

Since Gap 2 is the largest contributor to Gap 5, this example shows a police force which understands customer needs well, but is being prevented from achieving them due to policies which encourage different priorities. In this case study, both management and front-line staff responses were analysed separately but both identified Gap 2 as the major opportunity for improvement. Weighting the (E − P) results by Importance (I) also made no difference to this result.

SERVQUAL contains generic root causes for each gap (Appendix 7.4). Those for Gap 2 were tested with front-line staff revealing the following diagnostics shown in Figure 7.9.

When the Head of Organizational Services and his team at Sussex Police were presented with the combination of all the actual results, their view was that they were adequately reliable, since they compared closely to other existing customer and staff attitude survey results. However advantages of SERVQUAL were seen as being that the results were cheaper to obtain (standard questionnaire and relatively small sample sizes), provided a presentation that clearly demonstrated the key issues, and identified improvement solutions which front-line staff supported.

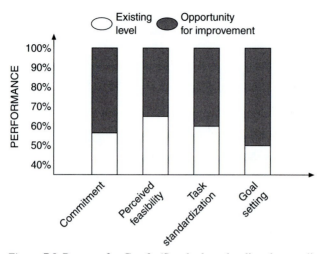

Figure 7.9 Reasons for Gap 2. (Standards and policy do not align with known require-ments; n = 67 police.)

Conclusion

Other customer surveys undertaken by Sussex Police had revealed very similar results from the general public but the outcome in terms of Quality Management initiatives had been an attempt to manage their perceptions and expectations through building closer partnerships with different customer social groups. The benefit of this very cost effective solution was confirmed by SERVQUAL results of Gap 1 (understanding of customer needs) and Gap 4 (communication to customers) both being small.

The particular benefit of SERVQUAL in contrast was the focus on the internal changes recommended. It also has the advantage that through involve-ment in data collection, staff support for the recommended changes is encour-aged.

Politically SERVQUAL is less helpful due to the size of the performance gap it can reveal. In previous applications in other organizations by these researchers, a gap of 20 per cent is not uncommon in companies with 'world-class' quality awards. In contexts where competitive pressure between different business units exists, and where funding is linked to performance, this does not encourage open publication and use of the results. The expectation of uses of SERVQUAL therefore needs to be carefully managed from the outset.

The presentation style of the results was welcomed by Sussex Police. They found that it clearly communicated the results and identified the recommended actions in a helpful visual layout.

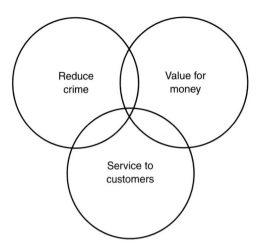

Figure 7.10 Scope of quality in Police Service.

The validity of the results in regard to coverage of the scope of Quality Management in this context is illustrated in Figure 7.10.

The police definition of quality given earlier in this chapter shows that its scope covers the three dimensions above. The results of this case study show that SERVQUAL covered the scope of service quality in the police context without any major modification to the standard questionnaire being required. However, in the method applied in this case, crime reduction and value for money was not assessed.

It would have been possible to amend the first four questions (covering the 'tangible' aspects of policing) to include more direct reference to success in reducing crime. Also the value or cost effectiveness of policing could have been an additional dimension of quality, with a few associated questions defined. Selective stakeholders with the necessary knowledge of performance in the aspects of policing could have been identified and SERVQUAL then applied to cover all three aspects of quality in Figure 7.10 above. However this would have required significant modification to the SERVQUAL questions.

To achieve a valid assessment of total quality, possibly more appropriate in the police context, would be to use SERVQUAL together with one or two other Quality Management methods in order to create a Balanced Scorecard (Kaplan and Norton, 1996) of total quality performance assessment. Whereas perceptual measures such as SERVQUAL have been seen to be applicable to assessing service to customers, other measures may be more appropriate to assess the technical service quality of reducing crime and the financial quality of reducing inefficiency.

The reliability of SERVQUAL in this context was judged by Sussex Police as the ability to identify the top priorities for improvement. In this regard the mean responses to two particular questions did consistently appear in the top five priorities identified by each stakeholder group (high importance and low performance). The responses to another two questions were consistently rated at the other extreme of not important but excellent performance. Due to variation in the replies, it was not possible to confirm statistically that these were higher priorities than any other question. But this was perceived by Sussex Police management as sufficient reliability to justify reallocation of resources to improve these issues.

Do customers know what is best for them? SERVQUAL is based on the premise that they do, and this case study shows that useful insights can be obtained by following this premise and using the tool. However, as illustrated in Figure 7.10, only one-third of the police definition of quality is addressed by service to customers, and customer opinion is not sufficiently knowledgeable to be used to guide improvement of the other two aspects.

The UK government's definition of 'Best Value' does not give exclusive priority to the customers' view. Consultation is only one of the 4 'C's, although it is the foundation for the other three.

In a service industry such as the police, it can be argued therefore that quality is not achieved solely by a customer focus. A customer-centred method such as SERVQUAL provided many useful insights in this case study, but its use is recommended only as a complementary technique. A balanced scorecard assessment (Kaplan, 1996) using SERVQUAL, together with other tools such as business excellence (Dijkstal, 1997) and process mapping (Hunt, 1996), is needed in order to support all the 4 'C' requirements of Challenge, Consult, Compare and Competition.

Acknowledgements

The authors wish to thank Peter Stock, Head of Organizational Services, Sussex Police, and Paul Whitehouse, Chief Constable, Sussex Police for their support in compiling this case study.

References

Association of Chief Police Officers (1998), Quality in the Police Service, Standards & Quality Sub-Committee.

Audit Commission Statistics (1999) *Police Review*, 29 Jan., 22–5.

Buttle, F. (1996) SERVQUAL: review, critique, research agenda, *European Journal of Marketing* Jan., v. 30, n. 1, p. 8(25).

Carman, J.M. (1990) Consumer perceptions of SERVQUAL: an assessment of the SERVQUAL dimensions, *Journal of Retailing* **66**(1), 33–50.

Cronin, J.J. and Taylor, S.A. (1992) Measuring service quality: a re-examination and extension, *Journal of Marketing* **56**(33) July, 55–68.

Cronin, J.J. and Taylor, S.A. (1994) SERVPREF versus SERVQUAL: reconciling performance-based and perceptions-minus-expectations measurement of service quality, *Journal of Marketing* **58**(1), Jan., 125–31.

De Sarbo, W.S., Huff, L., Rolandelli, M.M. and Choi, J. (1994) On the measurement of perceived service quality. In R.T. Rust and R.L. Oliver (eds), *Service Quality: New Directions in Theory and Practice*. London: Sage Publications, 201–22.

DETR (1999) *Preparing for Best Value*. Guidance note, London: DETR.

Dijkstal, L. (1997) An empirical interpretation of the EFQM framework, *European Journal of Work and Organisation, Psychology* **6**, 321–41.

Green and Srinivasan (1978) Conjoint analysis in marketing, *Journal of Consumer Research* **5**, Sept., 103–23.

Green and Srinivasan (1990) Conjoint analysis in marketing, *Journal of Marketing* **54**, Oct., 3–19.

House of Commons (1998) *Local Government Bill and Explanatory Notes*. London: The Stationary Office.

Hunt, V.D. (1996) *Process Mapping: How to Reengineer our Business Processes*. New York, Chichester: Wiley.

Kaplan, R.S. (1996) *The Balanced Scorecard: Translating Strategy into Action*. Boss, Mass: Harvard Business School Press.

Leigh, A., Mundy, G. and Tuffin, R. (1999) *Best Value Policing: Making Preparations*, Police Research Series Paper 116, Research Development Statistics Directorate of Home Office, UK.

Norusis, M. (1997) *SPSS for Windows: Professional Statistics*, SPSS Inc.

Parsuraman, A., Zeithaml, V. and Berry, L.L. (1985) A conceptual model of service quality and its implications for further research, *Journal of Marketing* **49**, Fall, 41–50.

Parsuraman, A., Zeithaml, V.A. and Berry, L.L. (1988) SERVQUAL: a multiple-item scale for measuring consumer perceptions of service quality, *Journal of Retailing* **64**, Spring, 12–40.

Parsuraman, A., Berry, L.L. and Zeithaml, V.A. (1993) More on improving service quality measurement, *Journal of Retailing* **69**(1)**,** Spring, 140–7.

Parsuraman, A., Zeithaml, V.A. and Berry, L. (1994) Reassessment of expectations as a comparison standard in measuring service quality: implications for further research, *Journal of Marketing* **58**(1), Jan., 111–24.

Richard, M. and Allaway, A. (1993) Service quality attributes and choice behaviour, *Journal of Services Marketing* **7**(1), 59–68.

Soutar, G.N., McNeil, M.M. and Maisey, G. (1995) Community satisfaction with policing: the Western Australia experience, *The Police Journal*, Oct, 351–67.

Teas, R.K. (1993) Consumer expectations and the measurement of perceived service quality, *Journal of Professional Services Marketing* **8**(2), 33–54.

Teas, R.K. (1994) Expectations as a comparison standard in measuring service quality: an assessment of a reassessment, *Journal of Marketing* **58**(1), Jan., 132–9.

Triplett, J.L., Yau, O. and Neal, C. (1994) Assessing the reliability and validity of SERVQUAL in a longitudinal study: the experiences of an Australian organisation, *Asia Pacific Journal of Marketing and Logistics* **6**(1, 2), 41–62.

Van Dyke, T.P., Kappelman, L.A. and Prybutok, V.R. (1997) Information systems service quality: concerns on the use of the SERVQUAL questionnaire, *MIS Quarterly* **21**(2), June, 195–208.

Wetzels, M., de Ruyter, K., Lemmink, J. and Koelemeijr, K. (1995) Measuring customer service quality in international marketing channels: a multimethod approach, *Journal of Business and Industrial marketing* **10**(5), 50–9.

Woodruffe, H. (1995) *Services Marketing.* London: Financial Times, Pitman.

Zeithaml, V.A., Parsuraman, A. and Berry, L.L. (1990*) Delivering Quality Service: balancing customer perceptions and expectations.* New York: The Free Press.

Zeithaml, V.A., Berry, L.L. and Parsuraman, A. (1991) The nature and determinants of customer expectations of service, *Marketing Science Institute Research Program Series* (May) Report No. 91–113.

Appendix 7.1
Summary of standard SERVQUAL questionnaire

(for full version, see Zeithaml *et al.*, 1990)

Dimension	Question number	Description
Tangibles (the appearance of physical facilities, equipment, personal and communication materials)	T1 T2 T3 T4	Has up-to-date equipment. Physical facilities are visually appealing. Employees are neat in appearance. Materials are visually appealing.
Reliability (the ability to perform the promised service dependably and accurately)	Rel 1 Rel 2 Rel 3 Rel 4 Rel 5	When promises to do something, it does so. Shows sincere interest in solving your problems. Performs the service right the first time. Provides services at the time it promises. Keeps accurate records.
Responsiveness (the willingness to help customers and to provide prompt service)	Res 1 Res 2 Res 3 Res 4	Tells you when the service will be performed. Gives prompt service. Always willing to help. Never too busy to respond to your requests.
Assurance (the knowledge and courtesy of employees and their ability to convey trust and confidence)	A1 A2 A3 A4	Employees can be trusted. Feel safe in your transactions with employees. Consistently courteous. Has knowledge to answer your questions.
Empathy (the provision of caring individualized attention to customers)	E1 E2 E3 E4 E5	Gives individual attention. Has operating hours convenient to you. Employees give personal attention. Has your best interests at heart. Employees understand your specific needs.

Appendix 7.2
SERVQUAL questionnaire
adapted for a police context

(used to measure both expectations and perceptions)

Expect/Actual Performance Questionnaire

Based on your experiences as a resident of Sussex and/or your contact with Sussex Police:

1 Please score each of the questions below for the extent to which you believe that feature is essential for an excellent police force.
2 Please complete an identical copy questionnaire for the extent that you perceive each feature below is currently being achieved by Sussex Police.

Question		Measure	
No.	*Description*	*Strongly disagree*	*Strongly agree*
1	Police use modern equipment (computer technology, radios, vehicles etc.).	1 2 3 4 5 6 7	
2	Stations and other facilities are visually appealing, clean, comfortable and accessible to all.	1 2 3 4 5 6 7	
3	Police appearance is smart and professional.	1 2 3 4 5 6 7	
4	Police forces produce written material such as stationary and public information documents that are visually appealing.	1 2 3 4 5 6 7	
5	When police promise to carry out a duty or conduct an enquiry by a certain time, they do so.	1 2 3 4 5 6 7	
6	When a complaint is made about a police force or officer, the police show a sincere interest in solving the problem or investigating the complaint.	1 2 3 4 5 6 7	
7	Police duties are performed right first time.	1 2 3 4 5 6 7	
8	When police promise to carry out a duty or conduct an enquiry at a certain time, they do so.	1 2 3 4 5 6 7	
9	Police forces insist on keeping totally accurate records.	1 2 3 4 5 6 7	
10	Police and support staff always keep appointments or inform members of the public, clients or officials of an alternative arrangement.	1 2 3 4 5 6 7	

11	Police and support staff always provide prompt service to any person requesting it.	1 2 3 4 5 6 7
12	Police and support staff are always willing and never too busy to help any person in need.	1 2 3 4 5 6 7
13	Police and support staff always keep a victim or client informed of progress on their case, and are easily contactable.	1 2 3 4 5 6 7
14	Police and support staff instil confidence in the people they serve.	1 2 3 4 5 6 7
15	Members of the public, clients and officials feel safe in their transactions with the police.	1 2 3 4 5 6 7
16	Police and support staff are consistently courteous with all the people they meet.	1 2 3 4 5 6 7
17	Police and support staff have the knowledge to answer questions asked of them by the public.	1 2 3 4 5 6 7
18	Police give people the individual attention they deserve.	1 2 3 4 5 6 7
19	Police stations have operating hours that are convenient and flexible enough to suit all those needing their services.	1 2 3 4 5 6 7
20	Police deal with the public in a caring manner, with tact and sensitivity.	1 2 3 4 5 6 7
21	Police have the public's best interest at heart.	1 2 3 4 5 6 7
22	Police understand the specific needs of all the people they deal with.	1 2 3 4 5 6 7

Appendix 7.3
SERVQUAL questionnaire to measure the importance of each dimension adapted for a police context

Importance questionnaire

Listed below are five features of the service provided by the police service. We would like to know how important each of these features is to you.

Please allocate a total of 100 points among the five features, according to how important each feature is to you. The more important a feature is to you, the more points you should allocate.

Please ensure that the points you allocate to the five features adds up to 100.

Tangibles	The appearance of police officers, support staff, police stations and other police facilities. This includes stationary, pamphlets and public information leaflets.	..........Points	Rank ....
Reliability	The police force's ability to perform the promised service dependably and accurately.	..........Points	Rank ....
Responsiveness	The police force's willingness to help those in need and to provide the service promptly.	..........Points	Rank ....
Assurance	The knowledge and courtesy of the police officers and support staff, and their ability to convey trust and confidence.	..........Points	Rank ....
Empathy	The caring, individualized attention the police force provides for those it serves.	..........Points	Rank ....

Appendix 7.4
Root causes of gaps

Please indicate to what extent you believe the following statements apply to Sussex Police:

Problem		Root causes	Strongly disagree				Strongly agree		
Gap 1	Qu. 1	Insufficient customer orientation	1	2	3	4	5	6	7
	Qu. 2	Lack of upward communication	1	2	3	4	5	6	7
	Qu. 3	Too many levels of management	1	2	3	4	5	6	7
Gap 2	Qu. 4	Insufficient management commitment to service quality	1	2	3	4	5	6	7
	Qu. 5	Lack of clear goal setting	1	2	3	4	5	6	7
	Qu. 6	Insufficient task standardization	1	2	3	4	5	6	7
	Qu. 7	Perception of infeasibility to improve quality	1	2	3	4	5	6	7
Gap 3	Qu. 8	Lack of teamwork	1	2	3	4	5	6	7
	Qu. 9	Poor employee-job fit	1	2	3	4	5	6	7
	Qu. 10	Poor technology-job fit	1	2	3	4	5	6	7
	Qu. 11	Lack of control	1	2	3	4	5	6	7
	Qu. 12	Insufficient supervisory systems	1	2	3	4	5	6	7
	Qu. 13	Role conflict	1	2	3	4	5	6	7
	Qu. 14	Role ambiguity	1	2	3	4	5	6	7
Gap 4	Qu. 15	Insufficient lateral communication	1	2	3	4	5	6	7
	Qu. 16	Propensity to over-promise	1	2	3	4	5	6	7

8   Quality in the NHS

Can we master the art of 'conversation'?

Harriet Jefferson

Introduction

The NHS has particular characteristics that raise interesting issues for the intro-duction of quality models originally developed for industry and the private sector. Traditionally health services have taken quality models from industry, namely the introduction of TQM in the early 1990s when the Thatcher govern-ment introduced the concept of the 'free market' to the NHS (DOH, 1989).

However over time it has become increasingly clear that the NHS is far from being a system that can be operated as a 'free market' and that even with succes-sive governments, there is not the political or public will to go full scale along this route. This has meant that the adoption, wholesale, of quality frameworks, tools and techniques from business and industry have not worked well and over time more appropriate techniques have had to be developed internally. However in attempting to measure and assess quality in the NHS over the last decade, more questions have been raised than answered. The introduction of quality assurance has meant that the fundamental principles of the NHS have been put under the spotlight requiring them to be revisited, re-examined and redefined.

This chapter provides an overview of quality in healthcare by examining the introduction of quality into health service policy and practice. The chapter will outline the main approaches, tools and techniques that have been introduced in order to attempt to assure the quality of healthcare delivery. However to date these approaches have continually failed to include the contextual and cultural dimensions important to health services. In the second part of the chapter an alternative approach to service evaluation is outlined and the case study sets the assessment of the quality of service delivery into context. Since conducting this work in 1996, others have also recognized that healthcare quality cannot be sep-arated from the value, meaning and context placed on the service by its stake-holders particularly users and already new quality frameworks are beginning to be developed to address this deficit (Wenger, 1999; DOH, 2000a; DOH, 2000b).

Background to quality in healthcare

The measurement of quality in the NHS has had a complex history (Humphris and Littlejohns, 1995; Lord and Littlejohns, 1994; Maxwell, 1992; Maxwell, 1984; Øvretveit, 1992; Pfeffer and Coote, 1991; Parsley and Corrigan, 1999) (see Figure 8.1). The formal development of quality assurance in the NHS came with the introduction of general management into the NHS in the 1980s (Griffiths, 1983). This was driven by the political agenda of the day and the need to control costs (DOH, 1989; Pollitt, 1993). It had long been recognized that little information was systematically collected and collated about the service allocation and delivery in the NHS, with almost no data available on cost of the NHS other than in gross terms, making decision-making and priority setting inconsistent and arbitrary. Attempts to address this were dealt with by the introduction of Körner (Fairey, 1986) and other data collection systems and was formalized in policy in the 1990 NHS reforms. This requirement to measure performance and provide a quality service at the lowest possible cost has been continued and strengthened in all following policy and statue, regardless of political persuasion.

It must be recognized, however that quality had been important to the NHS prior to this point in time. Indeed the fundamental quality standard was the creation of the NHS to provide a state run, universal healthcare system free at the point of delivery thereby delivering minimum quality by right of treatment and access to care (Rivett, 1998). Later the NHS, while supposedly maintaining minimum quality, started to develop higher quality standards of treatments and

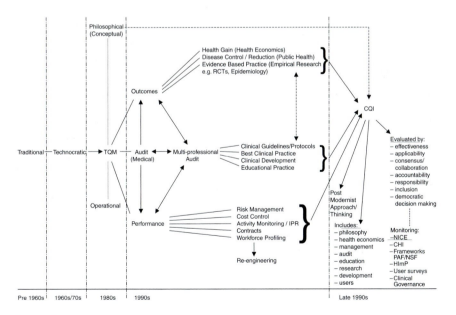

Figure 8.1 A history of quality in healthcare.

products in specialist areas, particularly in high technology medicine, often setting standards worldwide. However there was no consistency in the quality of healthcare service or practice provision at this time, and no concept that this was necessary or desirable. The quality of service was primarily based on the interests, status and personal practice of the medical profession responsible for local services. This generally had a positive effect for those healthcare professionals associated with high quality specialist medicine. However, over time, what emerged was an increasing gap between those who had medical conditions which could be treated or cured, thereby showing the NHS as successful in its function, and those who had chronic, degenerative or unattractive conditions which could only be controlled or ameliorated and with little or no hope of improvement. This was reflected in the amount of money, resources and service provision allocated in national budgets. Those services that were not attractive such as care of the elderly, those with learning disabilities and the mentally ill, received less money, even though the healthcare needs were considerable. They became known as the 'Cinderella services'. Such a term voiced the cultural values of the health services and was confirmed in action by the detrimental effect that working in these areas could have on your professional career. This all combined to create a 'status hierarchy' within the NHS. The quality gap continued to increase with the minimum quality no longer being maintained in these impoverished services. Despite a decade of more formalized and consistent quality monitoring and control, the legacy of this gap is still evident today.

Total Quality Management (TQM)

The first quality approach to be formally introduced across the NHS was that of TQM. This coincided with the interest in TQM in industry (Oakland, 1996) and was promoted via national road shows funded by the DTI as part of its Enterprise Initiative (1990) to 'encourage a vigorous reassertion of the UK's international reputation for quality' (DTI conference, 11 June 1991, Peter Lilley, Secretary of State for Trade and Industry). The values of TQM were to be identified in organizational 'mission statements' and the performance measures were to be outlined in service contracts between purchasers of health services (the health authorities) and providers of services (hospitals and trusts). Over time these were to become more sophisticated with internal contracts between departments or divisions.

The concept promoted was that of excellence; however, TQM was never actually defined in healthcare documents in healthcare terms. The Audit Commission used the accepted industrial understanding of TQM as 'a continuous striving, in "conversation" with the customer, towards an unattainable goal. In other words, quality is not an attainable feature of a product or a service. It is a "journey, not a destination"' (Audit Commission, 1992: 5–6). The NHS document, *The Quality Journey* (NHSME, 1993b) reinforces this analogy.

The problem here, as Seedhouse (1995) points out, is that these are not definitions of TQM but descriptions and are therefore ambiguous and open to interpretation and manipulation by any interest group. For instance the idea of 'a journey towards achieving excellence' has never been debated in healthcare. There are a number of assumptions here, first that patients receiving healthcare have experience of and information on healthcare services to know what is or is not excellent. If you are an elderly patient or have mental health or learning disabilities, the services you and your relatives receive may not be good but they are all that is available. As Seedhouse (op. cit.) notes, the assumption here is that 'NHS users are able to express their interests and views in the same way as buying a car'. It is also taken for granted that 'the act of "valuing" a service is done from an informed position, which is often not the case' (ibid., p. 48). The second assumption here is that patients have any influence over the quality of healthcare they receive. The evidence so far (Pfeffer and Coote, 1991; Pfeffer and Pollock, 1993; NHSE, 1994; DOH, 1999c; DOH, 2000a; DOH, 2000b) is that patients as consumers have little part to play in determining the quality of the service they receive and are still largely excluded from the consultation process. The 'excellence' of the service is in fact determined by the service provided (Seedhouse, 1995). Also the NHS can, when it deems necessary or feels threatened, take a powerful opt out position, namely that it is there to 'cure, treat and save life'. This does not necessarily need to be a quality experience. In fact in crisis the analogy of war, so commonly used in healthcare (Sontag, 1991), becomes actuality, and Beveridge's 'war on disease' has no place for quality. Indeed if there is any 'quality' in war it is minimum loss of life and victory over the 'enemy'. Healthcare professionals, as the 'experts', can change these rules as they wish and it is a brave person who challenges their right to do so, since they can also exercise ethical and moral arguments of autonomy (professional), preserving life, justice and beneficence (Phillips and Dawson, 1985; Seedhouse, 1988).

Quality, whatever the definition or description, has a different meaning for different stakeholders, whether they are external or internal to healthcare. Øvretveit (1992) asks the question 'whose quality?' and examines the different priorities and attributes of quality for different healthcare stakeholders. He concludes that common attributes are few, therefore emphasizing the divergent views on quality and demonstrating why a convergent view is difficult to achieve in practice. Parsuraman *et al.* (1985) showed that there is consistency among people about the attributes that make for a good quality service or product. Some of these such as courtesy, communication etc. may be relatively easy to observe and measure; however, there is a large intangible element to 'quality' (good or bad), characterized by being respected and feeling valued, which can be known but is difficult to describe, quantify or capture. This becomes particularly problematic when trying to measure quality objectively and numerically, particularly in healthcare where the 'service' and even the 'product' contains huge, personal, cultural and social variety and is context dependent. The intangible and personal dimension of quality is dominant here.

The NHS response to TQM was to largely ignore the contextual and personal aspects of quality. Many failed to understand that TQM is a concept not a tool, and chose to concentrate on measuring those parts of quality which could be tied to financial and activity performance, where the service could set the standards. This removed the difficulties of 'whose quality is this anyway?' and awkward questions about supply and demand, lack of finances, economic and social influences and inequity of access to service provision, all of which affected patient and public choice and control over the quality of the healthcare experience.

The concept of TQM has proved difficult to introduce throughout the NHS, was not supported by all levels of the organization (Berwick, 1992; Black, 1990), was imposed from the top on lower levels of the organization and did not fit in with short-term performance measurement requirements of the NHS or the yearly accounting procedures. There was reluctance to adopt a concept, which, in organizations where it has had a measure of success, has taken a 10–20 year programme to implement. TQM raised uncomfortable questions about the underlying values and conceptual understanding of those responsible for the provision of healthcare. These questions proved too difficult to deal with and a more reductionist method was adopted.

Audit

The need for quality measurement shifted therefore from all encompassing quality to the more tangible and objectively measurable idea of audit. This was outlined in the white paper *Working for Patients* (DOH, 1989) and defined as:

> 'medical audit' – a systematic, critical analysis of the quality of medical care, including the procedures used for diagnosis and treatment, the use of resources and the resulting outcome to the patient. (op. cit., p. 39)

Initially audit was aimed at the medical profession, hence the term 'Medical Audit'. This was in part a political move in order to get the medical profession to account for their practice and costs. To encourage this, the medical profession received funding for conducting audit; the ratio for funding of audit work was approximately 6:1 in favour of doctors (NHSE, 1992, EL(92)21). Nurses and other healthcare professions has already had a history of audit (Kemp and Richardson 1990; NHSE, 1991).

For a number of years Medical Audit and other healthcare professions audits were kept separate and uniprofessional. This meant that while the medical profession could put money into their audits and even employ audit assistants to conduct data collection and compile reports, other professionals had to continue to do this on an ad hoc basis and without help. This resulted in an imbalance in audit information across different healthcare professionals as some groups could carry out more audits than others. Also the uniprofessional approach meant that different audit methodologies emerged from different professional groups and perspectives (Wilson, 1987; Kitson, 1989; Richards and Higinbotham, 1989; NHSME, 1991). These methodological approaches evolved from the underlying philosophical viewpoints of the individual healthcare professions and, rather than resulting in a closer professional alliance, it emphasized the different and at times conflicting professional values. In addition it did not address the values of general management or users because it did not include management input (Buttery *et al.*, 1995), or the consumer focus (NHSE, 1994, EL (94)80).

In practical terms this resulted in duplication of effort and an inability to compare audits across professional groups because of the incompatibility of methodologies. There were conflicts where one professional group made recommendations for another group without their prior knowledge or inclusion in the audit design or process. This increased the tension between the professions rather than bringing clinical standards and practice closer. In addition to this, clinicians were designing audits without consultation with service managers, yet the solutions to the clinical problems required management support. Because of this lack of co-operation between professional groups, the recommendations made in the audits were seldom acted upon because there was no clear responsibility for action, highlighting the fact that professional groups did not understand their colleagues roles, priorities and responsibilities (Lord and Littlejohns, 1994; Buttery *et al.*, 1995).

Clinical (multiprofessional) Audit

In 1991/2 the concept of Clinical Audit evolved as an attempt to clarify the confusion created by uniprofessional audit (Clinical Outcomes Group, 1992) The idea was to bring the professional groups together to design and conduct audit, based on a collectively agreed clinical outcome. In principle, therefore, this should ensure that the right people were included in the planning and conducting of the audits and also in acting on the audit findings and recommendations (closing the audit loop). The concept was one of collaboration across professional groups to achieve clinical effectiveness (NHSE, 1993, EL (93)115).

Clinical Audit was defined as:

> A systematic, critical analysis of the quality of clinical care, including procedures used for diagnosis and treatment, the use of resources and the resulting outcome and quality of life for the patient. (Clinical Outcomes Group, 1992)

The problem with this definition is that in attempting to create a multiprofessional approach to audit it tries to be all encompassing, resulting in wide interpretation and adding to the confusion. Coupled with this it still fails to address the conceptual and holistic focus of healthcare, concentrating on resource management, cost effectiveness and utilitarian health economic measures of outcome.

Clinical Audit did, however, identify that one group of stakeholders had been consistently ignored, namely service users. Consumer satisfaction and choice should be key to clinical effectiveness and this was strengthened by the launch of the Citizens Charter (1991) and for healthcare the Patients Charter. This set national standards for service delivery and encouraged the citizens to complain if services did not match up to expectation.

The reality has been that the Charter has had limited success because the pressure that healthcare services have been under to deliver on it has lead to wide 'interpretation' and 'manipulation' of the standards, particularly those concerned with waiting lists. The game has been to hide deficiencies through manipulation and to maintain the status quo. The same issues appeared at the clinical level, where standards have been set by clinicians that were at best self-fulfilling due to standards being minimal (that being based on the current service provision) or re-interpreted if found to be failing.

Clinical Audit has suffered similar problems to Medical Audit in that the definition has been too encompassing, resulting in healthcare professionals reinterpreting it to suit their own requirements and making up their own rules. It has continued to emphasize high quality at the lowest cost, pressing for greater performance rather than necessarily the best and has had limited patient involvement, despite the membership being supposedly multiprofessional/agency and the focus being on the improved clinical outcome for the patient. In addition to this healthcare personnel have mistakenly equated Clinical Audit as equalling Quality Assurance (CA = QA) This is again a failure to understand that Clinical Audit is a part of Quality Assurance but as a subset of QA.

However, it must be recognized that this move towards Clinical Audit served an important purpose, namely it allowed healthcare professionals to collectively ask questions which were to be defined in objective outcome terms and therefore measurable. This had not been done before. For instance, detailed information on cost of care, types of treatment, appropriateness of treatment, effectiveness and efficiency had never previously been carried out in any systematic way. Audit enabled the questions: (a) *'what are you supposed to be doing and why?'* (defining purpose) followed by: (b) *'are you doing it properly?'* (level of compliance and consistency) and (c) *'is what you are doing effective?'* (meeting nationally determined requirements such as waiting times, as well as those determined locally, clinically, financially, competitively, professionally etc. – some of which may conflict), to be asked and data to be collected against the criteria. The idea then was that the audit cycle would be completed by changing practice in line with an agreed purpose and accompanying goals/objectives. This would, over time introduce consistency of quality and service delivery across healthcare, with examples of 'good practice' being shared locally and nationally for emulation.

Clinical Audit has worked well when there has been appreciation that the end result is important, not necessarily the means to that end. This has allowed different professional groups to recognize that they have different but important parts to play in the outcome. It has also strengthened collaborative teamwork, an increasingly important feature of future healthcare service delivery.

Health outcomes/health gain

Health outcomes/health gain attempts to pay lip service at least to context but in terms of economic gain (health economics), disease monitoring (epidemiology) and disease control/reduction (public health). The approach is to provide a package of core services, identifying what is included and excluded. Hunter (1997) notes that this approach has not worked as well in the UK as other countries, partly because the criticism of the outcomes approach is that it is based on utilitarianism at the cost of individual need. This is an approach which healthcare professionals used to working with individuals find uncomfortable and ethically and morally offensive as a way of deciding healthcare provision 'since such techniques place undue emphasis on community well-being at the expense of individual well-being' (Hunter, 1997).

The method of quality measurement used by health economists is the QALY. QALY stands for *Quality Adjusted Life Year*. It is a term developed by health economists for an approach that is concerned with evaluating both effectiveness of treatments and their cost-effectiveness. The outcomes are measured according to a generic scale whereby if a patient's treatment is felt to be effective and long-lasting as well as cost-effective, then the patient can increase his/her score on the quality-of-life measure. This technique supports treatments that show improved quality-of-life over a long time and for the least cost.

Hunter (op. cit.) notes that the problems with QALYs is that despite 'the considerable interest QALYs have attracted the scheme has had little practice impact'. As with TQM and Clinical Audit, there has been the intellectual interest but it has not significantly modified practice or priorities.

In discussing the limitations of QALYs, Hunter concludes that 'QALYs are seen to be ruthlessly and possibly unacceptably utilitarian. QALYs are also criticized for discriminating against elderly people and those with disabilities' (ibid., p. 71). Indeed this approach has some potentially controversial advocates such as eugenicists and those concerned with genetic engineering. Health economists and social scientists obliquely refer to concerns about such subjects, when they note that there are problems with the poor quality of data and research methods used, making this a less than safe way of decision-making. The fact is that the 'most fundamental objection to QALYs lies in the attempt to devise a common measure by which we can assign a qualitative value to disparate ingredient factors in quality of life ... They are incommensurable...' (Hunter, 1997: 72).

The legacy for health services of this way of prioritizing healthcare provision and quality of delivery is that it has forced the rationing debate into the public domain. With this, however, has come the recognition that much clinical practice and decision-making has been based on personal preference or on particular techniques taught as part of the 'apprenticeship training' that clinicians receive. A call for better research (evidence) based information on the most efficacious treatments and practice has lead to the rise in status of research as the new independent source for quality standards.

Evidence-based medicine

This is the current popular technique for assessing healthcare quality. It has grown out of health economics and Clinical Audit, both of which have now recognized that the missing link to practical and acceptable implementation of these methods could lie with the use of empirical research to determine effective clinical standards for practice and treatments. In reviewing the effectiveness of these techniques to improve the quality of service provision, the conclusion reached has been that overall they have failed because the one has proved too unreliable and the other has been compromised because the standards set have been internal and subjective. Late in the day, those using Clinical Audit techniques realized that they should not be determining the standards against which they measured themselves. At best auditors lacked sound independent information on which to set their standards and at worst they manipulated the standards to fulfil their requirements. In addition to this the audit loop can only be effectively closed if recommendations for action are based on the best available evidence on efficacy of treatment and practice.

The commissioning of new research and the systematic review and collation of existing research findings through use of such databases as the Cochrane Centre etc. has meant that local organizational quality provision has now been moved from a primarily internal and subjectively determined process to one characterized by independent, objective and nationally set clinical guidelines and benchmarks, derived from empirical research.

Current approach to quality in healthcare

The Labour government post-modernist welfare policy is characterized by the 'Third Way' and 'Positive Welfare' (Giddens, 1998). *The New NHS: Modern, Dependable* was launched in 1997, followed by legislation (The Health Act 1999) and in July 2000 the detailed plan was published (DOH, 2000a). It is too soon to assess the impact of the plan in practice; however, the 'New' NHS is to be focused on *equity, efficiency and effectiveness.* The NHS plan (DOH, 2000a) was launched by the PM in 'Bevanesque' style with the restatement of the founding five principles of the NHS, however these have been extended to ten. The new fifth principle states:

> The NHS will work continuously to improve quality services and minimize errors.

This suggests a desire to return to the philosophy of TQM. The expectation that services will continue to be shaped and evaluated locally will remain; however, a series of National Service Frameworks (NSFs) will be established to ensure the consistency and quality of service provision and the inclusion of a six point Performance Assessment Framework (PAF) to provide an overall assessment of NHS performance. In addition to this the government have set up a number of national bodies to set standards for and oversee the quality of service delivery. The main bodies are the National Institute for Clinical Excellence (NICE) whose purpose is to establish and monitor clinical and cost effectiveness of treatments, concentrating initially on reviewing the efficacy of drug treatments and surgery and the Commission for Health Improvement (CHI) who will oversee the delivery of clinical governance and service quality by reviewing all Trusts every four years.

The Government states that there will be 'a new relationship between the Department of Health and the NHS...' (DOH, 2000a: 11) characterized by a system of 'earned autonomy' where power will be devolved 'from the centre to the local health service as modernization takes hold' (ibid.). However both NICE and CHI have been given extensive power to intervene on behalf of the Government if local compliance with national standards is not met. These powers have already been activated thereby ensuring that the Government can resume centralist control if it does not like the way the NHS is progressing. In the guise of supporting local services by taking on centrally the costly task of setting standards for service delivery, this Government has, perhaps, promoted central intervention and control of the NHS to new heights.

The Government is committed to increasing the involvement of patients and users in shaping the NHS (DOH, 1999c; DOH, 2000a) and this will take place through conducting an annual Patient and Users Survey to assess how the public view NHS service delivery and the establishment of lay members on Primary Care Trust (PCT) Boards (NHSE, 1999a and b). However the Government is already alienating sections of the public, for example, through the refusal to accept key recommendations on financial arrangements for elderly people going into residential care made by the Royal Commission on Long Term Care (DOH, 2000b) and the recommended withdrawal from NHS use of Beta-interferon for Multiple Sclerosis sufferers (MS Society, 2000; NICE appraisal, www.nice.org.uk).

Evaluating health services

Evaluation in the NHS is a comparatively recent phenomenon. Historically, monitoring the implementation of health policy and evaluating the impact of the outcome has not been well developed. Up until the mid-1990s ministers were reluctant to evaluate health policy relying on self-regulation and peer review (Ham, 1999). Where evaluation was carried out prior to the 1990s, this consisted of measuring *inputs* such as staffing levels and expenditure, *activity levels* such as treatment of patients (usually recorded by condition/diagnostic group rather than success at meeting individual need) and bed occupancy rate and *outputs/outcome indicators* such as mortality and morbidity rates, which were rarely of practical use (Ham, op. cit.). The input, activity and output/outcome measures or indicators were seldom related to one another, thereby making it difficult to get a holistic or comprehensive picture of the day-to-day function of any service.

Even today, most monitoring and evaluation in health services concentrates on establishing whether there are specific systems and procedures in place for auditing compliance with legal, financial, managerial, professional and clinical performance indicators. Monitoring and evaluating these indicators tend to be conducted at different points in time, using different systems and incompatible criteria, thereby making it difficult to use the results since the information is not necessarily timely, accurate, complete or relevant (see Figure 8.2).

Approach 1

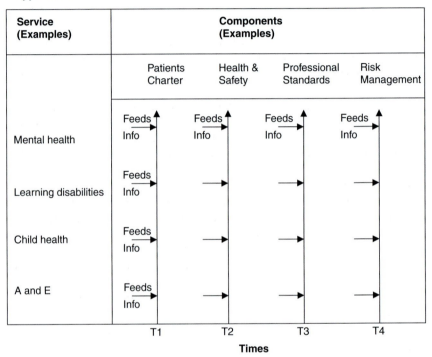

- Done in isolation
- Done at different times
- Done by different people
- Information not always communicated or shared with other interested parties
- Often done with incompatible criteria and information systems
- Not necessarily put into the context of the service, organisation or society
- Service contributes to specific components

It is not:
- Timely
- Accurate
- Relevant
- Contextual

In this model the components are driving the service decisions

Figure 8.2 Approach most frequently used in services.

Take as an example the following case study analysis of an audit set at a hospital in the Wessex Region in 1995. A standard was set on the topic: *time taken for patients to reach the admissions ward from casualty* (a measure of efficiency?). The hospital audited the standard (*maximum time to reach the ward was set at five minutes*) and found that it consistently failed to meet its own standard. The perceived actions for correcting this failure were to (a) revise the time standard because it was unrealistic; (b) ensure that the standard was measured at the point at which the patient was put into the admissions ward collection bay (not first put on to the trolley!); and (c) tell the porters to speed up their service to the admissions ward. The standard was once again measured and found wanting.

What the auditors and the staff failed to do was to look what was going on in the casualty department (the patterns and rhythms). If they had done so they would have established the following:

> There should have been five trolleys in the casualty department. There were four, but only three in use. One had gone for repair, one could not be used because its sides were missing (where they had gone and why no-one had bothered to report this, no-one knew!) and a third trolley had a broken wheel slowing down its progress. Added to this they were short of two of the three casualty porters and agency staff had been employed. Neither of these agency porters had worked in the hospital before and no-one had shown them where the admissions ward was (or any of the other wards, since between calls to ferry casualty patients they also had to take patients to and from other parts of the hospital). Other factors came into play such as the time of day when the audit took place, the fact that casualty staff and porters were unaware of the standard and had not be consulted, to name a few. No-one questioned whether the standard was relevant or useful and so the standard continued to be monitored, to fail and was eventually abandoned since the department did not want to continue to appear inadequate.

This method of evaluation has two major shortfalls, namely; that there is a heavily reliance on a unilateral process of information gathering which does not allow for cross-referencing to service context and relevance. Secondly, where assessment has been done by a department or team responsible for a particular quality performance measure, those responsible may have a vested interest in achieving a particular result.

An alternative, as proposed in this ethnographic service evaluation framework, is to use an integrated approach which allows for greater flexibility and understanding of how the service operates with legitimate examination of the inter-relationships between variables which effect service function. As already illustrated, failure to meet a particular standard or performance indicator may be affected by the inter-relationship between a number of functions of the service. If this inter-relationship is not understood, then actions to improve compliance with any one particular performance indicator/standard, has no guarantee of success.

This approach towards service evaluation is concerned with measuring the effectiveness of the human service, which includes that service's ability to deliver care to clients. The central premise is that the real needs and priorities of service users should drive the design and delivery of human services, not just the perception of the professionals.

An ethnographic approach to service evaluation

The 1980s and 1990s have seen increasing criticism of traditional empirical approaches to researching human behaviour, promoting the search for altern-ative qualitative ways of undertaking human research. The new paradigm philo-sophy is one of doing research *with* people rather than *on* people and is characterized by research that is collaborative and experiential (Reason and Rowan, 1995). The health arena lends itself to this new paradigm, particularly to evaluating the clinical environment (Rolfe, 1998; Streubert and Carpenter, 1999; Marks-Maran and Rose, 1999). Qualitative methodologies are particularly well suited for evaluating programme outcomes, their effects on individuals and for facilitating positive change (Bogdan and Biklen, 1982; Bardy and Cunningham, 1985) and micro-ethnography in particular for discovering and interpreting the organization of people's behaviour in specific social conditions (Spradley, 1980; Hammersley and Atkinson, 1997; Fetterman, 1998). With the focus of NHS quality once more being one of 'continuous quality improvement' (DOH, 2000a), an ethnographic based framework could become increasingly central to the future evaluation process (Lave and Wenger, 1994; Wenger, 1999; Oakley, 2000).

Service evaluation design and process

The evaluation framework was designed to achieve the following:

- to provide a comprehensive understanding of the service philosophy, purpose and cultural context through the development of a cultural picture (culturally valued analogue) of the service;
- to use methods applicable for analysing the needs of clients in residential services;
- to have an objective measurement (audit) of the service;
- to meet the requirements of the concepts of ethnographic research (Spradley, 1980; Fetterman, 1998).

To achieve this, the framework was based on the philosophy and principles of normalization (Wolfensberger, 1972, 1983). This was appropriate for the follow-ing reasons, firstly, that normalization starts from the premise that clients are both individuals and members of society and service delivery should be focused upon the uniqueness of the clients. However, institutionalization can result in a devaluation process that often occurs to those members of society who are vulnerable. Secondly, normalization proposes strategies for revaluation of clients. Thirdly, this philosophy has emerged out of work conducted in long-stay residential services. Fourthly, the work of Wolfensberger and Thomas (1983) has been validated and finally in the case study example, the service's own philosophy and principles were based upon normalization.

The evaluation tool *Compass* (Cragg and Look, 1994) provided the objective measurement in the evaluation. This is a tool designed to assess quality of life issues for clients in residential or other services who are at risk of being socially devalued. It uses a quality of life questionnaire that is administered through observation of the environment and interactions, interviews with clients and staff and completion of an audit tool (see analysis section below). This is based upon O'Brien's service accomplishments (1987), which is also derived from normalization theory and is an established audit tool for use in residential services.

Although *Compass* dealt with the language and imagery of record-keeping it did not address the professional dimension of client care and service delivery. Therefore the evaluators added record-keeping and drug/medicines administration to the evaluation framework. However, once combined with the culturally valued analogue, examination of the service philosophy and organizational policies the team had a comprehensive evaluation framework, which included both contextual and performance measures.

The evaluation needed to be comprehensive and include not only the physical qualities of the service but also the emotional, social and psychological factors which effect the service delivery. The following aspects were identified as fundamental in obtaining a comprehensive picture of services. These are adapted from Wolfensberger and Thomas (1983) and Cragg and Look (1994):

1   environment;
2   activity;
3   individuality;
4   privacy, dignity, respect and choice;
5   physical and mental health needs;
6   community access;
7   record-keeping;
8   relationships/staffing;
9   drugs/medications.

These nine aspects, as well as being individually assessed, should be reflected in the care plan/programme documentation used by the service. Combined, these gave a useful overview of the state of the service, its effectiveness in service delivery and service quality. They also provided the structure for the analysis and presentation of the results of the evaluation.

Although this framework draws heavily on approaches used to evaluate long-stay service for clients with learning disabilities or mental illness, this evaluation framework can be used generically and has relevance to all specialist areas across acute and community settings. This has been discussed elsewhere in the context of healthcare education (Astor *et al.*, 1998) and is outlined in Figures 8.2 and 8.3.

The evaluation process involved the following stages:

1　The preparation of the evaluators to ensure familiarity with the tools and techniques to be used and to establish inter-researcher reliability.
2　Analysis of the service philosophy and intent (documentation). Creation of the 'culturally valued analogue' (Wolfensberger and Thomas, 1983) – this

Approach 2

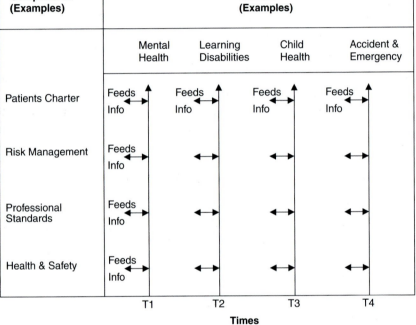

- All information collected at the same time
- It is in the context of the service and organisation
- It can be put into the context of policy and society
- It is designed to use compatible criteria
- The information gained feeds into the specific components (e.g. Patients Charter)

It is:
- Timely
- Accurate
- Relevant
- Contextual

In this model the service contributes to providing information on the components, but decisions are made for clients/service as a whole

Figure 8.3 Service evaluation framework.

takes the form of a description of the purpose of the service and has to be derived in consultation with all stakeholders in order to ensure that their perspectives are reflected in the evaluation. This then provides the baseline against which the service is assessed. This procedure not only reduces researcher bias, but also in itself tests the robustness and validity of the culturally valued analogue. It allows the evaluators to observe how far any part of the service deviates from what is considered culturally acceptable.

3   Data collection (fieldwork) through capturing of the evaluators first impressions of the service and then collection of data against the nine aspects. Data collection methods included:

- interviews with staff;
- talking to clients and relatives;
- touring the environment;
- observing care practices;
- assessing client records;
- participating in ward routines and client activities;
- narratives.

4   Analysis of data – this involved:

- triangulating the findings against the analogue, the service philosophy and the initial impressions of the service (the cultural and value dimension);
- assessing the service against the *Compass* criteria.

5   Presentation of results – this was done by:

- the production of interim and final reports for each individual area of the service evaluated;
- providing an overall summary of the findings;
- verbally presenting the findings to key service personnel and stakeholders.

6   Debriefing of evaluators and service personnel.

Conducting the evaluation: a case study

The following case study took place over a six-month period in 1996 and is based on a residential service, located in the south of England, which provides a long-stay service primarily for the elderly (over 65 years). Due to the sensitive nature of the enquiry and the chapter limitations, there are no direct quotations given; however, the details below are a summary of the interview, audit and observation findings and based on primary data.

Clients' dependency rating was determined as medium to high, meaning that they are heavily reliant on staff support to meet their needs. Staff work an eight-hour shift, 7.30am–3.30pm and 2pm–10pm and night staff work from 10pm–7.30am. There was usually one qualified nurse and a number of unqualified support care staff (between two and three) per shift. Contributions to the care come from other healthcare professionals such as doctors, physiotherapists, occupational therapists, social workers and some community-based staff. Relatives and visitors also made a significant contribution to client care.

The basis of the culturally valued analogue was determined as 'Home'. Exploration of this concept included physical components and the social and cultural image of home. For example, aspects of home included:

- security;
- comfort;
- right to invite people into your home;
- right to leave your home;
- ability to choose and/or negotiate with other 'members of the household' what to do in your home and when;
- choice of decor, furniture and furnishings;
- ability to access the community where your 'home' is situated for leisure, work etc.

Once the concept of home had been described and understood, this formed the basis of the contextual examination of the service, adding a 'rich picture' to the audit dimension.

The next stage was to agree the detail of the data collection and analysis. This was done over a five-day programme as outlined below.

- day 1 – observation and data collection;
- day 2 – an opportunity for collating personal notes/data for team analysis;
- days 3–5 – team debriefing and collation and analysis of findings ready for reporting (draft report);
- final evaluation reports within three months.

The evaluation team worked on a rota basis over a 16-hour period. Ideally it would have been best to cover a complete 24-hour period, but in this case resources meant it was not possible. The 16-hour period spanned the waking hours of the clients and provided sufficient observation of activity and behaviour of clients and staff. The beginning and end of the 16-hour period allowed some estimation of the night routines.

The evaluation times were between 6am and 10pm. The team rota comprising:

- Team member 1 – 6am–2pm
- Team member 2 – 9am–4pm
- Team member 3 – 2pm–10pm.

This rota allowed two evaluators to be present during the most active periods of the day.

One of the most important tasks for the evaluators was to capture their individual initial impressions of the service. The reason for this is that initial impressions give people powerful and often lasting views of a place/service and form the basis of their values and assumptions. However this impression is quickly suppressed (Wolfensberger and Thomas, 1983) as the 'unconscious' takes over the initial sensations are blunted. While this is a highly subjective process, it mirrors closely what new clients and visitors undergo when they first enter the service. When people work daily in a service or relatives visit frequently, the initial impression disappears yet some of that 'gut feeling' may remain, particularly if associated with feelings of security/insecurity, comfort/fear, belonging/isolation. Once these impressions are consigned to the 'unconscious' they are difficult to examine. For instance a residential setting may smell of stale urine. While staff and visitors might notice it initially and even comment on it, within weeks they 'cannot smell it any more'. There is a place therefore for examination of the 'unconscious' to remind people of these facts and look for resolutions.

For the evaluators recording and acknowledging their 'gut feelings' was important to the overall evaluation by contributing important information on context and values but also to ensure that the analysis was not biased by personal judgements.

Next the service function was initially assessed against the service philosophy and analogue to ascertain how closely they matched. This prompted further questions and information requirements to be examined under the nine aspects, helping to establish the type of data to collect.

Examples of what each aspect revealed and how this contributed to the overall evaluation are given below.

Environment

The environment is important to ensure that individual cognitive and physical functioning does not deteriorate to a faster degree than would be expected for that individual's age, physical or mental condition (Feil, 1995). Investigation of the physical environment produced important information on:

- state of decor – this provided information on how people are valued, whether there was choice over decor or whether it is decided by the institution;
- health and safety issues;
- cleanliness of personal and communal areas;
- state of the furniture, e.g. damaged, old, matching, appropriate, positioning;
- locking of doors, e.g. was this available for privacy or security? – to protect clients or to protect the public from the clients?;
- whether clients were segregated in day and/or sleeping areas;
- whether toilet and bathroom areas were well designed, had privacy, had aids, had doors!;

- availability of personal space and whether this was adequate or compromised.

The findings showed that while attempts had been made to improve the publicly visible places such as the lounge areas, most of the service areas were in a poor decorative state; bathrooms and toilet areas lacked privacy and were inadequate; personal space was limited and a stale smell of urine was commonplace. Some of these problems were compounded by external factors beyond the control of staff: the physical design of the old buildings requiring clients to sleep in communal areas. The findings proved helpful as services were being redesigned.

Activity

The efficacy of any activity programme is strongly influenced by staff attitude to the client group. Staff attitude must be moulded on the belief that people, whatever their age, have the right to engage in meaningful interaction with their environment. These activities should form part of the everyday working practice and routine of the service. This should be reflected in the service philosophy and policies and demonstrated in the care programmes/plans.

While activity might be taking place it is important to establish whether it is meaningful to the participants and that it has therapeutic value (Feil, 1995; Armstrong-Esther *et al.*, 1994; Turner, 1993; Godlove *et al.*, 1981). This aspect provided evidence about:

- lack of activity and associated behaviours such as picking at clothes, rocking and sleeping suggesting boredom;
- whether the activity taking place is related to client need and therefore meaningful rather than activity for activity's sake;
- whether clients have been involved in choosing to undertake the activity;
- whether the activity contributes to the process and programme of care or is merely a time filler.

Looking at who organizes and takes part in the activity can provide information on the level and understanding of the therapeutic processes and treatments employed. It is helpful to establish client understanding of the therapeutic value of the activity. Perhaps most importantly it gives a powerful indication of the real intentions of the service in terms of supporting personal independence. This is an area where the service philosophy and reality may be very different.

Here the findings showed that activity was usually ad hoc and not always appropriate to client need or desire. In one area an arranged activity required clients to be able to throw with accuracy in order to hit a target. The success of this required careful positioning; however, the clients were unable to move from their chairs or to position themselves to hit the target. This created great client frustration, but staff seemed unaware of the problem.

Individuality

In a human service, clients can easily be seen as a group of people who require similar treatments. However, it is important to recognize that clients are unique and that this should be reflected in individualized care programmes that are designed to meet the person's needs. The danger of ignoring this individuality can lead to service programmes being designed for clients that: (a) they do not need; (b) they have some need for but have other needs that are ignored; (c) that they have a need for but not to the degree that is being provided (Wolfensberger and Thomas, 1983).

In our society and culture people are recognized as individuals even though they have a collective identity. In residential service this might be reflected in the following ways:

- clients have named carers who know them well and understand their requirements. This should also be reflected in the care plans and documentation.

More obviously:

- clients have personal belongings;
- clients wear their own clothes;
- individuals have the right to make decisions concerning issues such as meal times, toileting, sexuality, activity.

The findings demonstrated that decisions were taken by the service providers and were designed to meet their desires, not those of the clients, for example the observed 'mass toileting' of clients at set times of the day was not according to individual need.

Privacy, dignity, respect and choice

This is about fundamental human rights and must be one of the most important areas for consideration within any human service. This aspect provided information about:

- availability of and access to private space for clients;
- communal areas such as bathrooms and toilets supporting or denying people personal privacy and dignity; in some areas there were no curtains or doors;
- staff knowledge levels and observation of clients religious and cultural beliefs;
- protection of individuals rights under the law, e.g. Data Protection Act (1984), Access to Records Act (1990) right to vote, power of attorney, consent to treatment etc. (Dimond, 1995).

In the case of choice there was wide variation in client involvement, (ranging from high level consultation with clients to none at all) in decisions about:

• the level of their involvement in personally planning their care;
• their ability to choose the activities they wished to undertake;
• their right to exercise choice over food, drinks and menus;
• their right to exercise choice over the routine of the day;
• their right to choose to go outside.

This aspect raised the dilemma between staff requirements and client need and it illustrated how close to the philosophy and analogue service operation really was. It raised issues of power and control and provided clear evidence about the status, value and respect accorded to clients. For instance, some service areas operated a secure system whereby ward areas are locked. While this may be in place to ensure that some clients cannot leave the area because of legal restrictions, or because they are diagnosed as 'at risk', this raised a dilemma for clients who were denied external access (de facto detention) and was at odds with the concept of home. For the sake of a few, the majority were denied their rights.

Physical and mental healthcare

It is well recognized that personal well-being is dependent on meeting needs, such as hunger and thirst or those which involve cognitive functioning and personal control (Maslow, 1954). Where these are properly met, then people can attain their full potential.

Examples of these needs being met should be evident from observation and client documents. Observation of the following physical needs provided clues to whether the service is responsive or neglectful of its duties:

• whether or not clients are incontinent, cold, in pain, nourished;
• incidence of infections and pressure sores in the immobile;
• safety of clients;
• positioning and availability of aids to help independence and comfort.

In general physical care was satisfactory for those clients who were self-caring or mobile, however this deteriorated as dependency increased due to the lack of specialist staff to help. Mental health needs should be fully assessed and documented including a programme of care where appropriate therapeutic treatments are identified and action taken. In this instance this proved very variable.

Community access

Access to the local community ensures that integration into society can continue for clients. This is important to ensure that people can either learn new skills or maintain their current skills for as long as possible. It is equally important for rehabilitation purposes, assessment purposes and community living.

This is a particularly interesting area for evaluation. Clients can spend large periods of time segregated from the general public because they are denied access to the community. However even when out in the community they can still remain segregated from the public because clients often go out in groups for organized events, but are not able to go to the shop/library/pub alone or with a friend. In one example, a young man was taken swimming by a member of staff, however the swimming bath was closed to the public at the time. Clients are in the community but not part of the community.

Record-keeping

In order to help clients meet their physical, social and psychological needs the service should provide accurate programmes of care that are highly relevant to each individual. These programmes must be part of an intended care plan. The recording of care should be in keeping with personal and legal guidelines (UKCC, 1993; NHS Management Executive, 1992).

Documentation is not only key to understanding individual clients needs but also to the care they receive. It also highlights the communication competencies of the service overall. Studying the service documentation revealed issues around:

- standards of care;
- confidentiality and access to information;
- language used in care plans with regards to the respect accorded to clients and value/image of clients by others;
- gaps in assessment of needs;
- progress of treatment and care;
- comprehensiveness of assessment and care delivery, e.g. the level to which documents were complete ranged from good to partial or non-existent. This in term raised questions over the usability of the documentation for clinical decision-making around client care and condition.

Staffing and relationships

In order to ensure that the atmosphere in the ward area is comfortable it is important that staff communicate appropriately and with respect. Also staffing levels in each area should be appropriate to carry forward the various care programme requirements for meeting individual needs.

Observation of the relationships between staff themselves, staff and other professional groups/agencies, staff and clients, staff and relatives can be very revealing, as can the relationships between clients. For instance the findings revealed complicated issues around:

- staff to staff co-operation/tension in teams, rivalry, power games;
- staff and professional groups/agencies – tension/co-operation where

responsibilities overlap, knowledge about referral procedures, appropriate involvement of others;

- staff and clients – information on values, e.g. how people are addressed and treated – ignored/patronized, included/consulted;
- staff and relatives – information on how relatives are viewed and supported by the service;
- clients to clients – ranging from personal friendships, common interests, to feelings of hostility, aggression, fear, indifference.

Drugs and medications

The responsibilities surrounding the administration of drugs and medicines are very clearly identified in the legal and professional acts, policies, and guidance documents and in professional codes of conduct (Medicines Act 1968; Misuse of Drugs Act 1971; Medicinal Products; Prescription by Nurses Act 1992; UKCC, 1992a; UKCC, 1992b). These were discussed with staff and clients to ascertain understanding of policy. The findings raised issues about:

- the types of systems used to safely identify clients, particularly when clients have communication problems or are confused;
- whether medication charts and documents complied with the legal require-ments, e.g. how they are written, who has authorized the treatment, dosage details etc.;
- whether staff have been assessed as competent to administer medicines;
- whether there were adequate systems for monitoring side effects of medica-tion;
- whether medicines were actually administered.

It is evident from all these examples that there is overlap between the aspects. This is extremely useful as it allows the same issue to be explored from different perspectives assisting with establishing a deeper understanding of service func-tion and variable interdependency.

Analysis

Once the complexity of the service had been examined against these aspects, the information was analysed by the team according to the outlined process.

For instance the *Compass* evaluation tool covered the following themes:

- choice and influence;
- status and dignity;
- individuality;
- relationships;
- community presence;
- continuity and progression;
- competence and experience.

There are 86 measures and each is assigned a numerical score between 1 and 4 (1 – high (satisfactory) level rating to 4 – poor (unsatisfactory) level rating). Each team collectively scored the service areas they had evaluated according to the *Compass* guidelines. This provided the objective measure of the success of the service to deliver client care in line with the principles of normalization.

The next stage of the analysis was to triangulate the evidence collected against the culturally valued analogue, the service's own philosophy and statements of intent and the first impressions to see how closely they matched.

Many of the aspects associated with the analogue were found to be missing or compromised. In some aspects physical environmental constraints (e.g. communal bedrooms) made achievement difficult; however, one area achieved a close match because of the staff attitude of valuing clients and colleagues as individuals. Despite the poor physical environment the atmosphere was one of harmony between clients and staff and a sense of welcome and security prevailed. This illustrates just how complex and multifaceted the idea of a good quality service really is. The physical manifestation was poor; however, the social, emotional and personal needs of clients were met and these transcended the other problems.

In other areas this match was not as close as the service thought it was. The closeness of fit between the analogue, the service philosophy and the evidence of service delivery were at odds. For instance some staff accepted the qualities of home as important and as the qualities they personally sought to achieve for themselves and their families; however, they seemed unaware (unconscious) that clients also held the same aspirations. Equally some staff professed to believe in the principles of normalization, yet their actions did not support this belief.

In summary, therefore this approach to evaluating health services produced many unsurprising results of which the service was already aware (e.g. environmental issues). What did produce surprise and discomfort for service personnel was that this approach made explicit the unconscious and ambiguous behaviours and attitudes that many of them exhibited towards their clients. Many thought they knew their service but now had to reappraise their views. It did, however, illustrate to service personnel at all levels the importance of tackling cultural change if service quality is to be really improved (see Preece, Chapter 9).

Conclusion

Evaluating the quality of healthcare delivery is relatively new to the NHS and it is still learning much about the concept of quality and how to progress the quality journey. The NHS started ambitiously with TQM and found that it was difficult to apply because the infrastructure for evaluating quality in any meaningful way, let alone improving it, did not really exist. Much of the last decade and more has been taken up with the painful process of trying to establish an appropriate and agreed framework to take the TQM philosophy forward. NHS quality has now been re-launched as Continuous Quality Improvement (DOH, 2000a). The definition of this remains problematic in terms of healthcare delivery; however, this may in future be increasingly defined by government action and intervention.

Research into the effectiveness of healthcare delivery is a growing area of interest attracting increasing amounts of independently commissioned research into establishing effective methods of evaluation. There is also a growing interest in qualitative methodologies, particularly ethnography. However the future stumbling block for evaluating health service quality is not likely to be the lack of a framework or infrastructure for assessment, but that the use of research methodologies which are able to examine the cultural and value-based dimensions of healthcare delivery prove too uncomfortable to face either at governmental or local level. As Ham (1999) notes, 'there is, of course, no guarantee that the results of evaluations will be acted upon' (p. 183), particularly if the message is unpalatable.

Finally there is no doubt that the NHS has made progress in its understanding of the quality concept and process; we may even claim to understand that 'quality' is essential to determining effective service delivery. However for an organization that is concerned with communicating with people, we have much to learn about the skills of holding a dialogue. This must be the next stage of the quality journey for health services – only then can we start to master the art of the quality 'conversation'.

Acknowledgement

The author is indebted to Mr K. Humphrys for his advice and support.

References

Armstrong-Esther, C., Brown, K. and McAfee, J. (1994) Elderly patients: still clean and sitting quietly, *Journal of Advanced Nursing* **19**, 264–71.

Astor, R., Jefferson, H. and Humphrys, K. (1998) Incorporating the service accomplishments into pre-registration curriculum to enhance reflective practice, *Nurse Education Today* **18**, 567–75.

Audit Commission (1992) *Minding the Quality: A Consultation Document on the Role of the Audit Commission in Quality Assurance in Health Care*. London, The Audit Commission.

Bardy, M. and Cunningham, J. (1985) Living and learning in segregated environments: an ethnography of normalization outcomes, *Education and Learning of the Mentally Retarded*, Dec., 241–52.

Berwick, D. (1992) Heal thyself or heal the system: can doctors help improve medical care? *Quality in Health Care 1*, Supplement, 52–8.

Black, N. (1990) Quality assurance in medical care, *Journal of Public Health Medicine* **12**(20), 97–104.

Birch, K., Field, S. and Scrivens, E. (2000) *Quality in General Practice*. Abingdon: Radcliffe Medical Press Ltd.

Bogdan, R. and Biklen, S. (1982) *Qualitative Research for Education: An Introduction to Theory and Methods* (2nd edn). Boston Allyn & Baker.

Buttery, Y., Walshe, K., Rumsey, M., Amess, M., Bennett, J. and Coles, J. (1995) *Provider Audit in England: A Review of 29 Programmes.* London: CASPE Research.

Cabinet Office (1998) *Service First: The New Charter Programme.* London: Cabinet Office (Better Government for Older People – BGOP).

Citizens Charter Unit (1991) *The Citizens Charter.* London: HMSO.

Clinical Outcomes Group (1992) *The Evaluation of Clinical Audit.* London: DOH.

Commission for Health Improvement (CHI) www.doh.gov.uk/chi/

Cragg, R. and Look, R. (1994) *Compass: A Multi Perspective Evaluation of Quality in Home Life.* Wolverley NHS Trust.

Crail, M. (1999) Never mind the quality . . . , *Health Service Journal,* 1 April, 12–13.

Dimond, B. (1995) *Legal Aspects of Nursing* (2nd edn). Prentice Hall.

DOH www.doh.gov.uk

DOH (1989) *Working for Patients.* London: HMSO.

DOH (1997) *The New NHS: Modern, Dependable.* London: The Stationery Office.

DOH (1998) *A First Class Service – Quality in the new NHS.* London: The Stationery Office.

DOH (1999a) *Working together – Securing a quality workforce for the NHS.* Wetherby: DOH.

DOH (1999b) *Saving Lives: Our Healthier Nation.* London: The Stationery Office.

DOH (1999c) *Patient and Public Involvement in the New NHS.* London: The Stationery Office.

DOH (1999d) *Health Act 1999 – Modern Partnerships for the People.* London: The Stationery Office.

DOH (2000a) *The NHS Plan: A Plan for Investment, A Plan for Reform.* London: The Stationery Office.

DOH (2000b) *The NHS Plan: The Government's response to the Royal Commission on Long Term Care.* London: The Stationery Office.

DTI (1990) *Managing into the '90s – The Enterprise Initiative.* London: HMSO.

Fairey, M. (1986) *A National Strategic Framework for Information Management in Hospital and Community Health Services.* London: DHSS, Oct., 1986.

Feil, N. (1995) *The Validation Breakthrough: Simple Techniques for Communicating with people with Alzheimer's Type dementia.* Baltimore: Health Professions Press.

Fetterman, D. (1998) *Ethnography: Step-by step* (2nd edn). London: Sage Publications.

Giddens, A. (1998) *The Third Way: The Renewal of Social Democracy.* Cambridge: Polity Press.

Godlove, G., Richard, L. and Rodwell, H. (1981) *Time for Action: An Observation Study of Elderly People in Four Different Care Environments.* Sheffield: University of Sheffield Social Service Monograph.

Griffiths, R. (1983) *NHS Management Inquiry.* London: DHSS.

Ham, C. (1999) *Health Policy in Britain* (4th edn). Basingstoke: Macmillan Press Ltd.

Hammersley, M. and Atkinson, P. (1997) *Ethnography – Principles and Practice* (2nd edn). London: Routledge.

Humphris, D. and Littlejohns, P. (1995) The development of multiprofessional audit and clinical guidelines: their contribution to quality assurance and effectiveness, *NHS Journal of Interprofessional Care* **9**(3), 207–25.

Hunter, D. (1997) *Desperately Seeking Solutions: Rationing Health Care.* London: Longman.

Hunter, D. (1999) Which way at the crossroads? *Health Service Journal* 1 April, 16.

Kemp, N. and Richardson, E. (1990) *Quality Assurance in Nursing Practice*. Oxford: Butterworth Heinemann.

Kinn, S. (1997) The relationship between clinical audit and ethics, *Journal of Medical Ethics* **23**, 250–3.

Kitson, A. (1989) *RCN Standards of Care Project* (Dysssy). London: RCN.

Lave, J. and Wenger, E. (1994) *Situated Learning – Legitimate Peripheral Participation*. Cambridge: Cambridge University Press.

Lord, J. and Littlejohns, P. (1994) Clinical audit: secret garden, *Health Service Journal* **25** Aug., 18–21.

Marks-Maran, D. and Rose, P. (eds) (1999) *Reconstructing Nursing: Beyond Art and Science*. London: Bailliere Tindall/RCN.

Maxwell, R.J. (1984) Quality assessment in health care, *British Medical Journal* **288**, 12 May, 1470–2.

Maxwell, R. (1992) Dimensions of quality revisited: from thought to action, *Quality in Healthcare* **1**, 171–7.

Maslow, A. (1954) Cited in Atkinson, R., Atkinson, R., Smith, E., Bem, D. and Hilgard, E. (1990) *Introduction to Psychology* (10th edn). London: Harcourt Brace.

Medicine Act (1968) London: HMSO (reprinted 1986).

Misuse of Drugs Act (1972) London: HMSO (reprinted 1985).

Medicinal Products: Prescription by Nurses etc. Act (1992) London: HMSO.

Millar, B. (1999) Clinical governance: carry that weight, *Health Service Journal*, 18 Feb., 22–7.

MS Society (2000) Not so NICE – the MS Society rejects the recommendations (Editorial), *MS Matters* **32**, July/Aug., 5.

National Institute for Clinical Excellence (NICE) www.nice.org.uk

NHS Executive (1992) EL(92)21, *Medical Audit – Allocation of Funds 1992–3*. London: DOH.

NHS Executive (1993) EL(93)115, *Improving Clinical Effectiveness in the NHS*. London: DOH.

NHS Executive (1994) EL(94)80, *Consumer Audit – The College of Health Guidelines*. London: DOH.

NHS Executive (1999) *Clinical Governance – Quality in the new NHS*. London: DOH. www.doh.nhsweb.nhs.uk/nhs/clingov.htm

NHSE (1999a) *Primary Care Trusts: Establishment and Preparatory Period and Their Functions*. Wetherby, Dec.

NHSE (1999b) *Working Together: Human Resources Guidance and Requirements for Primary Care Trusts*. Wetherby, Dec., 1999.

NHS Management Executive (1991) *Framework for Audit for Nursing Services*. London: HMSO.

NHS Management Executive (1992) *Keeping the Records Straight: A Guide to Record Keeping for Nurses, Midwives and Health Visitors*. NHS Training Directorate.

NHS Management Executive (1993a) *The A–Z of Quality*. London: DOH.

NHS Management Executive (1993b) *The Quality Journey*. Lancs, UK: Health Publications Unit.

Nolan, M., Grant, G. and Nolan, J. (1995) Busy doing nothing: activity and interaction levels amongst differing populations of elderly patients, *Journal of Advanced Nursing* **22**, 528–38.

Oakland, J. (1996) *Total Quality Management* (2nd edn). Oxford: Butterworth Heinemann.

Oakley, A. (2000) *Experiments in Knowing – Gender and Methods in Social Sciences.* Cambridge, Polity Press.

O'Brien, J. (1987) A guide to personal futures planning. Prepared for Thomas, G. and Wilcox, B. *The Activities Catalog: A Community Programme Guide for Youth and Adults with Severe Disabilities.*

Øvretveit, J. (1992) *Health Service Quality.* London: Blackwell.

Parsley, K. and Corrigan, P. (1999) *Quality Improvement in Healthcare: Putting Evidence into Practice* (2nd edn). Cheltenham: Stanley Thornes.

Parasuramen, A. *et al.* (1985) A conceptual model of service qualities and its implications for further research, *Journal of Marketing* **49**, Autumn, 41–50.

Pfeffer, N. and Coote, A. (1991) *Is Quality Good for You? A Critical Review of Quality Assurance in Welfare Services.* IPPR Social Policy Paper no. 5.

Pfeffer, N. and Pollock, A. (1993) Public opinion in the NHS – the unaccountable in pursuit of the uninformed, *British Medical Journal* **307**, 25 Sept., 750–1.

Phillips, M. and Dawson, J. (1985) *Doctors Dilemmas – Medical Ethics and Contemporary Science.* Harvester Press Ltd.

Pollitt, C. (1993) *Managerialism and Public Service* (2nd edn). Oxford: Blackwell.

Rappaport, J. (1981) In praise of paradox: a social policy of empowerment over prevention: residential address to the Division of Community Psychology of the American Psychological Association, *American Journal of Community Psychology* **9**, 1–25.

Rappaport, J. (1995) Empowerment meets narrative: listening to stories and creating settings, *American Journal of Community Psychology* **23**(5), 795–807.

Reason, P. and Rowan, J. (eds) (1995) *Human Inquiry: A Sourcebook of New Paradigm Research.* Chichester: J. Wiley & Sons.

Richards, H. and Higinbotham, C. (1989) *The Enquire System – A Workbook on Quality Assurance in Health and Social Care.* London: Kings Fund College.

Rivett, G. (1998) *From Cradle to Grave: Fifty Years of the NHS.* London: Kings Fund.

Robson, C. (1995) *Real World Research: A Resource for Social Scientists and Practitioner – Researchers.* Oxford: Blackwell.

Rolfe, G. (1998) *Expanding Nursing Knowledge – Understanding and Researching Your Own Practice.* Oxford: Butterworth Heinemann.

Sachs, J. (1999) Sachs on development – helping the world's poorest, *The Economist* 14 Aug., **352**(8132), 16–22.

Sale, D. (1991) *Quality Assurance* (Essentials of Nursing Management Series). Basingstoke: Macmillan.

Seedhouse, D. (1995) *Fortress NHS: A Philosophical Review of the National Health Service.* Chichester: J. Wiley & Sons.

Seedhouse, D. (1988) *Ethics – The Heart of Health Care.* Chichester: J. Wiley & Sons.

Sontag, S. (1991) *Illness as a Metaphor/AIDS and its Metaphors.* London: Penguin Books.

Spradley, J.P. (1980) Cited in Bardy, M. and Cunningham, J. (1985) Living and learning in segregated environments: an ethnography of normalization outcomes, *Education and Training of the Mentally Retarded*, Dec., 241–52.

Streubert, H.J. and Carpenter, D.R. (1999) *Qualitative Research in Nursing: Advancing the Human Imperative* (2nd edn). Philadelphia: Lippincott.

Turner, P. (1993) Activity nursing and the changes in the quality of life of elderly patients: a semi qualitative study, *Journal of Advanced Nursing* **19**, 239–48.

United Kingdom Central Council (1992a) *Code of Professional Conduct.* London: UKCC, June.

United Kingdom Central Council (1992b) *Standards for the Administration of Medicines.* London: UKCC, Oct.

United Kingdom Central Council (1993) *Standards for Records and Record Keeping.* London: UKCC, April.

Wallace, L. and Stoten, B. (1999) The Late Show, *Health Service Journal*, 4 March, 24–5.

Wenger, E. (1999) *Communities of Practice: Learning, Meaning and Identity.* Cambridge: Cambridge University Press.

Wilson, C. (1987) *Hospital Wide Quality Assurance.* Philadelphia: W.B. Saunders.

Wolfensberger, W. (1972) *The Principles of Normalization in Human Services.* Toronto: NIMR.

Wolfensberger, W. (1983) Social role valorization: a proposed new term for the principle of normalization, *Mental Retardation* **21**, 234–9.

Wolfensberger, W. and Thomas, S. (1983) Programme Analysis of Service Systems Implementation of Normalization Goals (PASSING), *National Institute of Mental Retardation.* Ontario, Canada.

9 Quality Management in public house retailing

A case study

David Preece, Valerie Steven and Gordon Steven

Introduction

The public house retailing sector has been seriously neglected in the Quality Management (and, indeed, other) literature as a 'research site'.[1] This is despite the fact that many thousands of people are employed there and that it forms part of the growing service sector, which is projected to continue to expand in the present century. We find this surprising, for public houses are businesses in which the quality of customer service provision is a key ingredient in their success and continued viability. One important reason for the lack of interest (until the early-to-mid 1990s at least) in TQM/customer-oriented initiatives, and for the predominance of a control-oriented culture and management style, was the strong focus in the public house retailing sector upon the products produced by the relevant breweries, that is to say an orientation which saw the pub as the 'shop-window' for the beer and other liquid outputs of the same company's breweries. As some pub managers commented in Johnston and Bryan's (1993: 127/131) study of service industry strategies:

> I believe that seeking a competitive edge through service as opposed to products could have a substantial impact on volume. I really believe that we should differentiate ourselves by concentrating our time and efforts on the way the service is provided; how the customer is dealt with ... However, I believe that to achieve real and lasting service improvement is relatively difficult and requires changes not only in the pub itself but to overall company culture and central control systems.

And, later, another pub manager commented:

> The problem is that our performance measurement of the licensed house manager is very much financially orientated ... and our control systems mirror this.

It is important to understand, on the basis of empirical research, what has been happening during a period of significant change and restructuring in the sector during the 1990s, and to determine whether and if so to what extent, Quality

Management (QM) has been adopted. Specific illustrations of the questions which might be asked of the data include 'What form of QM is involved?'; 'Why was it introduced?'; 'How was it introduced?' (i.e. the process of introduction); 'How was it received – by both external and internal customers, and managers and employees?' Our view is that in order to do this, a 'contextual-processual' perspective needs to be taken, that is, one which is sensitive to both the changing nature of external and internal organizational contexts over the period of time under consideration, the specifics of the change project(s) which were introduced, and the actions and orientations of the various actors involved (see, for example, Buchanan and Badham, 1999; Collins, 1998; Dawson, 1994; Pettigrew and Whipp, 1991).

The authors have conducted research into change and restructuring in the UK public house retailing sector over an extended period of time (see Preece *et al.*, 1999a, b). In particular, they have been examining both the unfolding and strategic changes which have occurred or been introduced into Bass Taverns (now called Bass Leisure Retailing), one of the UK's largest pub retailing companies. One of the change initiatives involved the adoption and promulgation of Quality Management. This can be viewed as much closer to Total/Strategic Quality Management than the other main forms of QM which had been in existence for some considerable time in the organization, namely Quality Assurance and Quality Control. The sectoral data base has subsequently been extended to cover other public house retailing/brewing companies (see Preece *et al.*, 2000).

Below, we first describe the main case study organization and then the organizational restructuring of the early-to-mid 1990s, of which the QM initiative was an important element. A Quality Assurance (QA)/Quality Control (QC) approach characterized the orientation to QM within the company until the major change initiatives of the early 1990s. There then follows a review and analysis of the company's two QM-related initiatives of the early to mid 1990s, one being aimed at public house personnel, and the other at senior managers and staff. We also outline and comment upon the reception given to the various QM programmes by the relevant organizational actors.

Bass Taverns

Bass Taverns was, during the period described, the name of the division of Bass PLC which operates public houses and restaurants throughout the UK (the other divisions were Bass Brewers; Britvic Soft Drinks; and Holiday Inns). The division emerged early in 1989 with the splitting up of the brewing and retailing interests of the PLC. Bass PLC is one of the UK's largest leisure industry companies, employing over 100,000 people worldwide during the time period of the research. The PLC takes a close interest in the performance of its constituent divisions, setting objectives and targets which they are expected to achieve over a given time period. Bass Taverns made a major contribution to the PLC's profits, employing over 30,000 people in over 2,500 managed public houses spread across the UK.

Before 1989, Bass was organized into six regional, vertically integrated companies, each region in turn being split into a number of trading areas. A managing director headed up each of the regional companies and there existed a strong regional identity, one which had been nurtured by Bass over a number of years, through devices such as distinct trading names reflecting each particular region. Each company had its beer brands and/or breweries, and regional brands of ales were positively marketed. Lager brands, however, were national, as was the organization and management of the Hotels Division. Territories and resources were jealously guarded, risk aversion was the predominant ingredient of investment decision-making, and accountability was thinly spread. All this added up, not surprisingly, to a conservative and slow-moving, gradualist organizational culture, which can be typified as follows:

1   Because of the two very liquid resources to be found in public houses, namely cash and drink, 'Pub managers are not to be trusted, therefore they must be controlled.'
2   'The pub is supply driven – the "shop window" for a range of ales and lagers.'
3   'Individual outlet performance is the key consideration.'

The organization structure was hierarchically based; business expertise was based upon function; managers acted predominantly as supervisors and the Board as a scorekeeper, senior management's priority being control over operations. Staff values were essentially defensive; and a customer focus was often missing (see Preece *et al.*, 1999a, b). Not surprisingly, given this culture and structuring, the predominant form of Quality Management to be found in the company was that of Quality Control, with some emphasis also upon Quality Assurance. However, from 1989 onwards, key changes took place in the outer contexts of Bass Taverns' operations, which were to have a profound effect upon the organization and its orientation towards customers and the market place, encompassing a radical programme of change and restructuring (see Preece *et al.*, 1999a, esp. chapter 2). These can be summarized as follows:

1   *Changes in consumer preferences.* Examples here include the impact of the health-food and drink lobby, and the shift away from the 'on trade' (buying drink and food in pubs) to the 'off trade' (people buying all or most of their wine, spirits and beer from supermarkets or off-licences for consumption at home).
2   *Economic recession in the late 1980s and early 1990s.* Many people had less discretionary spending power, and the lower prices to be found in some parts of the off trade and via beer and spirit imports became more appealing.
3   *The changing nature of competition.* For example, mergers and alliances were formed between brewing and retailing groups; foreign brewing

companies entered the UK market in a major way for the first time; many pubs were regenerated by smaller, independent companies, which focused much more effectively upon customer service and choice, and returned in some respects to the basics of a 'good local'.

4   *Legislative changes.* The UK government's 'Beer Orders' of 1989 was a watershed in legislating for the sector, bringing in as it did a number of regulative changes. One of these – if not the key one – was the ceiling placed upon the number of pubs which could be owned by a brewing group, where those pubs were tied in terms of supply to that particular group. For Bass Taverns this meant that it had to sell off over 40 per cent of its public houses during the period 1990–2 (amounting to some 2,750 outlets), in order to comply with the orders.

Change and restructuring in Bass Taverns

In 1992 the PLC set the division some extremely challenging targets to be achieved by 1997/8. They could not be achieved by cost-cutting alone, and senior management decided that the company had to 'start all over again'. At this time, these managers had not heard of Business Process Reengineering (BPR – see Hammer and Champy, 1993; Davenport, 1992, and, for a critical overview of and reflection upon BPR, Knights and Willmott, 2000), but they quickly came to understand what it was about, and what it might deliver. CSC Index Consultants were hired by the Taverns Board to facilitate the relevant changes. The Board took the view that BPR would help the company to achieve the 'quantum leap' which was seen as required, as it involved 'The fundamental rethinking and radical redesign of business processes to achieve dramatic improvements in critical, contemporary measures of performance such as cost, quality, service and speed . . . more succinctly it is starting over again' (Hammer and Champy, 1993). Subsequently three core organizational processes were identified: 'operate pubs', 'develop pubs', and 'manage cash', and henceforth the company was to be operated along these lines.

While, then, BPR was viewed as a key element in the organizational change programme upon which the company was about to embark, it was only one element of a series of strategic changes which were introduced from the early 1990s. Other change initiatives included the creation of separate public house and brewery divisions; major property disposals; infrastructural changes; new reward and remuneration structures; and major technological change in the form of the introduction of the 'Bass Retail System'(BRS). The latter involved a fully integrated electronic point of sale system in the pub, with checkout pads and touch screens, and with dispense monitoring linked to a back-office PC and, in turn, into the business. This meant that at any time, in every office, managers and staff could tell what was being sold in the pubs, at what price, to whom, at what time, who sold it, what their productivity was, etc, etc.

The New Retail Initiative (NRI), as the change programme came to be termed, was defined by the Director of Corporate Change as being about 'Delivering a quantum leap in outlet performance through increased turnover'. The key ingredients were as follows:

- Pubs were to be grouped in teams of five or six pub managers by type of trade (as against around 25 varied types of pubs previously), with a retail business manager (RBM) having responsibility for three teams.
- To encourage the development of team working, team achievements would be recognized and rewarded in addition to individual achievements.
- Two-day team training workshops were delivered for LHMs and their partners centred on team development activities.
- The RBM role was to be centred on business development, with the reduction in the number of outlets in each district enabling them to spend more time coaching individual LHMs on this aspect of their job.
- Local administrative and back-up support was to be more responsive and pub-focused. The number of routine operational reports and requests for information from the outlets was halved.
- The BRS roll-out had been completed by 1994, and enhancements and infrastructure developments resulted in a second PC being delivered to the managed houses in the Bass Taverns estate. This facilitated improvements in purchasing, personnel records and payment systems, financial reporting, productivity comparisons and business development initiatives.
- LHMs would be 'empowered', and would have a greater degree of autonomy and the freedom to make decisions based on the increased quantity and quality of information at their disposal from the new technology.
- Not only would LHMs be providing information to a central database, but they would also have access to shared market and customer information from this network.

The three core business processes were utilized as the central organizing principle for the restructuring. In order to illustrate how this incorporated an attempt to move the orientation of staff towards TQM, as against QC, let us take the main constituent elements and underlying principles identified for the 'develop pubs' core process:

- Cross functional and interdisciplinary teams with links between them were introduced in an attempt to break down the functional chimneys, improve communication and shorten process times. As an illustration of an output of this refocusing, the time taken to build a pub from scratch was reduced to less than 16 weeks and the number of 'new build' pubs was doubled in a single year.
- Measurement systems along the core process (as with the other two core processes) allowed performance to be assessed in such a way that it could be linked into team rewards (for example, measures relating to new sites acquired, new sites opened, and reductions in construction times were used to help determine the bonuses earned over a given period of time by Development Teams).

- There was an emphasis on the sharing of best practice so that quality improvements were not limited to one team or one RBM district.
- A constructively rather than destructively critical evaluation of performance was encouraged in order to break out of the 'blame culture' and motivate staff to innovate towards quality improvement.
- The process was to be streamlined and seamless, thus eliminating repetition and opportunities for error and giving individuals more responsibility for and ownership of their work.
- There was to be more focus on 'getting close to the customer' and using customer data to drive decisions on future development. This would be supported by a new 'Concept and Product Development' department.
- Strategic alliances were formed with core suppliers and other divisions of Bass in order to improve supply chain processes.
- To enable the above, management needed to place much more emphasis on the recruitment and retention of 'the very best people' and hence, *inter alia*, on their training and development. Assessment Centres were introduced for this purpose, and the key skills and knowledge against which people were now assessed included the ability to cope under pressure, experience of or willingness to work in teams, and ability to handle an extensive amount of complex data.
- New roles and activities were created of 'sector guardian', 'new concept operations', 'portfolio management', 'acquisition and development', 'marketing intelligence', strategic planning, and strategic alliance management. To take the 'sector guardian' role as an example, this was to be about the sharing of best practice and the casting of a critical eye over what was happening within the sector. An affinity with Quality Management benchmarking can be detected here.

There was a recognition that in order to improve and make fully effective the 'develop pubs' core process, there had to be elements of genuine innovation. Too often in the past, Bass had been innovators in terms of concept development but had then failed to innovate at the workplace level (that is public houses, but also head and regional offices) in relation to concept roll-out and implementation. However, with regard to themed pubs and catering concepts it was felt that there was a need for some 'blue sky' projects. According to the Operations Director for the 'develop pubs' core process activities, 'Innovation is not a dazzling leap in the dark, it has to be a series of trial and error experiments, all done in close contact with the customer and with the LHMs.' Failure had to be cheaper. He regarded low-cost experiments as being fundamental to future success, and his belief in a small number of people with a good idea outflanking an unresponsive giant, made sense to his team members. Everyone in the organization had to be empowered to innovate and he believed it was his job to get the message across that innovation is the key to growth, is a core process and not an event, and is an ongoing activity, sustained by continuous debate. We can see here many affinities with a cornerstone of TQM, namely continuous improvement.

A number of affinities can be seen above with TQM: 'everyone is involved', benchmarking, continuous improvement, quality measurements, a 'no blame culture', getting 'close to the customer', the need for an appropriate supporting infrastructure etc. (see, for example, Dale, 1994; Deming, 1986; du Gay and Salaman, 1992; Wilkinson *et al.*, 1998; Zeithaml *et al.*, 1990). Let us now focus more specifically, then, upon the elements of the Quality Management change initiatives which emerged. We outline and discuss these under two headings: the QM initiative in the pubs, and the 'Breakthrough' initiative for senior management.

Quality Management initiatives

'Succeeding with Customers'

The objective of the 'Succeeding with Customers' change initiative, as Bass Taverns labelled its TQM programme for the managed public houses, was to maintain and improve standards of customer service. It had both behavioural and attitudinal dimensions in that it was focused upon having bar staff put 'good' customer service at the top of their work priorities. Incremental improvements that could be measured and were capable of sustainability were to be the norm, as opposed to radical shifts in pricing policy or product mix or the physical environment of the outlet. It was made clear from the start that 'Succeeding with Customers' was unlikely to be accompanied by any substantial injections of supportive capital or revenue expenditure. 'Customer care', rather than, say, significant improvements in the amenities of the pub, was seen as the appropriate subject matter for team meetings and training sessions.

The training programme began with a one-day workshop where the pub managers were trained by their RBM on the principles of customer care, team working and continuous service improvement. This was followed by another one-day workshop where the pub managers were trained to deliver the 'Succeeding with Customers' initiative. There was minimal involvement of more senior operations management – 'Succeeding with Customers' was seen as a pub manager and staff training intervention, forming part of their on-going education and training programme. For newcomers to Bass Taverns this comprised a 14-week training course leading to membership of the British Institute of Innkeeping. 'Succeeding with Customers' was, then, the customer care component of this professional development programme for LHMs. Existing and newly appointed pub managers (including LHMs from other companies) all had to undertake the 'Succeeding with Customers' training programme, which included:

- the welcome and customer aspirations
- 'customers as individuals and groups'
- customer motivation
- customer complaints
- team working

- continuous service improvement
- 'Quality is free'
- the costs of losing a customer.

Typically, this discussion-based training, supported by a video and participant work books, was delivered in modules in a team meeting in the pub, prior to a working session, and usually lasted between 30 and 45 minutes. A familiar six-step continuous improvement methodology was prescribed for identifying problems and developing solutions:

- assess the situation or problem
- search for causes
- agree and target solutions
- take action
- measure the results
- provide feedback and communication at all stages and repeat the process.

A series of new measures of the quality of customer service provision were also introduced, designed to let everyone know how they were doing against the defined standards requirement. There were measures of customer satisfaction, measures of customer dissatisfaction via complaints, measures of 'good house-keeping', and attempts to measure the initial welcome given to customers when first entering the pub. How were these measures captured? Focus groups were run across the estate, attended by the relevant pub managers, RBMs and a selection of local external customers. 'Mystery customers' and 'Mystery drinkers' were also used to gather data. The former marked the outlet against a checklist which included external items such as outside lighting and car park cleanliness, and internal aspects like the welcome, the ease of placing a food order and the time between the order and the delivery of food, the presentation of food and wine, the 'selling on' of puddings and additional menu items, the cleanliness of the toilets, the billing process and the acceptability of credit cards or 'tabs', the presence of the manager or assistant manager, and the farewell. They also recorded the day and time of visit, the weather, and other conditions. 'Mystery drinkers' focused more on the range and quality of beers and lagers in wet-led pubs with little food. The reports which came out of these visits were then discussed by the LHM and the RBM in their business development meeting, together with the Quality Logs in which the LHMs identified and prioritized issues and problems in their pubs. This was, of course, with a view to exploring how the service provision could be improved and what actions were to be taken. One of the key elements of the company's wider strategic change initiative was the introduction of team working (see Preece *et al.*, 1999a, esp. Chapter 8), and Quality Management issues such as customer service and continuous improvement became regular items on the agenda of the LHM's and RBM's team meetings.

Once all this data had been collected, a comparison was made with financial data from the pub. This represented an attempt to correlate the so-called 'soft data' of customer service, customers' aspirations and feelings against the 'hard data' of sales turnover, takings per staff hour, labour costs and stock yield. One interviewee commented that, in Bass, 'if it moves measure it; if it doesn't move measure it anyway in case it moves'. 'Succeeding with Customers' was an attempt to implement continuous customer service improvements in the outlet via team working and a greater focus on customer wants and needs.

The use of 'mystery customers' and 'mystery drinkers' to help monitor and evaluate the quality of the customer experience is widespread in the sector, although it should be noted that it does not always take the same form. In another major public house retailing company, for example, the 'mystery customer' used to visit incognito, but recently this practice has been changed to a system whereby the evaluator makes him/herself known to the staff at the beginning of the visit and openly questions customers. The area managers are 'regularly swopped around [to new regions] in order to keep the standards up'(area manager interview). In some cases, it seems, in any event, the 'mystery customer' does not actually visit *all* the pubs he/she is meant to visit – e.g. missing out the 'rougher' hostelries or paying students to visit some of the pubs (but still writing up a report as if he/she had personally visited all the pubs listed). Across the divisions of Bass plc there have been variations in its use and in the way in which the scores have been linked to incentive schemes for staff. Sometimes other measures are also included, and there has not always been consistency of application across the estate. In Hollywood Bowls, for example (formerly a part of the Bass Leisure division), an external company was hired which had 'customers' visiting at random times, replicating the customer base at the time of the visit. They used a checklist in which they inserted ticks or crosses to indicate that certain clearly prescribed standards had or had not been met. From the data so generated, the company produced league tables which were communicated to all staff. They also devised an incentive scheme which (providing the scores indicated that certain criteria had been met) linked the employee's share of the bonus awarded to the outlet to the number of hours they worked.

These developments and attempts to improve service delivery in the pub were not occurring in isolation from other significant change project implementations. For example, the Bass Retail System (described earlier) was being rolled out across the whole estate, new catering concepts and brands were being implemented, and new products (including a completely new range of premium lagers) were being introduced into the outlets. At the same time the company was being forced to sell over one-third of its asset base of licensed premises in less than two years. Change, including much strategic change, therefore, was the norm.

As far as the pub manager and his/her staff were concerned, they were faced with the need to embrace new technology and new organizational and working arrangements, including not least working in teams for the first time, delivering new service offerings via new products, and developing a whole new range of skills associated with the technology and products. In the meantime, a

'Sword of Damacles' in the shape of 'Is my pub going to be sold or not?' was hanging over them and their staff. This is hardly a conducive environment in which to embed continuous service improvement in the culture of normal operations.

Our research data indicates (see Preece *et al.*, 1999a, esp. Chapters 8 and 9) that there was a positive relationship between the willingness and ability to embrace the new technology and the ability to get continuous service improvement and team working off the ground. Many LHMs and RBMs seemed to take the changes in their stride, in that they tended to be more consultative and open-minded anyway. In team meetings, where the 'Succeeding with Customers' philosophy was enthusiastically embraced, quality improvement became part of normal operations, with the RBM and LHMs feeding into these discussions not only the operational performance indicators, but also the results from the mystery customer and mystery drinker reports.

Although some people perceived the BRS as being mainly a control measure introduced by senior management to improve productivity, yields and profits, according to a senior manager responsible for the BRS implementation over 50 per cent of the benefits on which the project was in fact justified came from developmental applications. Yet, while these commercial goals were attained, the freedom that the technology gave LHMs to manage their business much less unfettered by the vagaries of routine stock control mechanisms was quite empowering. The (constrained) freedom which emerged from their consequent greater knowledge and control of their business (i.e. pub) resulted in a switch of emphasis from being the 'controller' of the outlet, to that of 'developer' and 'controller' and the builder of staff teams. Technology gave them a key enabling facility to build their business and thus to succeed with their customers. Baker *et al.* (1998) have observed that the EPOS/BRS 'enabled Bass to push through a sea-change in the culture of the company. It has allowed the company fundamentally to change the way it does business.' The focus was upon helping the pub managers to run their business, and by no means just upon using the technology as a control device.

It is, therefore, difficult, if not impossible, for us to attribute the improvements in performance that occurred, in terms of the hard and soft data measures, to the 'Succeeding with Customers' programme, or the BRS, or the new products. The performance of the outlets where 'Succeeding with Customers' became firmly embedded was compared with outlets where this did not occur to the same extent. The measures of customer satisfaction from the mystery customer and mystery drinker programmes highlighted the fact that there had been some improvement in the 'Succeeding with Customers' outlets, but the financial performance of these outlets as compared with the others showed no significant differences. It would appear, however, that the BRS was a much more powerful force in enhancing top-line productivity and bottom line performance than 'Succeeding with Customers' or any other element of the strategic change programme.

'Breakthrough'

The Taverns' Board had come to the view during the early stages of the strategic change programme that, if the company was to stand a chance of achieving the stretching targets set by the PLC in the context of the extensive outer contextual change outlined earlier, nothing less than a 'cultural transformation' was required. But culture, of course, is extremely difficult to change; indeed some authors would argue that it is unlikely to be changed at its deeper levels through an explicit managerial intervention (Anthony, 1990). Thus the Board decided that it was necessary to encourage the 'cultural transformation' through an education programme, and they decided to use the services of a behavioural consultant and an organization called 'Breakthrough'.

The Board and all senior executives took part in a three-day training and education programme designed to 'open up their minds' to the idea of and need for continual change. The goal was to 'break out' from defensive into creative cycles by concentrating on 'effective behaviour'. They had to focus less on the 'superficiality of immediate social relationships', and more on relationships which take into account the totality of 'background elements' which influence behaviour. They were introduced to a simple model, involving 'breaking out of the zone and crossing a personal edge'. This involved 'coming to an edge, flying off and creating a new zone'. The key behavioural questions to be addressed were 'Who am I?', 'What do I bring into the organization?', 'What's my edge?', 'What inspires me?' and 'What is my vision?' The consultant's argument was that what prevents people from 'crossing their edge' is that they are too firmly ensconced in their own 'comfort zone'. This is reinforced by the stories, myths and metaphors of the company (i.e. the organizational culture). For even senior managers within the company, there were a plethora of constraining rules and norms which were so all-embracing that to break out of a comfort zone could result in failure, 'not knowing' and uncertainty. Fear of failure meant that staff kept their heads down firmly within the boundaries of the status quo. There is a certain attractiveness attached to seeking solutions to problems from within existing repertoires and recipes, such as were to be found within Bass Taverns at the time (for an illustration, see the Sawyers case study in Chapter 3 of Preece *et al.*, 1999a). There also existed a 'blame culture', which made it even more difficult to escape from the confines of the comfort zone. There was the fear of 'losing control' and of losing a job, and the consequent loss of status or money and of thus being labelled a failure! The fear of loss of status was a powerful control mechanism in the company.

The consultants argued that these 'embedded' cultural phenomena, in order for them to stand a chance of being changed, demanded a flip in perception. This would change the senior managers' view of the business from being anchored in a capricious or predictable future to a view of a future which would come about by design. Perception of scarcity would change to a perception of abundance. Working relationships would no longer be rooted in a defensive morass, characterized by 'moaning and groaning', but rather by people working together in a task-oriented way. Above all else, instead of wallowing in a world of 'what we know we know' and mutual self-congratulation, staff had to arrive at a 'new world, whereby the whole company and every individual in it has access to a field of empowering knowledge' (consultant's literature).

Every executive in Bass Taverns was charged with the responsibility of creating a learning community. Knowledge could transform ability. The environment had to be supportive. The blame culture had to disappear. Enhancing the organization's skill base was to be every manager's responsibility. These were not pure types: they interacted and impinged upon each other. How *could* management create motivated teams? How *could* they create the supportive environment within which individuals could 'breakthrough' to operate at high levels of motivation without the constraints and shackles of the past? How *could* managers be motivated to breakthrough into 'Brave New Worlds' if they did not have the appropriate education and training support to improve their ability, knowledge and skills? What is more, they had to be given the opportunity to use their ability within an organizational context which was free from fear.

The parameters of the 'Breakthrough' projects were developed at the first workshop organized for the senior management team of Bass Taverns. It was agreed that there would be a follow-up one-day event to evaluate the implementation and the effectiveness of the project ideas. Individuals were assigned responsibilities, and first steps and structures were agreed for the specific projects. Four main projects were identified and agreed for implementation across the organization: the development of a customer charter, the production of a 'Breakthrough' video, the enrolment of new members into the 'Breakthrough' programme, and the design and holding of a national conference for all corporate and public house managers. This involved the recruitment of at least eight managers to each project.

In addition, a number of other projects emerged, each having a Board sponsor and a project manager; they included: (1) the establishment of a joint venture company, (2) 'good news communication', (3) 'adopt a pub', (4) proactive public relations, (5) 'information, not data', (6) the amalgamation of the Quality Management programme at the pub level with the higher level management 'Breakthrough' initiative, (7) 'walk the talk', (8) open-door policy, (9) the abolition of the Directors' car park, (10) becoming a first-name company, (11) the establishment of a new dress code, (12) teams to use peer group pressures, (13) agreement for the Bass Taverns' Management Committee to hold one of their meetings in a designated childrens' play area ('Deep Sea Den') of a pub etc.

The projects were seen as an opportunity to signal change and to highlight the supportive actions that every senior manager could take to facilitate that signalling process, and make it happen in the minds of the men and women who worked for them. Perhaps these projects come across as 'mere tinkering and window dressing', with a paternalistic or 'happy family' orientation, but be assured that for the senior management population of Bass Taverns, this was a *Cultural Revolution*. We know of one senior executive in Bass Taverns whose only direct social interaction with his staff came in the shape of the rather, according to him, 'boozy Christmas party'. The rest of the year he was never known to leave his office. He managed through his managers. Imagine his worldly view of Breakthrough! The idea of 'dressing down' on a Friday was quickly embraced by clerical and junior staff in several head office departments. However, of much greater significance in a policy sense was that Breakthrough led to the demise of the 'Succeeding with Customers' initiative in pub operations.

Senior managers appeared to be only too willing to take on board a new idea. If 'Breakthrough' was to be the brave new world, then it had to be embraced. 'Succeeding with Customers' was yesterday's god: ' "Breakthrough" would lead us to the new millennium.' It is as though senior managers need, nay demand, an ideology. They require a simplified view of the world which helps them accommodate to the complexity of organizational life. If this demands a bias towards action and purpose, then so much the better for them. In any event, these pub retailing managers have always been first and foremost men and women of action. 'Breakthrough' provided them with an ideology. The problem, however, was that 'Breakthrough' did *not* filter down to the level of the pub. The quality improvement initiative at the pub level, which, as we saw, had by this time begun to show signs of becoming part of the 'way we do things around here', had never been fully accepted by senior management. We have here a mighty paradox!

The Director of Quality Management and his team had been effective in gaining the commitment of a large number of pub managers to the 'Succeeding with Customers' initiative, and the great majority of them said (in individual interviews, through questionnaires and in focus groups) that they were fully supportive of all the key principles. Quality circles, for example, had been established throughout the estate, and pub managers accepted that the only source of sustainable competitive advantage in their outlets was their staff. Now the Bass Taverns' Board and senior management said, 'Look, let us merge the public house Quality Management initiative with the Breakthrough programme.' Breakthrough was understood and accepted by senior management; 'Succeeding with Customers' was understood and accepted by the pub managers. In practice, 'Succeeding with Customers' was killed off and the Breakthrough initiative never reached down to the level of pub. The King was dead and the heir apparent never did climb the steps to the throne.

Conclusion

What we see here, as we suspect is often the case (see, for example, Kelemen *et al.*, 2000) is a hybrid form of organizational changes initiated and introduced over a similar period of time into a given organization. There are no pure types in practice. While the QM change project was underway, so were other initiatives such as technological change, BPR, organizational restructuring, team working and new reward and remuneration packages. This makes it extremely

difficult, if not impossible, to separate out the contribution made to the performance of the company by any particular initiative, not least 'Succeeding with Customers'. However, the 'softer' measures do perhaps provide some indications,
and it was certainly becoming clear that many of the pub managers and RBMs
liked what it was doing for their pubs and the business. This did not, though,
prevent it from being killed off by senior management. The technological
changes, on the other hand, did become embedded in the organization, and most
if not all the stakeholders welcomed, supported and benefited from them.

The managed public house retailing sector, especially in the larger companies,
has a long history of focusing upon quality control (with respect to the predeces-
sor companies of Bass, going back at least to the late nineteenth century; see
Hawkins, 1978: 83; Bass Museum papers) and assurance, and we suspect that,
insofar as pub branding (such as Irish and Australian theme pubs, family outlets,
students' and young persons' venues) spreads more extensively across the
sector, QA/QC will come even more to the fore, due to the emphasis management gives to conformance with the 'templates' or elements of the brand. There
is much affinity here with Ritzer's 'McDonaldization of Society' thesis (2000).
This orientation is strongly associated with Tayloristic forms of job design and a
low-trust culture, connected to the quite substantial volume of liquid assets held
by and passing through the outlets. It was probably always going to be very difficult to shift such a focus to a higher-trust one based upon the real devolvement
of organizational control to public house managers, through higher level managers 'letting go', and encouraging and supporting them in acting in a more
innovative way through taking risky decisions.

There is, of course, an obvious reason why the 'Succeeding with Customers'
initiative fell by the wayside – top management support was withdrawn.
However, it seems to us that questions also need to be asked about how firmly
embedded within the organization – on the behalf of all managers, including
senior, middle and the LHMs – this form of Total Quality Management had
become. Yes, the majority of the pub managers and RBMs were telling us
through our interviews, the questionnaire returns etc. that they very much liked
many aspects of the strategic change programme, including the 'Succeeding
with Customers' initiative. Were they telling us what they thought we wanted to
hear? We think it far more likely that they were giving us their honest views on
the matter at the time, but that what was not so strongly pointed up (partly
because the questions were not designed to tap this dimension and partly
because this was part of their taken-for-granted world of working for a major
public house retailing company) was that the strong middle and senior management concern with control and surveillance was still there – it had never 'gone
away'. Pub managers and their staff could not escape this – it was not an
'option', and not something which needed to be developed or nurtured, as with
the attempt to move in the direction of (total) Quality Management. If anything,
given the parallel move towards pub branding over the same time period, the
control and compliance culture was becoming ever more pervasive.

And yet, as always, these public house managers, if they were to be successful in their own and the companies' terms, need to 'get close to their customers' and offer a quality product/service which is continually improved, whatever the latest offerings, discourses and edicts of senior managers. They are, in effect, responsible for mini-businesses, which can have sales revenues in excess of £2 million per annum. 'Managing customers' and managing their staff is a major responsibility, and can present some significant challenges and on occasions dangers to themselves and their staff (as well as to other customers). This requires the exercise of a range of skills in a situation where the public house manager and his/her staff are physically separated by some distance from the area and head office and the next tier of management. As a pub manager in Edinburgh observed:

> These days the most important aspects of running a pub are building a profitable business, and you can only do that with the right level of customer care, dedication, motivation and team building. The job has changed considerably since I first started – it is so much more than just talking to customers and being behind the bar. There's much more of an emphasis on running a business, with the corresponding numeracy skills and computer skills required. (Preece *et al.*, 1999a: 180)

Note

1 Apart, that is, from typically short, managerialist papers celebrating some aspect of the operations of a company – often written by a manager from that company. See, for example, Leech (1995), Pedrick (1994), Arkin (1997).

References

Anthony, P. (1990) The paradox of the management of culture, or 'he who leads is lost', *Personnel Review* **19**(4), 3–8.

Arkin, A. (1997) A new pub culture, *People Management*, 9 Jan.

Baker, M., Wild, M. and Sussman, S. (1998) Introducing EPOS in Bass Taverns: a report of the case and an exploration of some of the issues, *International Journal of Contemporary Hospitality Management* **10**(1), 16–23.

Bass Museum, Burton on Trent, Mitchells and Butlers papers, 95.2595.01, Managing Director's minute book 1888–1908, 8 January 1908, and 95.3099.01, Summary of Managed House Cash Books, No. 2, 1913–26.

Buchanan, D. and Badham, R. (1999) *Power, Politics and Organizational Change*. London: Sage.

Collins, D. (1998) *Organizational Change: Sociological Perspectives*. London: Routledge.

Dale, B. (ed.) (1994) *Managing Quality* (2nd edn). Hemel Hempstead: Prentice Hall.

Davenport, T. (1992) *Process Innovation: Re-engineering Work through Information Technology*. Boston, MA: Harvard University Press.

Dawson, P. (1994) *Organizational Change: A Processual Approach*. London: Paul Chapman.

Deming, W. (1986) *Out of the Crisis*. Cambridge: Cambridge University Press.

Du Gay, P. and Salaman, G. (1992) The Cult(ure) of the Customer, *Journal of Management Studies* **29**(5), 615–33.

Hammer, M. and Champy, J. (1993) *Reengineering the Corporation: A Manifesto for Business Revolution.* London: Nicholas Brealey.

Hawkins, K. (1978) *A History of Bass Charrington.* Oxford: Oxford University Press.

Johnston, R. and Bryan, R. (1993) Products and services: a question of visibility, *The Services Industries Journal* **13**(3), 125–36.

Kelemen, M., Forrester, P. and Hassard, J. (2000) BPR and TQM: divergence or convergence? In D. Knights and H. Willmott (eds), *The Reengineering Revolution?* op cit.

Knights, D. and Willmott, H. (eds) (2000) *The Reengineering Revolution: Critical Studies of Corporate Change.* London: Sage.

Leech, P. (1995) The importance of positive customer service to Ansells, *Managing Service Quality* **5**(4), 31–4.

Pedrick, C. (1994) Managing the critical processes that drive customer satisfaction at Whitbread, *Managing Service Quality* **4**(5), 31–5.

Pettigrew, A. and Whipp, R. (1991) *Managing Change for Competitive Success.* Oxford: Blackwell.

Preece, D., Steven, G. and Steven, V. (1999a) *Work, Change and Competition: Managing for Bass.* London: Routledge.

Preece, D., Steven, G. and Steven, V. (1999b) Changing organisation structures and processes at Northern Taverns. In K. Meudell and T. Callen (eds), *Management and Organisational Behaviour: A Student Workbook.* Harlow, Essex: Pitman Publishing.

Preece, D., Steven, V. and Steven, G. (2000) Quality Management in public house retailing: a case study. In *Fourth International and Seventh National Conference on Quality Management*, University of Technology, Sydney and University of MONASH, Melbourne, Feb.

Ritzer, G. (2000) *The McDonaldization of Society.* Boston, MA: Pine Forge Press.

Wilkinson, A., Redman, T., Snape, E. and Marchington, M. (1998) *Managing with Total Quality Management: Theory and Practice.* Basingstoke: Macmillan.

Zeithmal, V., Parsuraman, A. and Berry, L. (1990) *Delivering Service Quality.* New York: The Free Press.

10 Changing supervisory relations at work

Behind the success stories of Quality Management initiatives

Patrick Dawson

Introduction

This chapter examines Quality Management and supervision through drawing on a national programme of research on the introduction and uptake of Quality Management in a number of Australian organizations. Attention is focused on the important and yet often neglected position of the supervisor who may act as a major barrier or catalyst for change. It is argued that much of the prescriptive literature promotes unrealistic fairyland stories of the route to harmonious quality cultures. A brief history of the rise of Quality Management is provided and its place in the development of management thought is discussed. Although the human element is formally recognized as a central component of Quality Management, it is claimed that much of the literature tends to underplay the complex, ambiguous and multi-dimensional character of workplace change. It is argued that the win–win scenario of improved working conditions for all and quality output for employers is rarely, if ever, achieved in practice. Moreover, it is shown how supervision is often poorly conceptualized and the role of the supervisor misunderstood. As a result, these simple consultant recipes of success may appear attractive in their support of a planned staged rational process, while in practice, they may undermine supervisory relations through sidestepping the more complex processual dynamics of change initiatives. This mismatch between social science knowledge and the design of consultant packages is demonstrated in two Australian-based illustrations which briefly focus on Quality Management and the place of the supervisor. The chapter concludes by calling for a more critical appreciation of the problems and practice of managing workplace change and a broader contextual understanding of the development of supervision and Quality Management.

Quality Management: the new enlightenment?

There is nothing new about notions of quality. Craftsmanship and the development of expertise in the creation of items of value can be traced back to early empires in China, Babylonia and Egypt. It is around 3000 to 2501 BC that the first manufacture of iron objects is believed to have occurred and it was in the sixteenth century that the superiority of Japanese craft products were discovered by Dutch and Portuguese explorers (Grun, 1991). However, it is not until after industrialization with the growth of the factory system and the expansion of commodity markets, that attention has gradually shifted from low-cost competitive advantage to methods for achieving the large-scale manufacture of quality products. Apart from an early concern in the quality of mass-produced military products, Western manufacturing industries have been comparatively slow in the uptake of new Quality Management techniques. Although Armand Feigenbaum (1956) emphasized the competitive importance of quality in the 1950s, it was the Japanese who were the first to embrace many of the quality ideas promoted by Juran (1988) and Deming (1981). In part, the readiness of Japanese companies to embrace new methods of organization reflected their weak postwar position and their need to improve the quality of their products to compete on growing world markets. In the 1950s, Japanese goods were often viewed as cheap poor quality imitations of Western products and yet, by the 1980s they had become a dominant force threatening the competitive position of many Western companies. Over the last two decades, the views of Deming and Juran have been widely sought by Western management; for example, Deming ran a four-day seminar in America during 1987 which attracted some 50,000 executives (Allan, 1991: 30). Similarly in Australia, several visitations by Juran and Deming stimulated the uptake of Quality Management initiatives which culminated with the Australian Prime Minister Bob Hawke launching an *Australia for Quality Campaign* on 2 April 1984.

Since the 1980s, there has been a broadening of Quality Management in the development of initiatives which attempt to engage all employees in the systematic effort for quality. No longer is quality promoted as a simple operational manufacturing technique, but rather, it is seen as a potential strategic weapon for bringing about large-scale cultural change in the quest for competitive advantage (Dawson and Palmer, 1995). The definitional confusion and ambiguity of Quality Management (and various forms, such as, service excellence and Total Quality Management) has allowed it to accommodate new and emerging concepts, such as, benchmarking, and to incorporate non-manufacturing companies and areas of operation. On this issue, Chiles and Choi (2000: 186) claim that while as a body of practical knowledge TQM has had an 'unparalleled impact of modern business history' it has largely remained atheoretical, amorphous and conceptually hazy. The fluidity and ambiguity of terms also reflects the influence of different stakeholders who have a vested interest in differentiating their 'products' and 'services'. For example, competing consultant groups continue to advocate the benefits of their own 'unique' methodology for the successful implementation of quality schemes; quality organizations broaden and redefine their objectives in seeking to justify their continual existence and secure future funding (see Navaratnam, 1995: 83–91); and popular quality exponents argue for the adoption of their own 'distinct' set of principles (see for example, Albrecht, 1992; Crosby, 1980; Imai, 1986; Ishikawa, 1985). In short, the substance of Quality Management is composed of a number of elements which can be combined, redefined and implemented in a number of different ways. Part of the popularity of these programmes stem from their meaning different things to different people (Tuckman, 1994). For our purposes, however, there are a number of common characteristics which can be distilled from the work of some of the main exponents of the Quality Management movement (see also, Clark, 1995: 189; Hill, 1995: 36–40; Tuckman, 1995: 65–6).

One of the first common elements of many company quality initiatives is the notion of a comprehensive approach where quality is an integral part of all operations involving every employee of the company, as well as external operating practices and customer–supplier relations. Secondly, is the use of a range of statistical methods and group problem-solving techniques in applying a systematic approach to quality problems. Thirdly, is the call for strong senior management commitment to, and responsibility and support for, the achievement and maintenance of a quality system. Fourthly, is the importance of getting it right first time and developing a system based on prevention and not inspection. Fifthly, is the institutionalization of a system of continuous process improvement which ensures the steady commitment and ongoing involvement of all employees. Sixthly, is the development of small-group activities (through quality circles and TQM teams) where employees with different skills meet together to solve common quality problems. In practice, different combinations of these various elements characterize the typical features of company quality initiatives. However, within the popular and prescriptive literature there remains a view that such initiatives will not only improve company performance but also the quality of working life for employees. As Wilkinson points out in his discussion of empowerment, a common assumption is that:

> workers are an untapped resource with knowledge and experience and an interest in becoming involved which can be released by employers providing opportunities and structures for their involvement. It is also assumed that participative decision making is likely to lead to job satisfaction and better quality decisions and that gains are available both to employers (increased efficiency) and workers (job satisfaction), in short an everyone wins scenario. (Wilkinson, 1997: 45)

Since the middle of the 1990s, greater attention has been given to some of the failures of Quality Management projects and a growing body of critical material has emerged in America (Hackman and Wageman, 1995), Australia (Dawson and Palmer, 1995) and Britain (Wilkinson and Willmott, 1995). Hackman and Wageman (1995) argue that one of the main problems with Quality Management initiatives is that once new improved work practices are identified and documented they may be implemented throughout the organization, leaving a vast number of employees with no say over the new work arrangements. In their view, this is simply a new form of 'old-time scientific management' only in this case the new designs for work originate from peers working on cross-functional quality teams (Hackman and Wageman, 1995: 327). Similarly, the author has argued that in Australia, the solutions identified by a small group of employees may be imposed on others who may be unable to participate in group problem-solving due to English language difficulties (Dawson, 1995). More-over, through assuming the benefits (and need) for a common unitary culture, many of these quality initiatives are unable to accommodate or even account for the possibility of cultural heterogeneity – a common characteristic of many multi-cultural workplaces in Australia. As such, the unthinking endorsements of these programmes may exacerbate workplace conflict in spot-lighting the tensions and divisions between groups. As Valentine and Knights (1997: 84) conclude in their comparison of TQM and BPR 'there is too much prescription in the management and organizational literature and insufficient critical reflection'.

Supervision and Quality Management: some critical reflections

In this section it is argued that the tendency to forward simple notions of super-vision, to promote mythical shifts in emphasis from the so-called policeman to coach, or to make broad assumptions about the reaction of older supervisors to change, limits our understanding of processes of change. The tendency for neat prescriptions or simple solutions moves us away from critical reflection and the untidy nature of change. Taken on a broader level, it may lead us to package the historical transformation of supervision and quality in terms of a rational phased model of development and ignore the contextual, varied and emergent character of change. As such, it is argued here that it is often too easy to view the history of twentieth-century management thought as a rational, scientific and logical process and that attention should be given to more contextual historical analyses in making sense of current change initiatives.

A rationalist history of the changing role of the supervisor

For those who seek a rational account of the historical development of supervi-sion and Quality Management, the autocratic and 'undisputed' position of super-visor in the nineteenth century might be a useful starting place. During this period, autocratic supervisors were given free reign to hire and fire, set wages, and plan the allocation of work (Child, 1975: 72). As Marglin has described (1976: 29), the factory system allowed employers to gain greater control over the production process through the use of discipline and supervision. The problem of developing work disciplines (the quality and consistency of worker effort) was a major concern and the bowler-hatted supervisor was a logical solu-tion to this problem. However, by the end of the First World War autocratic supervision was identified as a significant problem (Lozonick, 1983: 124–5) and the supervisor was viewed as the culprit for much of the industrial unrest (Child and Partridge, 1982: 7). During the inter-war period, *scientific management* became attractive as it appeared to offer a solution to this problem by challenging the role of the traditional supervisor through the concept of 'functional foremanship' (Taylor, 1947: 95–109).

With the growing uptake of Taylorist forms of work organization a number of problems began to emerge centred on the impersonality of its scientific approach to job design, and the coldness of its strictly economic approach to human motivation. In response, the *human relations* approach developed which drew attention to the importance of the human side of the enterprise. Supervisors were taught to recognize the importance of non-economic, social rewards and motivators. Jobs were enriched to add variety and a sense of responsibility to the performance of work. At this time, the profession of personnel management developed and carried the ideas about human motivation into the growing industrial organizations.

In the 1950s, *socio-technical systems* theory was developed by the Tavistock group who recommended the creation of autonomous work groups in order to add democracy and flexibly to over-specialized and over-standardized work processes. The work of Trist demonstrated how it was possible to operate different systems of work organization in situations which had the same technological and economic constraints (that is, there is a degree of organizational choice), and that these different forms of work organization would have different social and psychological effects. The broader importance of contingent variables was highlighted by studies in the 1960s and the development of *contingency theory*. During the 1960s and 1970s, attention was directed towards situational variables and the need to find the right style of supervision to fit the circumstances. For example, Woodward (1980) in her study of a hundred manufacturing firms in south-east Essex argued that there has been a transition in supervisory emphasis and a change in the supervisor's span of control under different production systems. The movement from unit to process production is seen to represent a shift from traditional labour-oriented to more technical, machine-oriented supervision. In other words, rather than there being an appropriate style of supervision for all occasions the role of the supervisor is contingent on the prevailing set of circumstances or situation.

With developments in computer technology in the 1980s and 1990s, many of the control functions of supervisors were seen to be increasingly incorporated into the technology of production. This was being brought about through the machine pacing of operations and the automatic capture and analysis of production performance information (Buchanan and Boddy, 1983). The new century is seen to have witnessed a further erosion of traditional supervision with the development of self-managing teams, notions of empowerment and quality initiatives. It is claimed that what is needed is a coach rather than a policemen to enable highly motivated teams of workers to operate efficiently in the pursuit of win–win scenarios. This new breed of supervisor/team leader/facilitative coach is deemed to be central to the development of harmonious quality cultures. But does this rationalist history hold up to scrutiny?

Contextualizing the history of supervision and Quality Management

One of the major problems with a rationalist history of supervision is that it simply sidesteps the murky processual waters of change. The importance of context and history is simplified or downplayed as a complex shaper of the development, refinement, uptake and rejection of approaches to supervision in the organization and control of work. Under a more contextual analysis, the emergent unfolding and complex nature of these developments are highlighted. Our attention is drawn to the acceptance and influence that certain ideas may or may not have during different historical periods and how these may arise and be shaped in different situations. Under such an analysis, account may be given to the problem of management control with the rise of the factory system and the growth in large-scale manufacture (Littler, 1982); child labour and the abuses of the factory regime (Henriques, 1979); or the development of more intense and direct forms of supervision to reduce overall costs and improve output and effi- ciency (Melling, 1981: 74). During this period, although we may recognize how the mechanistic methods of Taylorism contributed to the development of mass production industries, cross-country comparisons illustrate how Taylorism was introduced in different countries in different ways and had different effects (Littler, 1982). Moreover, while Taylor advocated the abandonment of an hierar- chical militaristic type of organization and suggested its substitution with 'func- tional management' – the suggestion being to replace the traditional 'multi-purpose' supervisor who was held responsible for the successful running of the entire shop, with a number of different bosses, all of whom would perform their own particular function, for example, gang-bosses, speed bosses, inspectors, repair bosses, and shop disciplinarian (Taylor, 1947: 100–4) – in practice, this form of functional management was never fully adopted in either Australian or British Industry and is often absent in the more rationalist accounts.

If we turn our attention to the rise of Quality Management, it is possible to chart how Japan restructured and reconsidered methods of work following World War II. The shock of losing the war emerges as an important contextual factor which enabled new ideas to be heard. In contrast, Western management convinced of their own techniques continued to refine existing methods of mass production. In part, the uptake of quality initiatives among Western companies can be linked to the trauma experienced by the old industrial nations since the 1980s as competition, first from Japan and then from the newly developing countries, eroded their dominance in world markets. The globalization of busi- ness, and the evidence of Japanese success in coping with economic crises have stimulated an interest in Japanese managerial controls and an appreciation of different cultural assumptions underlying working relationships. In addition, the democratic idealism that followed World War II that gave support to pluralism and the collective representation of different interests as a means of managing conflict, has been weakened. Organizational change initiatives in many of the large-scale bureaucracies in the public and private sector have shaken confidence in centralized organizational structures and in the old prescriptions. In this context, assumptions of rational management practices are being recast to build flexibility and an easier response to continuous change into organizational life.

Developments in communication and information technology provides another contextual stimulus to the design, implementation and operation of Quality Management systems. Computer software permits the development of new methods for calculating and disseminating performance indicators. Information technology can be harnessed to eliminate much of the personal supervision once exercised by supervisors and middle managers. It provides the opportunity, both for more stringent monitoring of performance by senior management, and for the clearer communication of managerial expectations and requirements to workers. In this context, the greater involvement of employees in the management of their own work-processes can be seen to involve less risk for management. With concrete and statistically available performance indicators, the squandering of organizational resources should be apparent, and constant review should guard against the subversion of managerial intentions. This potential for increased surveillance and control over employee behaviour has been highlighted by Sewell (1998) and Sewell and Wilkinson (1992: 271–89), and might support the claim that traditional supervisory control functions are increasingly being incorporated into the technology of production. However, as our case material and the studies of others highlight, the outcomes of change on supervision are far more complex than indicated by a simple erosion thesis or transition from policeman to coach. The role of the supervisor has not remained static over time, but has continually adjusted and has variously been replaced, redefined, enhanced, eroded and reconfigured. Some studies have shown how new forms of control systems which minimize traditional forms of supervision may be applauded by workplace employees. For example, in a detailed monograph of innovation and change at Pirelli Aberdare, Jon Clark shows that while the new quality programme 'clearly served the interests of management', it also afforded a greater sense of involvement among employees than had previously been experienced (Clark, 1995: 235). In contrast, the work of Buchanan and Preston (1992) demonstrates how many of the traditional functions of supervision have remained. Again these studies spotlight the importance of clarifying what we understand by terms and concepts and studying processes of change within context and over time and as such, caution should be given to post-hoc rationalizations which over simplify these developments.

Making sense of supervisory change: concepts and terms

Before examining any case study material, it is important to clarify what we understand by supervision and how we can identify and define supervisors. Within the literature, supervisors are consistently cited as holding a peculiar middle position with a consequent problem of role conflict (with competing demands for subordinates and superordinates) and role ambiguity (confusion over job tasks, responsibilities and authority). From the marginal men thesis

(Wray, 1949) to the claim by Child and Partridge (1982) that supervisors have become 'lost managers', the so-called 'problem' of supervision remains (Dawson and McLoughlin, 1988). In part, this 'problem' is of management's making in reflecting an unwillingness to accept line supervisors as part of the management team and in a misunderstanding of what the job entails. The job of the supervisor has undergone significant and complex change since the historical emergence of the industrial supervisor during the nineteenth century (see Dawson, 1991). Management understanding have generally not kept pace with these changes and the inability of management to recognize and adapt to the changing responsibilities and skill requirements of supervisors has led to the implementation of inappropriate change programmes (Burnes and Fitter, 1987). For example, in redesigning work or implementing Quality Management programmes it is often assumed that supervisors will be a major problem. This assumption is often based on a misunderstanding of what the job of the supervisor involves, resulting in inappropriate decisions on the processes required to bring about change.

In conceptualizing supervision, the control of workplace operations is a useful starting point (as this goes beyond the simple notion of labour regulation and human surveillance to incorporate other elements of work). Operational control involves: directing and regulating operations; monitoring and evaluating operations; and correcting and adapting operations. These 'control responsibilities' can be carried out by designated supervisors, they may be built into the machinery of production, they may form part of computerized systems of control, they may be devolved to self-managing teams, or dispersed across several organizational levels.

In identifying supervisors (and not to be misled by simply following job titles which may differ across firms, industries and time), the criterion of 'authoritativeness' (formal authority accredited by management and the authority and status vested in an individual by their work group) is useful for differentiating supervisory roles from other organizational positions. As Etzioni (1964: 91) argued, whether one holds a position of power and authority over workplace employees is not simply determined by the location of that person within a formal organizational command structure. In other words, there will be individuals who hold a position of authority over fellow workers without being accredited authority by management (in part, their influence may even depend on them not holding a 'formal' supervisory position). Thus, within any workplace there is likely to be a network of interrelated roles, each with different supervisory elements and relationships, some of which may be designated as 'supervisors' and others who may hold 'informal' supervisory positions (in being neither recognized nor formally defined by management as holding 'supervisory' jobs). Furthermore, it is argued here that the job tasks which supervisors perform are neither 'universal' nor 'static', rather, they vary across organizations, under different contextual conditions of the same organization, and over time. For these reasons, an analysis of supervisory tasks can only be accomplished by a detailed examination of the job of the supervisor at his or her place of work (there is no exhaustive list of supervisory tasks). As such, supervisors should not be identified by their job titles or job tasks, but rather, according to the criteria that: first, they have control responsibilities for workplace operations; and secondly, authority is invested in their position by management and/or the workforce.

Ironically, the continuing 'problem' of supervision continues to be tackled on the basis of a narrow conception of supervision which promotes either an anachronistic perception of the need to abolish the traditional role of the supervisor, or the alternative view that there is a simple panacea to the problem of supervision through the development of team leadership training programmes under new workplace arrangements. Although supervisors can be a major catalyst or barrier to change, both in terms of the change process and under more stabilized operation, they too often remain a forgotten and misunderstood element at the workplace. In the case material which follows, the effects of this neglect on the implementation and operation of three Quality Management initiatives are outlined and discussed.

Quality Management and supervision in the Australian workplace

In this section, some of the human resource issues and supervisory problems of managing these types of change initiatives are illustrated through three Australian case studies on Quality Management at work. The first two case studies draw on data collected from an automotive component manufacturing plant and the Australian operations of Pirelli Cables. Material is used to illustrate how gaining supervisory and middle management commitment to the programme posed itself as a major problem and jeopardized the success of the initiative. The third case study (second sub-section) examines the introduction of a quality programme within an ophthalmic lens laboratory in Adelaide. Attention is again given to the process of implementation and the unforeseen consequences of downplaying the importance of supervisory tasks and relations in the management of day-to-day operations. Data from the case studies are used to show how supervisors can often be overlooked when discussing problems and suggesting change strategies. The case analyses concludes by claiming that there has been a general failure to recognize the importance of the role of the supervisor within both company programmes of change and in the prescriptive 'how to' literature on Quality Management; as such, a more critical appreciation is required of the place of the supervisor and the complex dynamics of workplace change initiatives.

The policeman to coach myth

A commonly held myth, which has been promoted in both the prescriptive and the more critical literature, is that there has been a shift in job of the first-line supervisor from policeman to coach. Although some studies have noted a peculiar absence of 'facilitative supervision' and the retention of more policing and directive functions (see Buchanan and Preston, 1992: 70), the argument forwarded here is that the job of the supervisor largely remains over simplified and misunderstood. Data from the case studies illustrate how the shifting nature of supervision and the precarious position of the older supervisor, frequently stood out as a major supervisory concern and organizational issue. For example, in an Australian automotive company which was restructuring work and introducing teams on the shopfloor, the role of the supervisor was formally changed from a task-oriented trouble-shooter and problem-solver role to a more facilitative people-oriented role. The traditional control responsibilities of the supervisor were devolved to team leaders (who held a supervisory relationship to other members of their group). For the most part, the new team leaders were far younger than the plant supervisors, who had tended to work their way up through the ranks and had attained their positions on the basis of the large stock of knowledge and experience they had gained in shopfloor operations. In this sense, the authority of the supervisor was based on their ability to deal with unforeseen events and to firefight in the case of a wide variety of production emergencies, such as, machine breakdowns. Today, the emphasis has formally shifted towards the management of people, as one interviewee recounted:

> Supervisors have to be more people-oriented than they have ever been in their entire careers, bear in mind that their training initially is task-oriented not people-oriented. Now we are trying to get a balance between the two, with perhaps a little more emphasis on people-oriented than task-oriented.

From the perspective of the supervisors, however, they maintained that the content of their jobs prior to change have never been fully understood by management. They noted how management have tended to downplay the traditional managing people skills aspect of the position. They explained that apart from technical contingencies, there have always been regular human contingencies which supervisors were expected to deal with on a day-to-day basis. In this case the supervisors (who were generally older workers) felt that they were often falsely portrayed as anti-change merchants, when in fact a central part of their job had always involved dealing with unexpected change situations. In other words, over time, supervisors had adapted their role to meet the changing expectations of other employees and the changing conditions of work. From a management viewpoint, this redefinition of supervision had largely gone unnoticed. Typically, managers talked about a clear, yet somewhat mythical contrast, between the traditional task-oriented and labour control function of supervision (the policeman) and the newly emerging co-ordinating role of enlightened supervision (the facilitative coach). Furthermore, due to the age of many supervisors (generally over 50 years old) they indicated that they would often find themselves ignored or viewed by others as a major source of resistance to new initiatives.

In cases where the supervisor gained early involvement in the change initiative, they could become a major catalyst and promoter of the change programme. Typically, a major obstacle to change occurred in cases where supervisors, or those holding a supervisory relationship to production, were not accounted for in designing training programmes and implementing change. For example, in the case of Pirelli Cables Australia, an early unforeseen problem centred on gaining employee commitment at the supervisory level. Resistance to their Total Quality Management (TQM) initiative was largely in the form of questioning its relevance to their area of operation. TQM, as a tool for solving process problems, assumes that problems exist, and that production workers are best placed for identifying solutions. However, the problem of dealing with unexpected operating contingencies, both technical and human, were central to the jobs of supervisors who would tackle these problems as part of their daily work routines. As a result, the introduction of a system that offered to take away the 'problem' of supervisory firefighting posed itself as a threat to the jobs of front-line supervisors. It is perhaps not surprising that good supervisory relations were threatened under this context and that supervisors became unsupportive of the change initiative.

Another issue that arose on the shopfloor was the question of the maximum number of teams that an employee should be able to join. Initially, the idea was to have lots of different teams and to continually move employees around. However, in practical terms this created supervisory problems, as employees could be in four different teams all of which met once a week. As the meetings are held in company time, employees were spending less and less time on the shopfloor and the allocation of labour in planning work became a significant supervisory headache. In short, by distancing supervisors from the change initiative and through undervaluing the importance of the supervisory role to maintaining good employee relations at work, the case highlights how the supervisor can be a critical yet misunderstood element in Quality Management programmes.

Circumventing supervisors: an unenviable middle position

Tecsol Pty Ltd is made up of five Divisions: Ophthalmic Laboratories, Contact Lens laboratory, Supply, Hearing Centres and the Industrial Division. The laboratories located in South Australia act as the manufacturing arm for Laubman and Pank and are the focus of this section. Within this manufacturing area, there has been a long history of Quality Management with the main emphasis being placed on quality assurance techniques and the setting of laboratory jobbing quality standards (for example, both spectacle and contact lens manufacture are based on documented Australian Standards). However, the move towards the 'softer' aspects of quality, in the form of a service excellence programme, was a relatively new development, which followed the growth in the companies core business (ophthalmic practice) through the acquisition of a large number of new employees and branch outlets.

On the question of work tasks, it was generally claimed that the quality programme had done little to change the nature of laboratory work. Many employees claimed that they were providing 'excellence' in service and that the programme merely highlighted what they were already doing. Although the programme did not have any major influence on the content of job tasks, the circulation of an anonymous attitude survey did spotlight a number of outstanding employee concerns. The survey was described by some employees as enabling individuals to 'go-to-town' and put all their frustrations down on paper.

> Of course, on the survey they don't even answer the question: they put what they want there. 'LISTEN' – just big letters, right across the form: 'LISTEN'. Because I was able to read them. 'Sack supervisors; you'll get results.' 'Get rid of Joe Blow' – really heavy stuff – real heavy; brilliantly presented, brilliantly fabricated – excellent. So, of course, it goes to the Board. They read it. My God! I mean, they read that information. What's their perception?... Anyway, to cut it all short, it came across very bad. We (supervisors) looked very bad, anyway. So, let's go along with what they want us to do. So, of course, they implemented a worker participation committee.

For some supervisory staff, the results from the survey created a great deal of anxiety and stress which was still present at the time of the interviews. It was felt that senior management over-reacted to the survey and as a consequence the WPC was causing as many problems as it was solving. As the manufacturing manager commented:

> See, people in Australia, they all think it's the management's responsibility. If anything goes wrong, that's their problem. Let's all laugh about it: it's pretty funny. They don't have the accountability; they don't want the accountability. They say they do, but they don't. If you start giving them the accountability they start to have all these harassment problems among themselves, and they fight among themselves, and bickering occurs, which is occurring at the moment.

The supervisor is the front-line of management and as such, must absorb and deal with a lot of shopfloor concerns and aggravations. In being the first line of formal authority, supervisors also tend to be blamed for conflicts which emanate from the shopfloor. In the view of one supervisor, this had been exacerbated by the formation of WPC which had by-passed the supervisor. He claimed that more time should be spent listening to supervisors who are dealing with problems on a day-to-day basis and that more effort should be made to ensure a balance of opinion from the shopfloor. Typically, supervisors felt that concerns were no longer being raised with them and that the WPC had resulted in far less communication between themselves and employees on the shopfloor. In this sense, the WPC was viewed as providing a forum which served to erode the position of the supervisor and in so doing, increased tension on the shopfloor.

Moreover, the removal of people from the shopfloor to attend meetings was seen to increase pressure on those employees who remained. As an employee explained: 'the main thing is if you're pulling people out of the production environment that area stops and somebody's got to work a bit harder to get that person covered. So there's a lot of pressure on people.'

In discussing the problem of supervision and the consequence of the WPC one technician commented that:

> It's certainly not easy to be a manager or a supervisor. I mean, I wouldn't want to be. Sure, the pay might be better but I don't know, you certainly lose friends. They've tried out quite a few chaps in the labs for supervisory sort of positions, but the same thing always happens. You know, they were one of the boys and now they've got to start giving a few orders and directions, and it never goes down too well. It ends up with them just getting totally frustrated and chucking it in, and getting back to being one of the boys again. You can't seem to be a supervisor and be a nice guy as well.

Although the WPC was set up with the intention of improving employee involvement on the shopfloor and tackling the issues raised in the anonymous attitudinal survey, in practice, it has become dominated by the vested interests of a particular group and as such, fails to address wider issues and concerns. In the case of supervisors, they feel undermined and claim that everyday issues which should be raised directly with supervisory personnel are now directed towards senior management through the WPC. On the shopfloor, employees outwith the new dominate group also claim that there is a lack of balance in the views of committee members and that the issues being raised do not reflect the 'real' concerns of all employees. In short, the WPC in tackling the problem of poor employee relations has unwittingly created other inter-personal problems, particularly among supervisory staff.

Conclusion

The major findings from the more critical contextual studies on Quality Management demonstrate how the consequences of change are varied and complex. There is no simple set of prescriptions to the development of harmonious quality cultures nor simple recipes for implementing new forms of industrial democracy at work. In some cases, change may represent a return to standardized work practices associated with earlier forms of Taylorism where variation is systematically designed out of new operational procedures; in other cases, employees may have a more positive experience of change and view the new working arrangements as an improvement over older methods of work. What is clear is that there is no rational linear development in management ideas and their implementation at work, nor are there simple outcomes which can be understood outside of the context and process in which they emerge and are shaped.

In the case of supervisors, who generally occupy a peculiar middle position between employees and management, the case material has highlighted how there is often a self-fulfilling prophecy of problems. In holding an unenviable middle position and in being cast at the outset as a 'problem' role, supervisors are often left with little room to manoeuvre. From their organizational location they not only find themselves having to absorb conflicting demands from above and below, but also often find themselves being marginalized in programmes of change. Moreover, this 'problem' is generally not of their own making but the result of a poor understanding of supervision and the role of the supervisor. Change agents – in not involving supervisors, in being quick to view them as obstacles to change and in often using old-fashioned and outdated assumptions about the nature of the job – may unwittingly create tensions and conflict which may serve to worsen rather than improve employee relations at work. The importance of the role of the supervisor has tended to be ignored both within company programmes of change and in the prescriptive 'how to' literature on Quality Management. As such, this chapter concludes that it is time to go beyond the 'fairyland stories' of Quality Management towards a broader and more critical appreciation of the problems and practice of managing workplace change. There is a need to integrate previous knowledge and theories of change in evaluating new initiatives and developing strategies which do not present neat marketable and simple solutions to what are complex problems. The supervisor is a central element within a wider whole and yet, they often remain overlooked and misunderstood during the uptake of Quality Management initiatives. Their position usefully demonstrates the complex and unfolding character of change initiatives which seek to transform workplace cultures and by so doing, draw attention to the need to break open many of the market-driven myths surrounding Quality Management as a simple recipe for creating harmonious quality cultures. They also draw our attention to the importance of history and context in any critical reflection on the emergence of Quality Management and supervision in the development of management thought.

References

Albrecht, K. (1992) *The Only Thing That Matters: Bringing the Power of the Customer into the Centre of your Business*. New York: HarperBusiness.

Allan, C. (1991) The role of diffusion agents in the transfer of Quality Management in Australia. Unpublished honours thesis, Brisbane: University of Griffith.

Buchanan, D. and Boddy, D. (eds) (1983) *Organizations in the Computer Age: Technological Imperatives and Strategic Choice*. Aldershot: Gower.

Buchanan, D. and Preston, D. (1992) Life in the cell: supervision and teamwork in a 'manufacturing systems engineering' environment, *Human Resource Management Journal* 2(4), 55–76.

Burnes, B. and Fitter, M. (1987) Control of advanced manufacturing technology: supervision without supervisors? In T. Wall, C. Clegg and N. Kemp (eds), *The Human Side of Advanced Manufacturing*. Chichester: John Wiley.

Child, J. (1975) The industrial supervisor. In G. Esland, G. Salaman and M. Speakman (eds), *People and Work*. Edinburgh: Holmes McDougall.

Child, J. and Partridge, B. (1982) *Lost Managers: Supervisors in Industry and Society*. Cambridge: Cambridge University Press.

Chiles, T. and Choi, T. (2000) Theorizing TQM: an Austrian and evolutionary economics interpretation, *Journal of Management Studies* **37**(2), 185–212.

Clark, J. (1995) *Managing Innovation and Change: People, Technology and Strategy*. London: Sage.

Crosby, P. (1980) *Quality is Free: The Art of Making Quality Certain*. New York: Mentor.

Dawson, P. (1991) The historical emergence and changing role of the industrial supervisor. *Asia Pacific Human Resource Management* **29**(2), 36–50.

Dawson, P. (1995) Managing quality in the multi-cultural workplace. In A. Wilkinson and H. Willmott (eds), *Making Quality Critical: New Perspective on Organizational Change*. London: Routledge.

Dawson, P. and McLoughlin, I. (1988) Organizational choice in the redesign of supervisory systems. In D. Boddy, J. McCalman and D. Buchanan (eds), *The New Management Challenge: Information Systems for Improved Performance*. London: Croom Helm.

Dawson, P. and Palmer, G. (1995) *Quality Management: The Theory and Practice of Implementing Change*. Cheshire, Melbourne: Longman.

Deming, W.E. (1981) *Japanese Methods for Productivity and Quality*. Washington: George Washington University.

Etzioni, A. (1964) *Modern Organisations*. Englewood Cliffs: Prentice-Hall.

Feigenbaum, A. (1956) Total quality control, *Harvard Business Review* **34**(6), 93–101.

Grun, B. (1991) *The Timetale of History*. New York: Simon & Schuster.

Hackman, R.J. and Wageman, R. (1995) Total Quality Management: empirical, conceptual, and practical issues, *Administrative Science Quarterly* **40**(2), 309–42.

Henriques, U.R. (1979) *Before the Welfare State. Social Administration in Early Industrial Britain*. London: Longman.

Hill, S. (1995) From quality circles to Total Quality Management. In A. Wilkinson and H. Willmott (eds), *Making Quality Critical: New Perspective on Organizational Change*. London: Routledge.

Imai, M. (1986) *Kaizen: The Key to Japan's Competitive Success*. New York: McGraw-Hill.

Ishikawa, K. (1985) *What is Total Quality Control? The Japanese Way*. Englewood Cliffs, NJ: Prentice Hall.

Juran, J.M. (1988) *Quality Control Handbook*. New York: McGraw-Hill.

Littler, C. (1982) *The Development of the Labour Process in Capitalist Societies*. London: Heinemann.

Lozonick, W. (1983) Technological change and the control of work: the development of capital–labour relations in US mass production industries. In H. Gospel and C. Littler (eds), *Managerial Strategies and Industrial Relations: An Historical and Comparative Study*. London: Heinemann.

Marglin, S. (1976) What do bosses do? The origins and function of hierarchy in capitalist production. In A. Gorz (ed.), *The Division of Labour: The Labour Process and Class Struggle in Modern Capitalism*. Harvester Press.

Melling, J.I. (1980) Non-commissioned officers: British employers and their supervisory workers: 1880–1920, *Social History* **5**, 184–221.

Navaratnam, K.K. (1993) Organizations serving the quality movement in Australia: a guide for human resource practitioners, *Asia Pacific Journal of Human Resources* **31**(3), 83–91.

Sewell, G. (1998) The discipline of teams: the control of team-based industrial work through electronic and peer surveillance, *Administrative Science Quarterly* **43**, 397–428.

Sewell, G. and Wilkinson, B. (1992) 'Someone to watch over me': surveillance, discipline and the just-in-time labour process, *Sociology* **26**(2), 271–89.

Taylor, F. (1947) *The Principles of Scientific Management*. New York: Harper & Brothers.

Tuckman, A. (1994) The yellow brick road: TQM and the restructuring of organizational culture, *Organization Studies* **15**(5), 727–51.

Tuckman, A. (1995) Ideology, quality and TQM. In A. Wilkinson and H. Willmott (eds), *Making Quality Critical: New Perspective on Organizational Change*. London: Routledge.

Valentine, R. and Knights, D. (1998) Research note: TQM and BPR – can you spot the difference? *Personnel Review* **27**(1), 78–85.

Wilkinson, A. (1998) Empowerment: theory and practice, *Personnel Review* **27**(1), 40–56.

Wilkinson, A. and Willmott, H. (eds) (1995) *Making Quality Critical: New Perspectives on Organizational Change*. London: Routledge.

Woodward, J. (1980) *Industrial Organization: Theory and Practice* (2nd edn). Oxford: Oxford University Press.

Wray, D. (1949) Marginal men of industry: the foremen, *American Journal of Sociology* **54**(4), 298–301.

Index

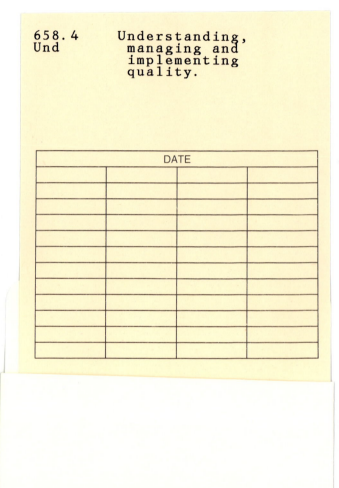

658.4 Und   Understanding, managing and implementing quality.

DATE			

BAKER & TAYLOR